Governor's Race

Governor's Race ★

A TV Reporter's Chronicle of the
1993 Florio/Whitman Campaign

Michael Aron

Rutgers University Press
New Brunswick, New Jersey

Library of Congress Cataloging-in-Publication Data

Aron, Michael, 1946–
     Governor's race: a TV reporter's chronicle of the 1993 Florio/Whitman campaign / Michael Aron.
     p.   cm.

ISBN 0-8135-2072-X

     I. Governors—New Jersey—Election—History—20th century—Chronology. 2. Florio, James J., 1937–   . 3. Whitman, Christine.
4. Elections—New Jersey—History—20th century—Chronology.
5. New Jersey—Politics and government. 1951– —Chronology.   I. Title.

FI40.A76   1994
324.9749'043'0202—dc20   93-37996
                                          CIP

British Cataloging-in-Publication information available

Interior design by Judith Martin Waterman of Martin-Waterman Associates

For Carolyn,
with love

★ Contents ★

He saw elections as heroic clashes of men and ideology that offered insight into the nation's mood.

—Tom Rosenstiel, writing about Theodore H. White, in
Strange Bedfellows

Fifteen years ago, through the sort of happenstance that life stories re-volve around, I moved to New Jersey with my wife, Carolyn, and our one-year-old daughter. I had lost my job as an associate editor of *Rolling Stone* magazine in a staff shakeup, and one of the young writers I had dealt with there had joined the staff of a magazine called *New Jersey Monthly*. He told me the magazine was looking for someone to be the editor, and I ended up getting the job and moving to Princeton, where the magazine was published. I had spent two years in Princeton as a graduate student at the Woodrow Wilson School of Public and International Affairs in 1969 and 1970, but I had never expected to return.

From that time on, I have poured myself into learning about New Jersey. At first, I had to learn the geography and the ethos of various places. Later, I would concentrate on state politics and issues. The reces-sion of 1982 cost me my job at *New Jersey Monthly* as the magazine's staff was pared down to make it a more saleable property to some new owner. In May of that year, I hooked up with New Jersey Network (NJN), the state's public television system, as an interviewer and special correspondent. Since then I have been churning out pieces and interviews on aspects of New Jersey public life almost daily. Around 1985 my title at NJN became senior political correspondent, and I have been covering New Jersey politics and government ever since.

This is the third governor's race I've covered for NJN. In 1985 I covered Tom Kean's re-election rout of a Democratic whiz kid named Peter Shapiro. In 1989 I covered Jim Florio's methodical march to mandate-ville over Republican Jim Courter, who cooperated by self-destructing on questions of abortion and homosexuality. Nothing in New Jersey politics is as compelling as the quadrennial contest to determine who will be the Big Cheese in this state for the next four years. We accord our governors a status, I believe, higher than governors in most other states enjoy. In other states there are celebrities in many fields, not to mention big-city mayors, overshadowing the governor. Somehow here, in this small, fragmented state pulled magnetically in opposite directions, the celebrities tend to be regional figures. Only the governor and perhaps a U.S. senator or a super-star like Bruce Springsteen command statewide recognition and identifi-cation as symbols of the whole state. Our governor is also said to have more appointive and executive power than any other state's governor, by virtue of the way we redesigned the office in the Constitutional Conven-tion of 1947.

The idea to keep a journal of the 1993 race grew out of an interview I did with Bill Clinton in the fall of 1992. Although he passed through New Jersey many times during his election year, and I covered him most of those times, the only time I got a one-on-one with the future president was on his visit to Drew University for a hastily arranged campaign stop on September 30. I got it through the good offices of Susan Thomases, a New York lawyer who had managed Bill Bradley's first U.S. Senate campaign and who was the scheduler for the Clinton campaign. I was granted five minutes with Clinton, which I used to ask three ques-tions: one about Ross Perot, who was about to jump back into the race; one about Jim Florio, because this was a local interview for local television, and because Republicans here were trying to link Clinton to Florio's tax policies; and one about what it felt like to be on the verge of the presi-dency (my "Barbara Walters" question). On Florio, my follow-up ques-tion was whether Clinton regarded Jim Florio as a courageous politician. Clinton thought for a second and said, "Well, he's not uncourageous," an answer, I would later learn, at least one Florio aide was not pleased with.

Clinton was on a tight time leash, so my producer and I hustled out of the room as quickly as we could. But the cameraman stayed behind to pack up his gear. He came out a while later and told us that after we'd left, Clinton had turned to Harold Hodes, his New Jersey advisor and a big-time lobbyist here in the state, and asked, "How did I do on the Florio question?" Hodes assured Clinton that he had done fine. "I don't want to come off like a chickenshit," said Clinton. Hodes assured him that he had not.

It was stories like this that I enjoyed telling to friends and co-workers. But there was no way ever to tell such a story on television. Around that time, either my wife or I (we don't remember which) suggested to the other that a backroom account of the upcoming governor's race would make for interesting reading. And so this project was born.

As a story, the governor's race would have a number of things going for it. The lead character, Jim Florio, is a complex mixture of idealism, pragmatism, and opportunism. Elected by 61 percent of the public in November of 1989, he fell so far so fast after hiking taxes in 1990 by a record amount that his quest for re-election became also a quest for redemption and vindication on an almost epic scale. For a few shining months after his inauguration, Florio took bold steps on auto insurance, gun control, and ethics, and was hailed on the cover of the *New York Times Magazine* as a model Democrat for the '90s. Then, after hiking the sales tax by a penny, extending it to new items, doubling the income tax on the wealthy and using the proceeds for a new education funding system that favored the poor districts and capped the rich ones, his approval rating went from 42 percent in March of that year to 18 percent in October. Regardless of who his Republican opponent turned out to be, the election would be "about" Jim Florio's first term, his effectiveness, his leadership style, and whether a majority of the people now agreed with him that he made the right decisions.

The outcome of that referendum would conceivably send a message to politicians throughout America. If Florio were to win, it could mean that raising taxes is not the kiss of death that conventional wisdom said it was throughout the late 1980s and early 1990s. If Florio were to lose, it could make American politicians more gun-shy about raising taxes through the remainder of this century.

Although readers would know how the story ended before they even picked up the book, there were other thing that would make this race a compelling tale: the presence of two smart Republicans battling for the nomination from the beginning, one of them a "glamour" candidate ("the woman who almost knocked off Bill Bradley"), the other a solid practitioner of the art of government; the possible entry of a Ross Perot-like businessman, either Republican or independent; the likelihood that two highly respected Washington political consultants, James Carville and Ed Rollins, would end up matching wits against each other here if Christie Whitman, as expected in many quarters, were to win the Republican primary; and the unpredictability of any campaign for high office conducted under modern media scrutiny.

Covering the race almost daily, for the television station that takes it more seriously than any other, I knew I would have the equivalent of a ringside seat. My aim in this journal has been to tell you what I saw and what I thought as the story unfolded. I want to give you a sense of what it's like to cover one of these races, especially as a television reporter. And while I don't intend for this to be a complete record of everything that happened, I do want it to be a living document of the 1993 governor's race, so that it becomes the best way for fans of New Jersey politics to capture the moment and the best single source about this election for future students of New Jersey politics. I've tried to write it so that aspiring TV political reporters in Iowa or Alaska might also find it of interest.

A word about my method and my biases. I wrote most of this on the day an event happened, usually at night, at home, after covering the event for NJN. Sometimes I include statements that were made to me "on background" or off the record, on the assumption that the person didn't want to be quoted at the time in the heat of battle but will not mind being quoted after the fact. I also occasionally divulge here something I chose not to share with viewers of my reports—such as the second time I saw Cary Edwards get emotional and fight back tears—in the interests of a full and unfettered presentation.

Readers may wonder about my own political leanings as they read this. If you can figure them out, be my guest. My aim here, as in my television reporting, is to be neutral, balanced, and at the same time honest with myself and with you. The ultimate accolade you can bestow on a reporter is "fair," and on a political reporter, "I don't know which party he supports."

Finally, a heartfelt thanks to Carolyn and our three daughters, Leah, Nina, and Alexa, for their love, patience, and support.

★ Acknowledgments ★

Like a political campaign, a book involves teamwork. Marlie Wasserman, editor-in-chief of Rutgers University Press, embraced the concept, nurtured it, and did a wonderful job of pruning, shaping, and sharpening the manuscript. Judith Martin Waterman copyedited and designed the book with as much sensitivity and precision as any writer could ask for. I also want to thank Marilyn Campbell, Kate Harrie, Tricia Politi, Steve Maikowski, and Kenneth Arnold of RUP for their support and effort.

The book also would not have been possible without the help of my colleagues at NJN. Many of them are mentioned in these pages. Those who are not and who helped me cover the race include Ray Cardoza, Maureen Duffy, Harvey Fisher. Frank Foley, Peggy George, Judy Goetz, Jim Hamilton, Scott Kremer, Sandy Levine, Tim O'Sullivan, Joy Purdy, Ed Rodgers, Kent St. John, Pat Sangimino, Rich Scott, Margie Smith, Bob Wick, and John Williams.

I also would like to thank my sister-in-law, Linda Braun, for her generous enthusiasm and her advice about the ways of the book industry; my mother, Joan Aron, for being a great fan and an active clipping service; Frank Capece, for sending clippings from the papers I don't see; Charles Arbogast of the Associated Press for giving Carolyn useful tips about jockeying for position among photographers; and all of the people who talked to me.

PART ONE

Warming up

Tomorrow, it appears, Bill Clinton is going to be elected the forty-second president of the United States. Among those who will benefit is Governor Jim Florio of New Jersey. Florio has to stand for re-election in 1993. He has had a tremendously difficult time in his first term, because he raised taxes early on and got frozen in an image-warp as The Governor Who Tried to Be Bold and Ended Up Alienating His People. This reputation has carried far beyond the borders of this state. Florio has been trying to shed it for two years now. "President" Clinton could help.

In the eighties, the New Jersey Division of Travel and Tourism adopted the slogan New Jersey and You: Perfect Together. Though corny, it clicked and caught on. Since then, it has been played upon in numerous political speeches and rubber-chicken circuit after-dinner remarks (Florio and Taxes: Perfect Together). In its desperation this fall, the New Jersey Republican party tried to push the slogan Clinton and Florio: Perfect Together, thinking it would hurt Clinton in this state. Republican national chairman Rich Bond even came to the New Jersey Statehouse in Trenton and stood next to a cardboard cutout of the two men with Clinton's arm around Florio and proclaimed that Clinton, like Florio, would raise everybody's taxes. It didn't seem to work. Despite Florio's lingering unpopularity (which may not be as fierce as it once was), voters did not seem moved by the Republican tactic.

And then last night Florio got a "golden embrace" from Clinton.

The Brendan Byrne Arena in the New Jersey Meadowlands Sports Complex was the scene of a gala send-off for the Clinton campaign's final day. It was Bill and Al's excellent rock-and-roll finale featuring Michael Bolton, Bon Jovi, Glenn Close, Richard Gere, Gregory Hines, and other celebrities. All the big New Jersey Democratic politicians sat on stage behind the podium—Bill Bradley, Frank Lautenberg, Jim Florio, various congressmen, candidates, and camp followers. First Tipper Gore spoke, then Hillary Clinton, then Al Gore. When a hoarse Bill Clinton finally made his way up onto the stage (almost floating up from the force of the adulation in the hall), he started pumping hands as he moved along the front row of Jersey dignitaries. When he got to Florio, he threw his arm around the governor—in a gesture that seemed spontaneous and real.

Today I spoke to a Democrat who spent fourteen hours with Jim Florio yesterday. We both agreed that that embrace meant a lot. It meant that Bill Clinton is not afraid to link himself politically and karmically with Jim Florio two nights before the biggest election of Clinton's life. (The event was being carried on C-SPAN, where I saw it and, presumably, thousands of others did, too; it was also being satellite-fed to Clinton rallies in nine other states.) "The Clinton people aren't dumb," said this Democrat. "They wouldn't do this if it were dangerous." He saw it as a sign that Florio's image is on the mend. He and many others think a Clinton presidency would be a real tonic for the Florio re-election effort. "Clinton will be popular for at least a year," he said, "and fortunately that's our year."

★ Wednesday, November 4 ★

Clinton's win last night reverberated through the NJN studios in suburban Trenton, where we were putting on our election-night broadcast. I was in the conversation pit, doing on-air analysis with our regular Democrat and Republican duo, Jim McQueeny and Roger Bodman. Most of the sixty or seventy people who worked on the program were Clinton supporters (the liberal media, you know), and you could sense an air of excitement as the result unfolded.

New Jersey politicos are so hung up on gubernatorial politics, however, that it wasn't five minutes into the telecast before we were all speculating on the effects of a Clinton win on the '93 New Jersey race. It was the second question asked by senior correspondent Sandra King, who was at New Jersey Clinton headquarters in New Brunswick interviewing Senator Frank Lautenberg. When later she put the same question to Florio, the governor, who can be ever-so-humble and ever-so-modest when you're looking for him to crow about himself a bit, demurred and said it would be nice to have a "kindred spirit" in Washington. He would leave it to others to state the obvious: that this was a big boost for him.

Up at New Jersey Bush headquarters, in Parsippany, the two likeliest Republican gubernatorial candidates were each trying to spill water on this little fire, in interviews with Larry Stuelpnagel, NJN's Statehouse correspondent. Christie Whitman, the putative front-runner, was not particularly close to the George Bush apparatus; Bush had failed to campaign for her in her 1990 near-upset of Senator Bill Bradley. (A Whitman aide believes that was because Bush did not want to antagonize Bradley, who was seen at the time as a possible presidential candidate in '92.) So Whitman had very little at stake in Bush's re-election, and she sounded that way as she told NJN viewers that a Clinton win wouldn't affect her decision to run one way or the other.

The other leading Republican, former state attorney general Cary Edwards, was more combative. He made the peculiar leap in logic that the Republican Bush's loss meant bad news for Democrat Jim Florio—because just as the public had turned out an incumbent who was ignoring its economic plight, it would do so again next year. Bad news for incumbents, that was Edwards's spin on the night. Asked what solutions he might have for New Jersey's problems, Edwards asked for sixty to ninety more days to ponder them.

The presidential election ended last night. The race for governor technically begins today.

The New Jersey papers have been full of spin articles on how the Clinton victory will affect the gubernatorial race. It seems clear that it helps Florio, in the following ways. First, it means that a President Clinton can come in and campaign for Florio, or be the guest at a fund-raiser, or both. If Clinton is still popular next fall, that helps. Since New Jersey and Virginia are the only states that hold statewide elections after a presidential year, the New Jersey election may come to be seen as a referendum on Clinton's first year, giving the president that much more reason to help. The fact that James Carville, Clinton's campaign strategist, repeated this week his intention to come to New Jersey to work for Jim Florio means there will be a natural conduit between the political teams of each man. If Florio needs help, and Carville calls the White House for a favor, his call will at least get answered. No one seems certain whether Carville will actually come here and run the campaign on the ground, or advise it from Washington, perhaps dispatching his partner, Paul Begala, to run it day-to-day. We shall see. Psychologically, this is a potentially important factor in the race, because Carville is revered by Democrats, admired by members of the press, like me, who dealt with him during the 1988 Frank Lautenberg race, and genuinely feared by state Republicans, who saw what he did in 1988 to their Senate candidate, the former West Point All-American halfback and Rhodes Scholar Pete Dawkins.

A second way President Clinton can help Jim Florio is by freeing up federal funds for New Jersey, particularly the $450 million in Medicaid reimbursements the state feels it is entitled to but that the Bush administration continually withheld. Next year will be the fourth straight difficult budget year for the state; $450 million, in a budget of $15 billion, would help.

Florio aides and the governor himself press a third argument, the idea that a governor and a president "philosophically in tune" will appeal to voters. They say that an activist president will make an activist governor look more respectable, and less like a freak.

Although Clinton carried the state by only two percentage points (43%, to 41% for Bush, with Perot getting 16%), perceptually a win is a win is a win. The fact that Clinton won here is being seen as proof that the link to Jim Florio didn't work or that Florio's name is not the poison it once was thought to be.

At his post-election news conference on Wednesday, Florio seemed unusually relaxed.

★ Tuesday, November 17 ★

The Republican most people expect to get the gubernatorial nomination is Christine Todd Whitman, a forty-six-year-old upper-class woman of modern ideas but old-fashioned Republican cloth-coat style. She is the daughter of the late Webster Todd, who was Republican state chairman from 1964 to 1969, again from 1974 to 1977, and was a GOP potentate for several decades. But that's not what she's known for. She was virtually unknown until 1990, when she volunteered to be the sacrificial lamb who would run against and lose to Senator Bill Bradley, at the time still widely regarded as New Jersey's living legend. Instead, she came within a percent or two of unseating him. He spent $12 million. She spent $1 million. Polls never picked up how close the race would be, so we were all the more stunned on the NJN set that election night as the returns poured in and after 43 percent of the vote had been counted, Whitman actually led Bradley.

From that moment on, Christie Whitman has been projected, and has allowed herself to be projected, as a future candidate for governor. Her experience is relatively limited. She served for five years as a Somerset County freeholder (the New Jersey equivalent of a county supervisor). In 1988 Republican governor Tom Kean appointed her to the Board of Public Utilities, where, with his blessing, she became its president, a cabinet position. But that's about it. She is a graduate of Wheaton College in Massachusetts, tall and thin, with a short, no-nonsense haircut and a penchant for bright-colored, loosely tailored suits and flat shoes. She is married to an investment banker named John. They have two teenagers, Kate, fifteen, and Taylor, fourteen. A week before the 1990 election she took reporters to a rifle range to show off her skills as a marksman (and to energize voters who belonged to the National Rifle Association) and explained that she had grown up with a gun in her hand, shooting skeet in her father's backyard in the Somerset hills, the fanciest, or at least horsiest, section of the state. "Tom Kean in pearls," someone once called her, a reference to the patrician heritage she shares with New Jersey's former governor.

To build a gubernatorial candidacy, Whitman immediately got herself a radio show and a newspaper column. Then, in March of 1991, she and a few of her supporters created the Committee for an Affordable New Jersey, a Political Action Committee (PAC). Whitman was its chairman. For eighteen months it raised money and dispensed money to Republican candidates for office. Based in a nondescript office building in a vast wasteland of office-industrial space in the center of the state, it served as a base from which Christie Whitman could go forth each day and meet Republicans. That seems to be pretty much what she did for eighteen months. Then last week she announced she was stepping down as chairman of her PAC. Today she announced she's forming a new committee, People for Whitman '93, to raise money to help her explore the possibility of a candidacy.

Whitman's chief aide all this time has been Kayla Bergeron, a thirty-year-old operative who is good at talking up her boss and discrediting the opposition. Bergeron ran the 1990 campaign against Bill Bradley and has been at Christie's side ever since. Today Kayla asked me if I would be interested in working for the campaign, presumably as press secretary. She said my name keeps coming up in conversation. I didn't tell her that I had been approached with the same feeler at the Republican National Convention by another Whitman operative, Hazel Gluck, a former Kean cabinet officer and now a lobbyist who will either manage the campaign or play some other large role in it. In September I told Hazel I liked what I was doing and it would be difficult for me to argue that Jim Florio's attempts to shift school aid to poor kids in urban schools was misguided. Nonetheless, it's flattering that they're still talking about me.

Just when I thought Cary Edwards might be having doubts about running against the formidable Christie Whitman, the former state attorney general surprised everyone by declaring his candidacy today. He did it in strange fashion, putting out a news release this morning saying that he was filing campaign papers with the Election Law Enforcement Commission and, by the way, he would be a candidate. No exploratory committees, he said. No game playing. No gimmickry.

There was also no press conference. Instead, reporters had to troop to his law office across the street from the Statehouse in ones and twos for interviews. When I arrived for mine, two reporters from the *New York Times* were in with him, and two from the *Asbury Park Press* were in waiting.

Cary Edwards is fifty years old, outgoing, slightly overweight, and appealing to those who have observed him over the years. He's smart, aggressive, and likes to talk. Although he claims not to like the campaigning part of politics and to be more interested in governing, he's a pretty good glad-hander. He lives way up in Oakland, almost two hours north of Trenton by car—a commute he made almost daily as Tom Kean's chief counsel and, later, as his attorney general.

My first awareness of him was in 1980, when I was editing *New Jersey Monthly* magazine. We dreamed up a feature called "80 People to Watch in the '80s" (stole it, actually, from other city/regional magazines), and our writer Randall Rothenberg, who would later go to work at the *New York Times*, nominated Edwards for inclusion. At the time, Edwards was a relatively young state assemblyman from Bergen County, where Rothenberg also hailed from, which is how he knew about Edwards. The selection seemed prescient two years later when Kean was the governor and Edwards was one of his top aides. As chief counsel, Edwards was deeply involved in preparing the budget and was in charge of relations with the legislature. He was well regarded by almost all in the press.

Somewhere around the time of his landslide re-election in 1985, Kean made Edwards attorney general. It seemed a reward for good work done. As AG, Edwards was one of the great self-promoters. He called press conferences at the drop of a hat—to announce indictments, to announce reorganization plans for any of the eleven divisions, such as motor vehicles, that fall under the attorney general's purview. He was good on television, and came across as a forceful activist. He was also a moderate Republican in the Kean mold, more interested in pragmatic solutions to problems than in ideology or party positions.

Cary's drawbacks as a politician are stylistic. Although many in the press find him charismatic, he has a face that can look like an unhappy hound dog's. He speaks with a thick tongue and sometimes sounds like he was up too late the night before (maybe he was). He's about six foot one, and now that he's joined the Mudge, Rose, Guthrie, Alexander, and Ferdon law firm—Richard Nixon's old firm—he wears nice suits that don't show much gut, but there's a sluggishness about his bearing that could be mistaken for dullness.

But dull he's not. In 1989 he ran for the Republican nomination to succeed Tom Kean and finished second. There are some who feel Kean betrayed him by not endorsing him in the primary. There were five major Republican candidates that spring, and two others had almost equal claim on Kean's allegiance, including the eventual winner, Congressman Jim Courter. Then Courter got swamped by Jim Florio in the general election, after making some terrible blunders, and many people said that if Edwards had gotten the nomination, with his superior knowledge of state government he'd have possibly beaten Florio.

Which brings us to today. There was an oddly disorganized air around Edwards today. We were in a lovely old brownstone across from the Statehouse on West State Street, the Mudge, Rose, Trenton office. Two key campaign operatives were there, Jeff Michaels and Bill Palatucci—both young, aggressive Republicans with track records. But when I walked into the office that looks out onto the street, Edwards joked about how manic he was feeling. He said someone told him you have to be crazy to run for governor a second time, knowing how arduous it can be, and he admitted to feeling slightly crazy. There's something vaguely impolitic about these admissions. As a journalist, I appreciate it. If I were managing the campaign, I might want someone a little more buttoned-down. Subliminally, it suggests a lack of discipline.

From his statements in our interview, and from his news release, it is clear that Edwards will position himself as more experienced than Whitman and more in touch with the hardships of the working class ("I grew up in a single-parent household . . ."). He also plans to stress the crime issue and his background as the state's chief law enforcement officer. The state has been plagued with violent crimes of a shocking nature in recent months. Rape-murders and carjackings top the list. If Cary Edwards can hold out the promise of safer streets, he just might get elected. And that is exactly what he promised in my interview with him today. It was the last sound bite in my package. He mangled it a bit, stumbling over the words "street," "safe," and "state," but he got the point across, and, hey, it's still early.

He'll formally kick off his campaign sometime next month.

★ **Friday, December 18** ★

The Republican primary has its first flap. In a one-on-one newspaper interview the other day, Cary Edwards was critical of his old boss Tom Kean. He said the Kean administration had been good at policy but not especially good at "management." The Bergen *Record*, one of the state's four most influential newspapers, played it up. "Cary Edwards starts his run for governor," said the headline, and beneath it: "Criticizes both Florio and ex-boss Kean."

This morning Kean's old press secretary, Carl Golden, told me off the record that various Keanites around the state are furious at Edwards. They see it as disloyal. Edwards was Kean's right-hand man. The fact that he now appeared to be distancing himself from Kean is a sign of how Kean's near-godlike status has been tarnished during the Florio era. Under Kean state spending doubled, from $6 billion a year to $12 billion, in the years 1981 to 1989. In the current climate, such behavior has come to seem profligate in some eyes, especially to conservative Republicans, who were never as enamored of Kean as the rest of the state. Conservative Republicans can be important in a Republican primary.

Golden wondered whether Edwards's criticism was a calculated appeal to the right or a slip of the tongue. I soon had occasion to find out.

Jeff Michaels, who will be Edwards's campaign manager, was in our studio today, along with Hazel Gluck from the Whitman camp and former Democratic senate president John Russo, for a discussion of next year's race. I wasn't doing the interview, but I watched the taping and hung out afterwards to catch Michaels alone. I pulled him aside and asked if the Kean remark was intentional or a mistake. With surprising candor, Michaels said, "He talked too much. That's all it was, Michael."

This morning in the Newark *Star-Ledger*, the state's most influ-ential paper, Kean is quoted as taking issue with Edwards's remark, but, at the same time, saying Edwards would make a "superb" governor. Michaels touted that on the air and told me that Edwards had been mortified at how his stray comment had been blown out of proportion by the Bergen *Record* and had called Kean yesterday. I wondered if Edwards, or Kean, had called David Wald, the *Star-Ledger*'s political reporter, and planted this new story, or whether Wald just called Kean for reaction. It certainly seemed as if Kean were forgiving his wayward son.

Golden said it was stupid for Cary to have announced his candi-dacy the way he did, without a press conference. "A parade of one-on-ones is a mistake. You get trapped," he said. "Edwards hurt himself."

I called Hazel Gluck, the Whitman advisor, to ask if she thought Edwards's line had been intentional or a mistake. "I'm sure Cary never meant to disavow Tom, just to separate himself slightly." (Gluck and Edwards had served together in the Kean cabinet.) Off the record she told me that Whitman also had called Kean right away, and Kean had told her that, if asked, he would say the same thing about her—that she, too, would make a superb governor.

Maybe I'll try to ask him, on camera, next week. Meanwhile, I think we've seen that Cary Edwards has a tendency to shoot off his mouth. Or at least he likes to talk—like Bill Clinton.

Carl Golden told me that he, too, had been approached to be communications director for the Whitman campaign. Golden is a very savvy old hand, in his mid-fifties, a wiry, nervous little guy who was Tom Kean's press secretary and gets some of the credit for Kean's good image. He now is chief spokesman for the New Jersey Supreme Court and the rest of the judicial system. He said he was interested in the Whitman job (interesting that he would work against his former fellow Kean inner-sanctum member Edwards), but that after Whitman hired Ed Rollins to be her consultant, things changed. Rollins is the Washington operative who managed Ronald Reagan's campaign in 1984 and served briefly as Ross Perot's ticket to respectability in June and July of this year. Rollins apparently made up a budget for the Whitman campaign, and it didn't include much for a press secretary. "There are three things Ed Rollins wants to spend that money on," Golden cracked. "TV advertising. Direct mail. And Ed Rollins."

On the Democratic side, there was a sighting this week of James Carville, the hottest political consultant in America right now. Dan Weissman, a veteran reporter in the *Star-Ledger*'s Statehouse bureau, saw Carville crossing West State Street from the Statehouse toward the headquarters of the Democratic State Committee. He wrote a short item about it, which appeared on an inside page of the *Ledger*, but for political people it was the most intriguing story in the paper that day. It said that Carville and his partner, Paul Begala, had slipped into town quietly, had met with Florio at the Statehouse, and that the meeting had then moved across the street. The story said that strategy was not discussed, just "themes." Carville apparently wouldn't say much to Weissman. The only quote in the story from Carville was in response to the question of why he had come. "Because Joe Salema called me," was the answer. Salema is Governor Florio's chief of staff and chief political advisor.

Later Weissman told me another quote had been cut from his story. When Weissman asked why Salema had called him, Carville, whose mother published a Cajun cookbook, said, "I'm here to give Joe Salema a recipe. Elephant stew."

★ Monday, December 21 ★

Today Governor Florio nominated 16 women lawyers to be judges. When you're running against a woman—or could be—it helps to have some women in your corner.

If confirmed, the 13 going to superior court will bring to 62 the number of women in the state's main court system, out of 377 judges total.

And counting the tax court and other courts, Florio will have appointed 44 women judges in three years' time, as compared to 34 appointed by Tom Kean over an eight-year period.

Last spring the New Jersey chapter of NOW (the National Organization for Women) held a press conference to give the governor a grade of "F" for his record on appointments of women to high positions. The criticism didn't really ring true; Jim Florio has four women in his cabinet, has a key woman advisor, and has named plenty of woman judges. But the charge was made, and Florio must not want to go into an election year with it hanging over his head. His staff billed today's announcement as "the greatest single advancement of women in the history of New Jersey," and it probably was.

The appointments were my story on tonight's newscast. At a press availability in his outer office this morning, another TV reporter and I asked the governor about them. In television, you try not to ask a question that can be answered yes or no, because that way you may not get much elaboration and, therefore, no sound bite. So I asked "to what extent is this move a reaction to the recent criticism by women's groups?" "It's not," Florio said in a very clipped fashion. "To what extent is it based on an awareness that you may be running against a woman next year?" I asked. "It's not," was all he said again.

But I found the exchange revealing, and I wanted to demonstrate to the governor that giving short answers wouldn't necessarily protect him, so I included the exchange in my report. As we were assembling the piece in the edit room and came to that bite, my editor, Cindy Carpenter, watched it on the screen as she laid it into the master tape and said, "Oooh, Michael. He doesn't like you." "Naaa," I said confidently, hoping she was wrong.

★ Tuesday, December 22 ★

On Sunday the *Star-Ledger* and Trenton *Times* had articles about Edwards's criticism of Tom Kean. Today it was my turn to do the Kean story, except as a TV reporter I can't just pick up the phone, I have to actually go see him. Which is fine. You get to experience more that way.

It takes nearly an hour and a half to drive from our station in suburban Trenton to Drew University, where Kean is president. Drew is a lovely little college, in the lovely little town of Madison, in heavily Republican Morris County.

At fifty-five, Kean is still the big, affable gentleman who presided over this state in its boom years and rode the boom to record popularity. He is a moderate Republican, maybe even a liberal Republican in the old, Nelson Rockefeller mode. As governor, he was slightly more standoffish, in my experience, than Jim Florio is—but the public didn't see that. The public took to Tom Kean and his big grin and his New England-patrician accent acquired at prep school, because he was decent and down-to-earth, as well as clever and lucky. The public finds Jim Florio a cold fish, or arrogant, or out for himself—at least much of the public does. They don't get to see the gracious side of Jim Florio, who is always polite and solicitous of others in public. Somehow it doesn't come through the media quite as readily as it did with Kean. In my eight years covering him, Kean never let me and a camera crew into his small private office. Florio does routinely, and Florio is more inclined to make a little small talk. It's stiff, but the attempt is made.

Today, however, Kean was pretty talkative. We spent about ten minutes on camera, talking about the Edwards flap. He was totally forgiving of Edwards, praised him to the skies, and did the same for Christie Whitman. Yes, she, too, would make a "superb" governor, he told me, and of course I used that in my piece tonight. It advanced the story. I suspect he was privately a little miffed at Edwards, but he certainly didn't let on. On the key subject of which one he might endorse, if either, he naturally said he would probably not make an endorsement—unless one of them clearly outperforms the other. If that happens, he said, he might endorse the one with the best chance of winning in the general election. My guess is that he won't endorse. It's not like Tom Kean to stick his neck out. He didn't in '89. There was no compelling reason then, or now, for him to risk alienating half the people in his own party.

While the set-up shots were being taken and after the camera was turned off, we chatted for about half an hour. That's something you can do with an ex-governor that you can't do with a sitting governor. He told me about the feeler he had gotten from the Clinton camp about being secretary of education, which he said he discouraged, just as he had turned down a strong offer, he said, from President Bush, of the same job about eighteen months ago. (The president doesn't ask if you're interested unless he knows you'll say yes, Kean said. Intermediaries always ask first, so you never have to say no to the president.)

I asked him how tough it will be for a Republican to beat Jim Florio. Very, he said, sounding like he meant it. He named three factors. The first was money. He said Florio can raise great sums of money, and that even though there's a ceiling on what candidates can spend on themselves, there is no limit on what the parties can spend on generic promotion. Next, the governor has a built-in media advantage. He has direct access to the press. "He can open his door and the press will be there," Kean said. Third, the governor has a built-in staff. Technically, they are not supposed to do political work on state time, but, of course, to one extent or another, many do; the Republican candidate will have to pay his staff of ten or twenty out of campaign funds, while the governor's regular staff of eighty or ninety is subsidized by the taxpayers.

To hear Kean talk about Florio is to be reminded of the intense rivalry the two have engaged in for more than a decade. Both ran for their party's gubernatorial nomination in 1977 and lost. In 1981 they opposed each other in the governor's race. Florio was expected to win, but in the final six weeks Kean caught up, and the vote on Election Day was so close that a recount was required. After several excruciating weeks in which no one knew who would be New Jersey's next governor, Kean was declared the winner by 1,797 votes out of 2,290,201 cast. It was the closest election in state history.

Kean would go on to preside over New Jersey for eight years during a period in which the economy soared and the state's sense of identity cohered. Kean's approval ratings at one point hit 81 percent. Florio went back to Congress, nursed his wounds, and plotted his revenge. He sat out the 1985 race. In 1989 Florio came back with a softer voice than the shrill technocratic lecturer of 1981 and with a new wife, a photogenic blond elementary-school teacher named Lucinda, whose hand he held almost perpetually, for support and, perhaps, as well for the image it conveyed of a warmer man.

Since 1989 Florio and Kean have danced the peculiar dance of two men who have shared a unique experience. They will still speak critically of one another, but circumstance throws them together in public every few months, and they show deference and understanding toward one another in such circumstances.

Kean had told me about the technical advantages a sitting governor enjoys in his re-election year. How about policy, I wondered, and attitudes toward Florio? Kean said he thinks Florio's standing is "certainly better than a year ago, but still not great." He said, "A lot of people tell me they still don't like him. You've got to overcome that. One way to do that is to go on television. But he's not good on television. If people look at you on television and say, 'I don't like the guy,' it probably helps to stay off television. I hear people say that when he goes on television, he hurts himself."

Well, of course, that is in the eye of the beholder. I have heard people say Florio is weak on TV, but I don't see that. I have watched dozens and dozens of hours of Jim Florio on videotape over the years, and I think he comes across reasonably well. Except, of course, when he gives a weaselly answer, like he did to me yesterday.

★ Friday, January 1, 1993 ★

The campaign took some time off in late December, and so did I. Jim Florio went to Florida during the week after Christmas. He has taken very few vacations since becoming governor. He is not the sort who likes to lose control of anything for very long. Cary Edwards and Christie Whitman exchanged one round of hostile press releases about ten days ago, and then they kept quiet. The releases were silly. Edwards charged that Whitman was misleading the public by filing candidate papers with the Election Law Enforcement Commission while continuing to say in mailings to Republicans that she is exploring a "possible" candidacy. Actually, Edwards himself didn't make the charge. It was his campaign manager, Jeff Michaels, who harrumphed about the voters of New Jersey being "tired of political double talk." It was met with return fire from Congressman Dick Zimmer, a Whitman campaign co-chair, who called it a "desperate" ploy for attention and a "personal attack." The flap produced a round of stories on how "nasty" the GOP primary has become already, but I don't think anybody took it very seriously. Reporters are eager to write about the race, and will seize on the slightest conflict at this early stage. Later, when there are differences of substance, these tactical cries of foul over flying elbows will be ignored in all but the most egregious cases.

Another round of year-end newspaper stories has been devoted to Jim Florio's good positioning heading into the election year. It is quite remarkable that Florio and the Republican legislative leaders, after a year of feuding, sniping, and serious partisan game playing, have come together and reached quick compromises on some major issues. On health care, for example, they met a self-imposed November 30 deadline and significantly redesigned the health-care system in this state. A week later they unveiled a major bond refinancing scheme designed to free up some money for next year's budget. It was the kind of thing they'd have screamed at each other about last year. This year they agreed to it in a week and made it law in ten days.

Both houses of the legislature were controlled by Democrats in Florio's first two years as governor. Then the Republicans swept to veto-proof majorities in 1991 on the strength of voter backlash against the 1990 tax hikes. In 1992 the two parties jockeyed over taxes and spending more fiercely than ever. The legislature overrode Florio's veto in order to cut the sales tax by a penny and overrode another veto to cut a billion dollars out of the budget. No governor had ever vetoed a state budget before.

Now, in '93, Governor Florio is trying to get the fiscal issue off the table. He is trying to craft a 1993–94 budget that Republicans will buy into and be part of, so that they can't attack it, or him, once the campaign gets going in earnest. He has already gotten the health-care issue off the table. And by a stroke of luck—or maybe not—the auto-insurance issue is also leaving the field of play, by virtue of Allstate Insurance Company's sudden announcement that it has reversed its decision to leave New Jersey and will stay after all. Auto insurance is a political fireball in New Jersey. It was probably the number-one issue in the 1989 gubernatorial campaign. Florio got elected on a promise to do away with the state's massively indebted assigned-risk pool, the Joint Underwriting

Association (JUA), which he did. But his Fair Auto Insurance Reform Act of 1990 enraged the insurance industry, which was assessed for much of the JUA debt. Allstate, the state's largest auto insurer, sued the governor. Florio, in one of his more colorful and memorable bits of repartee, said, "They call themselves the 'good hands' people—only trouble is, they don't tell you which part of your anatomy they have their good hands around." In mid-1991 Allstate announced it was leaving the state of New Jersey because it was impossible to make a profit here. The company said it was losing tens of millions of dollars a year. The Florio administration said, baloney, the company was actually making money, and promised to drag out Allstate's withdrawal for five years. Then, last month, Allstate, in a stunning case of "never mind," said it had decided New Jersey was not such a bad state after all, the company could make money here, and had postponed its decision to withdraw. As part of a deal with the Florio administration, Allstate would kick in $65 million for its share of the JUA debt, and the state Insurance Department would give Allstate a 6.5 percent rate increase. For Governor Florio, it meant that another potential adversary in '93 had been neutralized.

So Florio is being seen in the media as "on the rise" and heading into the election year in better shape than he has been since that fateful first six months of his governorship.

It is in the area of school funding that the governor and the Republican legislative leaders have reached their most stunning compromise of all. For one year only—just this election year—they have agreed to a new school-funding formula that increases state aid to every school district in the state, while a study commission devises a new permanent formula. The commission is to report by next November 15, a week and a half after the election! Florio, who has been portrayed as an urban Robin Hood, willing to rob from the rich and cripple some good school systems in order to prop up the "corrupt" inner-city schools, and the Republicans, who have been portrayed as selfish protectors of their suburban fiefdoms and somewhat racist when it comes to thinking about inner-city schools, have made peace. And education—the most volatile of all issues in this state, even more so than taxes—is also off the table for '93. At least legislatively.

All this fence mending is getting high marks in the press and in the hallways of the Statehouse. Credit for it is going to Joe Salema, the governor's chief of staff, and Bob DeCotiis, his relatively new chief counsel. Some say the idea originated with James Carville and Paul Begala, who supposedly saw while running the Clinton campaign how the public was fed up with gridlock. For all we know, Florio himself is the driving force behind this shift in strategy; I often suspect his aides and advisors are getting credit for moves Jim Florio himself concocts. The presidential election of '92 seems to have convinced Florio, and many politicians and political operatives, that the public is tired of partisan bickering and wants action, or at least cooperation. Ross Perot made gridlock the scourge of American politics, and the conventional politicians have gotten the message.

Jim Florio has been a conventional politician virtually all his adult life, from his first run for state assembly in 1969 through fifteen years as the congressman from the First District, centered in Camden County, through his three years as governor. During that time, he has tried to be adaptable. He is a progressive, liberal Democrat at heart, an activist who believes in governmental solutions to social and human problems. But the experience of 1990 has forced him to try to remold himself. His liberal instincts got him in hot water, and he has been trying to keep them in check and become more of a populist ever since. Thus, in early 1992, he embraced "initiative and referendum," a populist cause that would give citizens here direct law-making power the way they have it in California and other states, a cause Jim Florio had vigorously opposed for twenty years. And now, heading into his re-election year, he is trying to play the statesman, to rise above politics and make compromises with Republicans for the good of the people.

Florio is fifty-five, stands about five foot nine, and has the tight, taut body of a runner and former boxer. He is always meticulously groomed and conservatively dressed (almost always black shoes, hardly ever brown). His still mostly black pompadour is the salient feature that cartoonists like to embellish. Once, from behind a podium, I saw him stand on his toes for the duration of a speech, presumably to look taller.

Born in Brooklyn, the son of a shipyard worker, he dropped out of high school after his junior year in 1955 and joined the Navy. It's been observed that Florio, whose Navy boxing career ended when his left jaw was shattered, is best when he's in a fight. Suddenly, he's making peace with Republicans, and the spectacle is something to behold. The governor seems happy to have hit upon it.

Another quality Florio has displayed over the years, to varying degrees, is intensity. A hard worker to begin with, he has had to work even harder to try to dig himself out of the hole his tax hikes have put him in. One imagines him reading briefing papers after hours, and when those are done, reading the newspapers, and then, when it's time to relax, turning on the television and watching news and public affairs programs or picking up the latest volume of fashionable political theory. Right now, for example, as I write this, it is very late New Year's night, the Bowl games are over, in my house the children are asleep and my wife is upstairs, and I'm pretty sure that neither Christie Whitman, Cary Edwards, Joe Salema, James Carville, or any other Americans are working at the moment. Jim Florio, who lives two miles from me in Drumthwacket, the big white colonial governor's mansion in Princeton, I'm not sure about.

★ Monday, January 11 ★

Tomorrow Governor Florio delivers the annual State of the State address to a joint session of the legislature. NJN will carry it live at two o'clock, and we will rebroadcast it at night, followed by a Republican response.

This morning I got to interview the governor for about ten minutes for a State of the State preview piece for tonight's newscast. The theme of this year's address—as blasted across the front pages of newspapers for the past two days, leaked and parceled out in bits and pieces—is Planning for the Economic Recovery. Jobs is the number-one concern right now, nationally and here in New Jersey, and the governor is trying to ride that wave rather than have it crash over him.

He said some predictable things on camera, and when I tried to get him to state, for the first time, that he will be a candidate for reelection, he continued to play coy. I had prepared six ways of asking the question and used two of them. ("The newspapers keep saying you're 'expected to be a candidate.' Since you don't write letters to the editor saying they are wrong in that assumption, can we assume you are indeed going to run?" "You mean you might *not* run?") He fell for neither but was kind enough to assure me on camera that when he does decide, "you'll be the first to know, because of my high regard for NJN." That always looks good on the air. At least one imagines the bosses like it.

Off camera, he told me he thought he was the underdog, and that he really still had an open mind about the whole proposition, implying he might not run. I expressed skepticism. He tried to convince me he was sincere. He said the decision will depend on how "things play out" in the next couple of months. I thought he meant the economy, but he said, no, he meant how some of what he was doing would be "received" around the state. He spoke in cryptic terms. Later it hit me that he may have been talking about polls. Maybe he needs to see a few more poll results before knowing for sure. Maybe he was just playing with me.

The interview was in the cabinet room, right off his small office. The cabinet room has a large oil painting of former New Jersey governor Woodrow Wilson above a mantelpiece. Florio's office sports a small framed print of FDR, Florio's role model. The Wilson portrait is there permanently; FDR will leave when Florio does.

I was alone in the cabinet room when the governor walked in. He walked right over to me and told me had seen this weekend's "Reporters' Roundtable," a weekly program I host. "Immediately afterward I went to my dictionary," he said, "to look up the word 'fawn.'" This was the week we had invited onto the show as a special guest assembly speaker Garabed ("Chuck") Haytaian, one of Florio's rivals and former nemeses. It had been a good show, I thought, but Florio said the reporters were fawning all over Haytaian, me included. I wasn't sure how serious he was—or whether he was just giving me the needle—but I brushed it off as needling and told him we could start the interview and I would fawn over him.

Cary Edwards is launching a three-day, twenty-one-county bus caravan on Wednesday, to unroll his candidacy formally. If it worked for Clinton and Gore, maybe it will work for him. Edwards has been promising some "scathingly brilliant ideas" for New Jersey for months. That's a direct quote from an interview I did with him at the Republican convention in Houston last August, and it was not said tongue in cheek. The time has come for him to deliver.

Today was one of those days when the Statehouse buzzes with camera crews and political figures—the day of a Big Speech or a Big Vote. The governor gave his address at two o'clock, speaking for about fifty minutes. Florio's speeches over the years have tended to be disappointments, from my vantage point, but I thought this was one of his better ones. David Wald of the *Star-Ledger*, on the other hand, thought it was lousy, or so he told me in the hallway afterward. Reaction to speeches is subjective, I guess.

In my analysis piece on the news tonight I called the speech "future-oriented, conciliatory, and populist." I was impressed by Florio's call for a seven-point plan to make New Jersey the world leader in environmental clean-up technology. It's a clever idea for promoting high-quality jobs with a progressive public policy twist. I don't know how realistic the seven points are, but taken together they sounded good and forward thinking. The speech also contained plenty of homages and appeals to the Republican-controlled legislature, and the governor reiterated his new-found belief in initiative and referendum. He spoke of "empowering" the citizenry, employing this year's most popular political buzzword.

My assignment for the news tonight was to look at the speech as an election-year document. Another reporter would deliver the substance of the speech; I was to analyze its political content. For that I wanted the reactions of Christie Whitman and Cary Edwards. Whitman entered the Statehouse right after the speech to give interviews in the hallway. She noted that today's speech sounded like a "new" Jim Florio, a more "Republican-sounding" Jim Florio, but that the voters wouldn't be fooled.

Cary Edwards was supposed to come over to press row at the Statehouse at four, but when he didn't show up on time, I went across the street to his law office for a quick interview so I wouldn't back up any closer against my six o'clock air time. Edwards gave me a warm greeting. "Just talking about you," he said, as I walked in. Again, as with Florio yesterday, I wasn't sure if he was serious or just toying with me. He, too, reacted to the speech by talking about the "new" Florio, whom he proclaimed just like the '89 Florio, that is a "campaign mode" Florio. He, too, said the voters would remember "the Florio of 1990, '91, and '92."

Off camera, in talking about his preparations for the three-day bus caravan he begins tomorrow, he said he doesn't like to read speeches and prefers to speak extemporaneously. He described himself as a "candid" person, and said that candor sometimes got him in trouble. Like the Kean remark? I asked. Exactly, he said.

In conversations with others around the Statehouse today I got varying opinions of Jim Florio's chances for re-election. The consensus is, he's got a chance, maybe a good chance, maybe he'll even be tough to beat. Dick Leone, a very smart man who is chairman of the Port Authority of New York and New Jersey and once ran for U.S. Senate, said he doesn't know what this election is going to be fought over. It can't be the tax hikes of 1990, he said; that's too old. Something will emerge, he said.

George Norcross, the thirty-six-year-old Camden County Democratic chairman who is reminiscent of an old-style boss, told me he didn't think Florio would win if the election were held today. But Norcross, who is very astute and not terribly fond of Florio, also told me that the "alliance" between Florio and the Republican legislative leaders is working well, in his opinion, for both sides. Norcross understands the finer points of political motivation. In his view the Republican legislative leaders, Chuck Haytaian and Don DiFrancesco, actually want Florio to win re-election, because, assuming they hold onto their majorities and their leadership positions, they'll have more power than they would with a Republican governor. I had not thought of this before, but it makes sense. Right now they are the top Republicans in Trenton and get a lot of attention as the foils of the Democratic governor.

What I like about talking to Norcross is that he's usually two steps ahead of me.

★ Wednesday, January 13 ★

Cary Edwards's wife, Lynn, and their daughters, Kari Lynn and Marci Lynn, were the first Edwardses I saw today. They were in room 319 of the Statehouse, the best room in the building for a press conference, with a whole bunch of Edwards supporters and media and a big red, white, and blue banner saying "CARY EDWARDS, GOVERNOR '93" hanging on the front wall.

This was the fourth stop of the day on the Edwards bus caravan, in the fourth county of the twenty-one Edwards will visit over the next two and a half days. The daughters were cute, suburban, and heavily made up. Kari Lynn, whose name is a combination of her mother's and father's, is twenty and a student in Arizona. Marci Lynn is fifteen. Their mother, Lynn, talks fast, laughs loud, and looks warm. "I'm Lynn and I'm forty-six," she said after hearing me ask the girls their names and ages. "And if you use that on the air I'll kill you."

"The state is broken and needs to be fixed!" Edwards intoned at the beginning of his prepared remarks. Actually, the first thing he said was, "I have a propensity for verbosity . . . and today I'm going to try to keep it short." As I would later see when videotape was fed down to me of his earlier stops in North Jersey, he had made the same supposedly off-the-cuff remark up north.

With about a hundred people looking on, most of them supporters riding a bus for three days around the state, Edwards bashed Jim Florio over the poor condition of New Jersey's economy, promised tough law enforcement from this former law enforcer, and made favorable comparisons between the background and experience of Edwards and the wealthy background and lack of experience of Whitman.

To underscore the difference in backgrounds, Edwards had done his big stop up north this morning in Fair Lawn, in front of a modest house that he and his mother once lived in. Standing in front of the house, with reporters and supporters looking on, he told the story of how his mother had tried to get a mortgage for the house but, being a single woman, was only able to get one if a male cosigned. The male was him, a nineteen-year-old kid cosigning a mortgage so that he and his working mother would have a house.

"The pressures, the pain, and the demands of that time," Edwards said, and then he started flicking a finger at his chin to keep himself from crying. For the longest time he kept flicking—seven, eight seconds maybe. Watching the tape, I thought of Edmund Muskie crying in the snow in 1972 because a New Hampshire newspaper had insulted his wife.

Edwards caught himself and continued on. "None of it was too great for my mother. She's standing behind me." At this point his face contorted again. "She made me what I am." There was relief in the audience that he had gotten through it.

Obviously the man has heart—or else he's a real faker—because at the Statehouse five hours later he did the same thing. He started talking about the house and his mother, and started to lose it again. "I did this this morning, too," he blurted out, shaking his head in apparent surprise at his own emotionalism.

After the speech Edwards asked if the media had any questions. I had one. An NJN North Jersey cameraman, Kirk Sohr, had told me over the phone that after the Fair Lawn event all the people had climbed onto the bus except Cary, who had climbed into a black Lincoln. It was on tape, Sohr said. So I asked.

"Cary, I'm told by one of our cameramen that after an event this morning, everybody else got on the bus, but you got into a black Lincoln Town Car. Is that true?"

I could feel the tension in the room, but Edwards had a good answer. "First of all, it was a Lincoln Continental not a Town Car. And yes, I got into it because several weeks ago I made a commitment to the mayors of Ocean County to speak at their luncheon today, and there was no way I was going to be able to keep that commitment and still get here on the bus. I knew it might give the wrong appearance, but I didn't want to disappoint the mayors, so I took a car. Okay?"

Okay. So much for today's attempt at gotcha.

After a half-dozen more questions from the media—all of which my cameraman, Joe Macklin, rolled on, so that we can replay the event tonight at eleven—I did an interview with the campaign consultant, Jay Smith. Then, in the milling around, I found myself crossing paths with Edwards.

"Feelin' good?" I asked.

"I'm starting to," he said. He looked beat, like a man in the wringer, a wisp of his soft graying hair slightly askew. But he was pumped full of adrenaline and had just given a pretty strong speech. With people around us, he started talking as if he were confiding in me.

"For three years I had one foot in the business world, while the other part of me was still on the front page," he said. "I was trying to build a law business, but I couldn't stay away from what was on the front page. The issues—I just care about them. Nine months ago I started thinking, should I do this? The more I thought and people encouraged me to do it, the more I just had to do it, and here I am. It's my passion."

"Follow your passions," I said, as if it were a mantra we both should live by.

For Edwards, this race is probably his last grab at the brass ring. Whitman could lose and theoretically try again in 1997. But Edwards has been around once before, in 1989, when he finished second to Jim Courter. There is the sense about him that running for office is somehow a confining experience, as if the consultants had asked him to squeeze an outsized personality into a straitjacket. After his 1989 second-place finish, he said to me more than once that he is better at government than at campaigning. He is loquacious and gives long answers to simple questions. There is the tendency he seems to have of saying something that will get him into trouble. The next five and a half months are going to test his intelligence, acuity, and sense of timing.

★ Thursday, January 21 ★

Yesterday Bill Clinton took the oath of office and became the forty-second president of the United States. A contingent of several hundred New Jersey Democrats went to Washington for the four-day extravaganza that Clinton set up for himself—a kind of populist coronation. NJN News went there, too, to look at the inauguration through New Jersey eyes.

My first night there, I went out with a cameraman to the Washington Convention Center, where one of the inaugural dinners was being held. Media were not allowed in, and I was there to get an interview with Bill Bradley on his way in. Instead I interviewed other New Jerseyans as they stepped out of limousines and taxis. Bradley did not show up while I was there, even though his printed schedule said that was where he would be. That Bill Bradley keeps his own timetable is almost a cliché, although it's usually meant in the larger sense.

One New Jerseyan I spoke to was Clay Constantinou, a short Greek-Cypriot-American lawyer, about forty years old, who had been the chief fund-raiser for Clinton in New Jersey. After some serious schmoozing, he said, "Here, you can have this." It was a ticket to a party for James Carville later that evening. "It's good for two people. You can't take your camera in there, but have a good time."

"The Hottest Ticket in Town," said the printed invitation, and indeed it was. The party, at Duke Ziebert's, a popular Washington watering hole, was glitzy. About five hundred people showed up, most of them dressed in their formalwear, having come from one of the inaugural dinners. Carville was the center of attention. He had a constant pool of people around him. Some celebrities were there—Chevy Chase, Kathleen Turner, Christie Brinkley, Catherine O'Hara, Ed Begley, Jr., Senator John Kerry. It was a well-heeled, pretty crowd of yuppies and politicos.

"Hey, Michael," Carville said when he spotted me. I introduced him to my colleague, Larry Stuelpnagel, then hung around and watched the guests flow toward Carville like lava flowing down a hill. Carville's mother, "Miss Nippy," and Virginia Kelley, the mother of Bill Clinton, squealed and hugged as they were introduced to one another for the first time.

"We've got a ways to go, but I think we can pull it out," said Carville, when someone at the party asked about the Florio campaign. All week in Washington I saw a new optimism among Democrats about Florio's chances for re-election.

The first poll of the year had come out on Sunday. It was done by the *Asbury Park Press* and showed that in a head-to-head matchup against Christie Whitman, Whitman would get 36 percent to Florio's 31 percent, with the rest undecided. In a head-to-head match-up against Cary Edwards, Edwards would get 32 percent to Florio's 31 percent, with the rest undecided. These numbers were seen as very good news for Jim Florio. "It completely changes the dynamics of the race," said an aide to one of Florio's rivals in the Democratic party. "It shows that Jim Florio is viable!" Interestingly, the poll also showed that Florio has 97 percent name recognition. Whitman has 38 percent and Edwards 28 percent. That means everyone in New Jersey has heard of Florio. If only a third say they'd vote for him, that's not great. But there is a large bloc of undecided voters.

Florio himself liked the poll. He also liked an article in the Sunday *New York Times* by Wayne King, one of the *Times*'s two Trenton correspondents, that mentioned the poll and called Florio "a phoenix rising from the ashes." It ran on the front of the Metro section. I am sure there is no paper Florio is more concerned about seeing himself portrayed positively in than the *New York Times*. It's the one seen outside New Jersey. It's the one people in Washington are likely to see. Floriocrats said that the poll and the article had buoyed the governor's spirits, and indeed he looked rather self-satisfied when I first saw him in Washington. This was at a breakfast in his honor at the ANA Westin Hotel, the unofficial New Jersey hotel for the week. The breakfast was hosted by the law firm of Clive Cummis, another big Democratic fund-raiser. When Florio and his wife, Lucinda, stepped up to the lectern, the roomful of two hundred or so people got to its feet and chanted, "Four More Years! Four More Years!" It may have been someone on the governor's staff who got the chant started, or it may not have been, but either way the chant worked, because I used it as the opening of my piece on the news that night back in New Jersey.

"Jim's really feeling good," said a PR man who's part of Florio's inner circle of forty or fifty top supporters. "You should have seen it last night at the dinner. Clinton comes in, goes right for the microphone, and guess whose names he mentions? One of them is Nelson Mandela. Who's the other?"

I went out on a limb. "Jim Florio?"

"Jim Florio! Clinton must have scanned the room and those were two faces he recognized near the front of the room where the light was good. Florio and Mandela. You think that makes him feel good?"

Florio does seem to anticipate benefits from his connection to Clinton. Political benefits and governmental benefits. He told me in an interview after the breakfast that his top priorities with Clinton are transportation money, health-care reform, and getting the administration to reverse a Bush administration position and free up $450 million in Medicaid reimbursements that Florio seems truly to believe New Jersey is entitled to (others have their doubts). He told the breakfast audience that Clinton was for activist government, just like he is, and "We're all going to benefit, in New Jersey particularly, because there is a compatibility in philosophy."

Florio talks like that. The *Times* story called him a policy wonk "with about as much charisma as a flow chart." Nonetheless, he touted the *Times* story to his breakfast audience. It seemed a vindication of both him and their support of him. "As you know, I've had close relatives who were not particularly thrilled to have the name Florio two years ago," he told them with characteristic self-deprecation bordering on self-pity. "I've had people visiting from out of state think my first name must be 'Dump.'"

A labor leader I met at the Trenton train station on my way down to Washington told me the "guy on the street" still hates Florio. I had said I thought Florio had a fifty-fifty chance of being re-elected, my standard safe answer to all who inquire (and also my honest assessment). He said, "Who are you talking to, insiders or the guy on the street?"

"I talk mainly to insiders, I guess," I admitted. "I probably should talk more to average people, but I suppose I don't. Why, what do they think?"

"They hate him," he said.

"Taxes?" I asked.

"Taxes, auto insurance. They're seeing those things go up, and they blame him," he said.

"Didn't they see their JUA surcharge disappear and their auto insurance rates go down by $200 per car?" I asked.

"Tell it to the guy who's paying $4,000 to insure two cars and sees it go down to $3,600. It's expensive to insure a car in this state! You have a teenager who becomes a driver and your rates go through the roof."

So the Floriocrats are feeling optimistic, the labor insider is saying watch out, and James Carville is saying he "thinks" he can pull it out.

★ Saturday, January 23 ★

It was Jim Goodman of the Trenton *Times* who pointed out in his column last Sunday that political campaigns often hinge on a mistake. I gave Goodman some good-natured ribbing on "Reporters' Roundtable" this week for thinking that the candidates' records and positions on issues would not count for anything in the Republican primary. Suddenly, Goodman is looking prophetic.

The Republican primary has taken a dramatic turn in the past twenty-four hours. Both candidates have revealed that they once employed illegal aliens as housekeepers or child-care workers, and that they failed to pay taxes for these workers. The shock of this revelation is reflected in the front-page treatment it is getting today. "ILLEGAL ALIEN FLAP HITS GOP GOVERNOR'S RACE," says a bold headline on page one of the Trenton *Times*. "WHITMAN, EDWARDS ADMIT EMPLOYING ILLEGAL ALIENS," says a three-column headline on the left front of the *Star-Ledger*.

Just yesterday President Clinton's first nominee to be U.S. attorney general, Zoe Baird, was forced to withdraw from consideration by the Senate after an uproar over her having employed illegal aliens as child-care workers in her New Haven, Connecticut, home, while she pulled down $507,000 a year as general counsel at Aetna Insurance Co. and her husband was a star faculty member at Yale Law School. The media— particularly the talk-radio programs—have been giving Baird's behavior a thorough public laundering. Three weeks ago, nobody had ever paid attention to the legal status of the domestic help of public officials. Suddenly, it is the sin du jour, and not only has it taken down the first woman attorney general-designate, it has spread to the New Jersey governor's race.

How the news came out, and how I learned about it, are worth telling. Yesterday morning, right after Zoe Baird's withdrawal became public, I got a call from Jeff Michaels, the Edwards campaign manager. I was putting a piece together on the Clinton inaugural for one of our weekend shows, "Front Page: New Jersey," and told him he had to make it quick.

"I'll make it real quick," he said. "Since you were the guy who asked Cary that unusual question about the limousine [at his announcement speech], I think maybe you ought to ask Christie at her kickoff next week whether she's ever employed illegal aliens."

"I'm not going to ask unless you have some shred of evidence," I said. "Do you?"

"I have reason to believe it's a legitimate question," he said.

My deadline was approaching, and I was exhausted from the inaugural, and told him I'd call him on Monday. It occurred to me that news of this sort, if true, would not keep until next Wednesday when Whitman kicks off her campaign, but at that point I didn't care.

I left the TV station early and went home to rest. I was sleeping when the first phone call came in from the newsroom. It was one of my co-workers sharing with me the shocking news that had just come across the Associated Press wire: Christie Whitman has admitted that, like Zoe Baird, she and her husband, John, had employed illegal aliens from 1986 to 1991, and had not paid taxes for them during that time. I thought to myself, so Michaels has leaked the news to someone else.

All night I wondered what impact this revelation would have on the race. I felt sorry for Whitman; she has worked so hard to get to this point. Would this be fatal? It was for Zoe Baird, but her situation was special; as attorney general, she was going to have to administer the very immigration law that she had violated.

It wasn't until this morning, Saturday, that I learned about Edwards. And I didn't learn about it from the *New York Times*, the first paper I see each day. The *Times* had a Wayne King story on the front page of the Metro section headlined "G.O.P. Candidate Says She Hired Illegal Aliens." It was only about Whitman. The last sentence of the article said, "An aide on the Edwards campaign who insisted on anonymity said that Mr. Edwards . . . said he had never employed illegals."

Either Edwards lied to his aide, or the aide lied to Wayne King, because about an hour or two after King filed his story last night, Edwards consented to several brief telephone interviews with reporters in which he confessed his situation. (A third possibility is that Edwards didn't know he had a problem until very late in the day.)

Whitman made her admission via written statement around four on Friday and refused to elaborate on it. She had employed a Portuguese couple in 1986 and began right away trying to get resident-alien status (green cards) for them. She said she and her husband had advertised for child care in several newspapers, gotten few takers, and had hired the people they felt would do the best job of caring for their children. By 1991, she said, the couple had obtained green cards, and at that point the Whitmans began reporting their wages to the IRS and seeing to it that taxes were paid. The couple still works for them, said the statement. The Whitmans would pay back taxes on the unreported income as soon as their lawyer apprised them of the amount, probably next week, it said. "I fully acknowledge that the hiring of this couple before they received their legal residency and the delinquency in filing tax payments on their wages was a serious mistake, and one which I deeply regret," said her statement.

After this news came out at four o'clock, Cary Edwards declined to take phone calls until about nine-thirty. For those brief hours, it appeared to the outside world as if Edwards had just been handed a key to the gubernatorial nomination. My newscast, "NJN News," led with the story. "Christie Whitman dropped a bombshell today," is how anchor Kent Manahan introduced it.

But inside the Edwards camp there must have been some furious churning and debating going on. By half-past nine Edwards revealed that he, too, had a problem. In his case, his late father-in-law had hired a Portuguese woman as a housekeeper in 1987. After the father-in-law died in early 1989, Edwards told several reporters, he and his wife "took her over" for about eighteen months. They tried to get her a green card all that time, and she was working in several relatives' homes during the week as well as theirs. Finally, she got a green card, and at that point Edwards said he tried to start paying social security for her and reporting her wages to the IRS, but the woman insisted she was an independent contractor and that no reporting was necessary. He persisted, and she resigned, he said. He hasn't seen her since.

So, as Bill Clinton casts about for a replacement for Zoe Baird, Christie Whitman and Cary Edwards ponder the impact of their upper-class "crimes." If it had been Whitman alone, as poor Jeff Michaels must have thought when he called me yesterday morning, it would have played right into Edwards's charge that Whitman is a rich heiress out of touch with the common people. But, alas for Edwards, he is now a Mudge, Rose, Guthrie, Alexander, and Ferdon attorney pulling in $300-500,000 a year and capable also of hiring a housekeeper, and for this he loses what would have been a brilliant advantage.

Meanwhile, Jim Florio is saying nothing, and his spokesman Jon Shure is saying nothing, though they must be licking their chops, or chortling, or at least enjoying the spectacle of somebody else taking the heat for a change. For Whitman the timing is terrible, coming right before she formally launches her campaign with a three-stop kickoff ceremony next Wednesday. The state Democratic chairman, Senator Raymond Lesniak, is already calling for Whitman to do the "honorable" thing and "do what the nominee for attorney general did . . . withdraw from the race." Lord knows what he'll say once he takes cognizance of the fact that Edwards, too, has a problem.

Will a third candidate emerge in the Republican field? Assembly speaker Chuck Haytaian perhaps? I don't think so. The fact that both Whitman and Edwards sinned in the same fashion (with the same nationality!) ought to cancel it out as an issue between them. I've been in New Jersey fifteen years now, and I don't think this is the sort of transgression that will set New Jerseyans on their ears. Raise their taxes, their insurance rates, or fiddle with their schools, and you'll hear from them. But if Bill Clinton can survive Gennifer Flowers, I think Christie and Cary can survive Emma and Antonio Franco (Christie's couple) and an unnamed Portuguese housecleaner.

★ Tuesday, January 26   ★

Everyone is trying to assess the impact of the illegal-alien confessions. The Sunday papers had front-page stories full of spin and speculation. The state Democratic chairman, Ray Lesniak, now is calling on both Whitman and Edwards to withdraw from the race. Monday was my first shot at the story.

I started at the Statehouse, because the senate was in session and it would be a good place to gauge the reaction of other politicians, particularly Republicans. The first person I interviewed, however, was a Democrat, U.S. senator Frank Lautenberg, who was there doing a transportation-funding news conference. A multimillionaire himself, he took a hard line on the hiring of illegals, saying it was a serious violation of the law, and you just can't run for governor and be a law-breaker at the same time. From there I must have interviewed eight or nine other politicians and got mixed reactions. Some think it's very damaging. Others think it will dissipate. But nobody was saying this is inconsequential, like breaking a traffic law.

The Monday morning *Star-Ledger* said state senator Bill Gormley of Atlantic County is now reassessing his erstwhile candidacy. Gormley is a strange bird. About forty-five, with a big, round, boyish face, he looks and acts like a prankster or the class clown. Yet, he is an effective legislator who ran for governor in 1989 and finished fourth in the Republican primary, a respectable fourth. I saw him in the hall underneath the Statehouse rotunda and asked for an interview.

"Aw, *now* you want to talk to me!" he shouted, waving his arms wildly. "You've ignored me for the last seven or eight weeks, and now all of a sudden I'm hot stuff. Forget it, Aron." It was a put-on.

On camera he said he'd have an announcement to make in two or three weeks, but he was careful not to criticize Whitman or Edwards. "I don't care for circumstances where some people have had bad press and others take advantage of it," he said, full of self-righteousness at how virtuous he was being. "I'm going to do my job and leave my options open."

"Gormley's just stirring the pot," said a Republican I speak to often, a former Kean administration official. "He'd rather be king of South Jersey than governor." Gormley does seem to have a lock on all appointments and public works projects in Atlantic City, which is one of the "capitals" of South Jersey.

"You seen Gormley?" a lobbyist asked me. "He looks like the cat who swallowed the canary."

To get Governor Florio on camera reacting to the "Alien Uproar," as the NJN assignment editor slugged my story in our computer, we went into the governor's outer office for a bill-signing ceremony. The governor was signing a bill mandating that clemency grants to prisoners be fully disclosed and explained to the public. With him were the bill's two sponsors, Gormley and senate president DiFrancesco (another name bandied about that morning as a possible surprise third candidate), plus two crime victim advocates, Jim O'Brien and Richard Pompelio, men who had lost teenage children in highly publicized murder cases. I found it hard to pay attention to the ceremony; I was thinking about my story, although it occurred to me that the bill signing might actually be more important to the people of the state than the sensational news I was pursuing and that would surely lead our newscast that night.

When the governor opened it up for questions, no one asked about clemency. The first question was about illegal aliens—so if my priorities were wrong, at least I had plenty of company. Consistent with his "no comments" of the weekend, Jim Florio tried to say as little as possible about a situation that he is probably relishing. The reporters kept trying.

"I'm really trying to minimize the partisanship in a political year for as long as possible," Florio said, adding he wanted to be able to get things done with the Republican legislature, like today's bill and next month's budget presentation. That made sense, and explained why the governor is delaying his own announcement of re-election until late March or early April.

I tried one more time on the alien issue and managed to wrest this slightly critical line out of Florio: "From the Washington perspective it was serious enough to have someone withdraw, but you have to have a case-by-case evaluation of the circumstances." That would be my sound bite.

Bill Bradley passed through the Statehouse as I was leaving, but he was on his way in to see Florio and said he didn't have time to stop for an interview. I had interviewed him extensively in Washington last week for our weekend show "Front Page: New Jersey." He had declined to take a position on the Zoe Baird question, "until I hear everything." Within twenty-four hours, she had resigned, before the interview even aired! Now I asked him if he'd caught that interview on TV ("it's on tape," he said, implying he might watch it at some point), and told him I'd ask one of my colleagues to get a comment from him later about illegal aliens for my story tonight because I had to run.

They say TV news is a glamorous business. Not this day. I got a lift back to the station, then got in my own van for a one-hour drive north to Clark, N.J., where I would meet a Newark-based cameraman for an interview with Christie Whitman. I debated stopping for a slice of pizza to go, but reckoned it would make me late, so I skipped lunch.

Whitman's campaign headquarters in Clark is as nondescript as her old Committee for an Affordable New Jersey suite of offices. Republicans in this state favor low-slung generic little office buildings adjacent to major-highway on- and off-ramps for their campaign headquarters, and this was another one. I was surprised at how many people were in there, however—maybe thirty, of whom twelve were paid staff. That's sizable for this early in the race. The little rabbit-warren offices offered nothing visually interesting, so we didn't bother shooting the headquarters.

Whitman's office is an airless little room without windows, very spare and spartan, without pretension, which might be a clue to her personality. Dave Marziale, the press secretary, escorted us in there to set up and spun me for awhile about how Christie had never realized she'd had a problem until Zoe Baird's disclosure, and how candid she's been about "Emma and Antonio."

"She released this on her own. We hadn't received one inquiry from anybody," Marziale said. "We *created* the story. Contrast that with Edwards, who came out only because we came out."

Christie came in and gave me a little kid-caught-with-hand-in-cookie-jar expression of guilt. She joked about the number of high public officials who must be worrying about their domestic help at the moment. "There's gonna be a lot of high grass and dirty windows in Arlington, Virginia, this summer," she said, a tart, country club–class remark.

The interview she handled well. She admitted her error, explained how well intentioned it had been, and expressed regret. She didn't think it would ruin her candidacy, but that was for the voters to decide. "The difference between Zoe Baird and this is that hers was an appointive office," she said. "In this case, the people will get to make the ultimate judgment as to whether this is the critical issue or there are other things more critical, like the state's economy and the management of state government." I had heard her make the same statements on the radio on my way up to her headquarters. Nothing varied. She had her story down straight, and she delivered it with feeling each time. She would pay the back taxes and social security on Tuesday, and go ahead with her formal announcement on Wednesday.

After the interview, as we kept talking, she confided off the record that she had reason to believe that in the 1989 Republican gubernatorial primary, three of the five candidates, including Edwards, knew they had illegal aliens at home and kept it quiet. "They observed the eleventh commandment," Whitman said. "Don't beat up on fellow Republicans. I won't tell if you don't tell."

She also said that getting her own secret out had brought her a measure of relief. "I'll tell you, I wasn't sleeping too well there after the Zoe Baird thing broke. Since Friday, I've been sleeping well. It was good to get it out."

I left Clark at two-thirty for a three o'clock interview with Cary Edwards in our Newark bureau. Still not a moment to spare for a quick stop for food. Upon arriving, I learned that Edwards had changed the time to three-thirty. That gave me time to return a call from Jeff Michaels, Edwards's campaign manager, who had called me last Friday with the tip on Whitman.

Michaels tried to tell me that Cary's problem is less serious than Christie's. He only employed a woman *part*time and she didn't live in the house, Michaels said. Christie's couple, on the other hand, "worked seven days a week, morning 'til night, cleaning the house and cleaning the stables." C'mon, Jeff, I said, one of them also took care of the children. But Jeff was convinced that "most people can relate to Cary's circumstances better than Christie's."

"I thought of you on Saturday," I said.

"Oh?"

"Obviously you didn't know when you called me Friday morning to plant the seed about Whitman that your guy had a problem, too."

He admitted he hadn't, and I enjoyed hearing a trace of embarrassment in the voice of this aggressive, pugnacious twenty-eight-year-old Republican bulldog.

Edwards bounded into our newsroom, and we sat him down for an interview. He was a little less contrite than Whitman, more eager to rationalize and explain how an illegal alien had come to work in his home. He also contradicted himself, saying that when the woman had started work for his father-in-law he had raised a red flag because she was illegal and he knew that was against the law, then saying that when she came to work for him a year later, he didn't know it was illegal to employ her and that he immediately undertook the process of legalizing her status. His story was a little less linear than Whitman's. It had more twists and turns and explanations, like a man who doth protest just a little too much.

After the interview, Edwards said, "What do you think, Mike? What's your professional opinion of all this?"

Taken aback at being asked for advice, I answered the only way I know how: honestly. I told him, personally, I didn't think it was a serious offense, but the people might. He seemed concerned.

"Do you think it softens it when people hear the circumstances?" he asked. "If I try to explain . . ."

"The details were in the Saturday papers," I said. "People who want to know the circumstances already have them."

A producer in Trenton had gone out and interviewed people in the street for my piece, and had left me a message in our computer that the reaction was overwhelmingly critical of the two Republicans. The radio station I'd listened to had done a listener poll: 120 callers thought Whitman and Edwards should quit the race, 98 thought they should stay in. There were already jokes about the situation ("Have you seen the latest bumper sticker?" someone at the Statehouse asked me. "It says, 'CHRISTIE—WHO'S WATCHING YOUR KIDS?' "). Political cartoonists were having a field day.

I put my piece together with breakneck speed, just barely making the air at six o'clock, then drove home to Princeton, an hour's drive (stopping for that slice along the way).

And now today I led the newscast with another piece on the flap, this time looking at the immigration law and interviewing lawyers. Whitman was on our newscast live, interviewed by one of the anchors. A *Star-Ledger* editorial today says, "Overnight, there has been a development which significantly improves Jim Florio's prospects for re-election."

An editorial in the Trenton *Times*, which generally has much better editorials, says, ". . . the voters will decide whether they should be nominated and elected. Our own judgment, based on last week's revelations, is that they should not."

So, obviously, the flap is not about to go away overnight.

And Whitman kicks off her campaign ten hours from now, tomorrow morning.

★ Wednesday, January 27 ★

Christie's Big Day began with a handful of protesters in the lobby of the Cherry Hill Hyatt carrying signs, one of which read WHITMAN ECONOMICS—GOOD FOR PORTUGAL, BAD FOR NEW JERSEY. She got past them good-humoredly and into a small ballroom, where perhaps two hundred supporters and media awaited her.

Her speech, which she read in a slightly halting fashion, was okay, but light. It promised a new direction, "a new way." It attacked Jim Florio for "the tragedy of the past three years in New Jersey." It promised to bring New Jerseyans together again, and bring them into government. Employing that Republican buzzword that even Democrats like Jim Florio are using now, Whitman promised to "empower the people of New Jersey [by] bringing more citizens into government, limiting terms of office and giving the people of New Jersey a direct voice in their government through initiative and referendum."

There was much in her statement that rang false, however. She accused Jim Florio of dividing the state into rich and poor, urban and suburban. He did that by trying to correct the inequity between them; to scold him because the "haves" got a little restless is to take their side. She promised to "abolish the perks and privileges of office," an ironic comment given the uproar over her domestic help. It could be argued that her whole life has been one big perk. She and her husband are multimillionaires. Finally, she came down hard on the recent debt refinancing package, which she blamed on Florio when, in fact, the Republican legislative leaders were every bit as responsible for pushing it.

On the biggest issue of all, state taxes, she offered an untenable position. She said she was committed to trying to roll back all of Florio's $2.8 billion 1990 tax hike ($600 million of which was rolled back when the Republican legislature cut the sales tax in mid-1992, bringing it back down to 6 percent). That is impossible, and she knows it, and everyone else knows it. She called it a "goal" when I questioned her about it in a Q&A session after her speech, but it's an empty gesture. To roll back all the taxes, she would have to cut aid to public schools by 25 percent or lay off 10,000 of the 70,000 state workers, at the very least.

Her second stop was the Statehouse, where about two dozen unemployed workers were waiting for her with picket signs that said things like Recent Events Have Reminded Me I Forgot to Pay Back Taxes; and Whitman's Minimum Wage—$1.50 an Hour; and I'm American, and I Need a Job. It was easy to imagine someone in the state Democratic party office calling a friendly labor union and arranging for this visual display, but the union guys assured me they were here on their own.

At this stop, many of the same supporters who had been in Cherry Hill were bused in, but this time Whitman abandoned her script and spoke her lines instead of trying to read them. It came out shorter and less halting, but she left a lot out. Then came the question-and-answer session. The Statehouse press corps went at her. With about ten TV cameras in the room and twenty to twenty-five reporters, the pressure was on. For the first twenty minutes, all the questions dealt with the illegal-alien flap. Reporters who had had one-on-one interviews with her several times wanted to run over the same ground all over again. Reporters who were new to the story were even more eager to hear her explanations. She answered the reporters gamely, but the intensity and duration of the questioning were a signal to everyone that this candidacy is in trouble.

This morning's papers had been full of stories about how Whitman had paid $25,000 in back taxes yesterday and Edwards would soon pay $3,000. The Bergen *Record* story said that Roger Bodman, the hotshot Republican lobbyist who doubles as an analyst on some of NJN's shows, was trying to get former governor Kean to call a summit of party elders to figure out what to do next. Bodman was quoted as calling the two principal Republican candidates "wounded," a remarkable admission from a Republican insider. And Jim Ahearn, one of the best columnists in the state, weighed in with his thoughts on the Whitman-Edwards affair. He called it "a double train wreck."

Whitman supporters are clinging to the hope that the voters will be more broad-minded than the media, and that Christie is showing the public great presence, strength of character, and grace under fire.

★ Sunday, January 31 ★

A week after the revelations, the big question is how badly damaged are Whitman and Edwards.

"Dead meat," is what David Blomquist, the Trenton bureau chief of the Bergen *Record*, called them on "Reporters' Roundtable" Friday night. Those were the first words out of his mouth, and he usually knows what he's talking about.

Others are not so sure, including me. I still think they can both get past it. On Friday, as part of my story for the day, I went to the Trenton train station and asked ordinary people what they thought. Of the two dozen or so I asked, about half didn't know what I was talking about. Of the other half, perhaps eight thought it was an egregious violation of law that seriously tarnished the candidates; perhaps four were more understanding and forgiving.

Oddly, Whitman and Edwards are now boxed into a corner together. To some extent, their fates are intertwined. They will sink together because of this scandal—which is acquiring a name that seems to be sticking, Nannygate—or together they will convince the public to look past it.

Conventional wisdom says that if they are not, in fact, dead, they are at least damaged. There is a vacuum now for a Republican or independent politician to fill, if the right one decides to fill it.

Names are being bandied about. Mike Kelly, a feature columnist for the Bergen *Record*, wrote an entertaining column Thursday urging assembly speaker Chuck Haytaian to run ("Bring On the Kahuna").

"The one person who can get in and blow away the field is Tom Kean," said Alan Marcus, a highly successful lobbyist with good ties to the Republicans. Kean has not been heard from at all this week, and some wonder if maybe he has an illegal-alien problem, too. "I remember Ruby from Jamaica," said Marcus, referring to Kean, "but she was probably in the family for years and probably legal."

"Bill Gormley's phone has been ringing off the hook," he continued, "but he doesn't want to run." Why not? "He's just not psyched for it."

"Donnie D. would like to do it, but he's waiting for a draft," he said of the senate president from Westfield, who's got the integrity and likability to run, but may not have the oratorical skill or dynamism.

Other names mentioned are Congressmen Dean Gallo and Chris Smith, former Bush booster and businessman "Bo" Sullivan, and former congressman Matt Rinaldo, who has let it be known he would accept a draft. On Friday, a has-been state senator named James Wallwork, who's sixty-two and has been out of public life since 1982, sent a letter to GOP state chairman Ginny Littell (she insists on calling herself chairman) and the forty-two state committee members indicating his interest in running, but he was very conservative, and it's hard to take him seriously. Same for Rinaldo, who seems over the hill and nongubernatorial.

Christie and Cary were going to face off on national television over Nannygate Friday morning, but "Good Morning America" canceled them late Thursday night in favor of other news (a federal judge's decision on the gays-in-the-military issue that consumed America last week, President Clinton's first full week in office). Both candidates appeared, back-to-back, Friday afternoon on "Inside Trenton," a rival program to ours that Channel 13 in New York just started recently. I was a bit upset to see that "Inside Trenton" had them, whereas we were going with the campaign managers on our Friday night show "Front Page: New Jersey." But when I remembered that I had interviewed both of them Monday, and each had done a live Q&A with our anchors on Tuesday and Wednesday, I felt better.

My colleague Kent Manahan hosted "Front Page" this weekend.

I hung around the studio during the taping to pick up the vibes and whatever information I could. Dave Murray of the Whitman campaign showed up first. He's an engaging fellow, about forty, tall, with a ruddy complexion, a mustache, and the looks of someone who could model a rugby shirt in a sportswear catalogue. He's been a Republican operative for years—specializing in campaign advertising and direct mail—and this is clearly his biggest shot. He is a good talker. I poked at him for about fifteen minutes, and he gave me a lot of good spin back. Notably, he defended Whitman's call for rolling back the entire $2.8 billion tax hike. In his view, it's fresh and bold; the only reason we reporters think it's preposterous is because we're part of the inside crowd that doesn't believe taxes can be cut back.

Jeff Michaels, Cary Edwards's campaign manager, is ten years younger, five inches shorter, and more baby-faced and pudgy than Murray, but he's just as smart. He seemed somewhat uptight before the taping— either because it's been a horrible week or because the prospect of appear-ing with Murray intimidated him. The televised match-up was a dud— too short (ten minutes) and no fireworks. I chatted with Michaels after-wards, and he admitted to me the past week's turn of events was particu-larly frustrating for him.

"I took this job because it was supposed to be a very uphill thing," he said, implying that if he could work a "miracle" and get Edwards nominated it would do wonders for his career. "Things were going great. We'd managed to get across some of the things we needed to get across, and we were damaging Christie. Then this." He seemed genuinely agitated but philosophical for a young man.

Later in the day I interviewed Edwards, briefly, to get something fresh for my Friday night story. Whitman was too far away for me to get to her, so I knew I wouldn't use too much with Edwards for the sake of balance, and I kept it short. I interviewed him outside the Channel 6 Trenton studio, where he had been taping a weekend talk show for that Philadelphia station. He seemed upbeat for a man who'd just been through a battering. He and Whitman are both hewing to the line that their transgression becomes part of the record the public will judge them on, but that it's only one part, and they hope the voters will consider their total beings and presentations.

"I know you'll find this a little hard to believe, but in a way this has been good for me. The public knows who I am now. Name recognition is less a problem," he said. And that part is true.

Every day this week I either reported on the illegal-alien flap or talked about it on a talk show. The irony is, I don't personally think it's a very serious offense. Why, then, am I riding it? Because it's the talk of the newsroom where I work. Because my news director, Bill Jobes, thinks it's an important development. Because the newspapers are playing it on the front page almost daily. Are the media making more of it than it warrants? Such stories are what we imagine the public wants to hear. We arrive at this conclusion by asking ourselves what *we* would rather hear about or read about. A scandal or something more neutral? The misadventures of a candidate for high office or his position paper on some issue? Thus does a story like Nannygate build and endure and get the suffix "gate" affixed to it. We will beat the issue to death until we have examined all the angles. When there are no more angles and we are thoroughly bored by the subject, we will assume the public is bored by it as well, and will move on.

The headline on David Wald's news story in the *Star-Ledger* today says, "Experts unable to gauge 'nannygate' impact on Whitman, Edwards run." That about sums it up. Some people are drawing comparisons to Bill Clinton's scandals of sex, marijuana, and draft dodging, and arguing that if he can survive those, Christie and Cary can survive a little illegal-alien flap.

Some of the best lines this week have come from state Democratic chairman Ray Lesniak, who knows what it's like to be on the receiving end of critical news coverage, having been featured in a famous Bergen *Record* series called "The Politics of Greed." He branded Whitman "New Jersey's Leona Helmsley," i.e., a rich bitch who exploited the hired help and evaded taxes. And he said, "I knew Bill Clinton was going to help Jim Florio. But who ever imagined it would be by choosing Zoe Baird as his attorney general?"

Wald's article also said there's a story circulating in Washington that James Carville sent Jim Florio a bottle of champagne this week to "celebrate the change in the political climate."

So far, this has been another good week for Jim Florio. From Sunday to Tuesday he was in Washington for the National Governor's Association winter meeting. He chaired the welfare reform committee, and on Tuesday President Clinton named him to a White House task force that will devise the administration's welfare reform plan. This morning, a photograph at the top of page one of the *New York Times* showed a smiling Clinton at the governors' meeting pointing at something and Jim Florio next to him, applauding, and nearly in stitches at whatever Clinton was saying. Two chums on page one, for all the world to see.

Then this afternoon in Trenton Florio announced that the Clinton administration has agreed to release $412 million in Medicaid reimbursements that New Jersey had been trying to squeeze out of the federal government for a year. The Medicaid money has been a political hot potato all that time. Florio included it in his last budget but could never get it. The Republicans blasted him for counting on it, but when they went to Washington to try to get it themselves, George Bush and his health and human services secretary, Louis Sullivan, first said no, then offered $62 million if the state would drop the rest of its claim.

Florio and many others had made it a test of the new relationship between Florio and Clinton that New Jersey would get the money. And sure enough, two weeks after Inauguration Day, and six days before Florio has to unveil next year's budget, Clinton came through for his fellow Democrat. Perhaps more impressive, Clinton has accepted Florio's invitation to drop by the annual state Chamber of Commerce dinner in Washington tomorrow night and say a few words to eighteen hundred assembled New Jersey politicos and businesspeople.

At his news conference today announcing the Medicaid agreement, Florio downplayed the idea that the release of the money was a political favor. He insisted the claim was honored on its merits and "the only favor was in getting somebody to look at it quickly with a sharp pencil and a green eyeshade. This was not a gift." But he also was quick to let the press corps know that "the president came up to me on Monday, unsolicited, and said 'I'm aware of your Medicaid problem and I want to help.'"

He wanted us to know that his connections helped, but not to think of it as a political payoff. After all, Clinton is trying to cut the deficit and is thinking about raising taxes. It might not look good to be giving one state a $400 million windfall as a thank you for victory or as a boost for the governor who shares your political consultant. Four hundred million dollars is what the United States owes the United Nations in unpaid assessments, and somehow we haven't been able to find the money for that.

In the meantime, Whitman and Edwards continue to try to fight off the lingering scandal. They campaign. They make appearances. Whitman was endorsed today by Phil McConkey, the former Giants football player who has become a semirespected right-leaning Republican politician. The newspapers keep checking with the INS, and the IRS, and the state Labor Department, for holes in the candidates' stories. One day they find them. The next day the holes close and the papers backtrack. Republicans around the state are clearly concerned. A businessman in South Jersey is trying to start a Draft Matty Rinaldo movement, which is like trying to bring on a washed-up movie star of the 1960s because Richard Gere and Kim Basinger have suddenly backed out of the picture.

For diversion this week, the tabloid *Trentonian*, a scandal-sheet that occasionally does some good reporting, has run a five-part series alleging that Florio's chief of staff, Joe Salema, and his policy chief, Brenda Bacon, who own nursing homes, have influenced the state Health Department's policy on nursing homes in a way designed to enrich themselves. The series is so full of innuendo and facts that go nowhere, it's hard to know how much credence to give it. The blistering headlines certainly tried to shift the spotlight away from Whitman and Edwards: "Florio's Top Aides—USING THEIR JOBS TO GET RICH," "FLORIO AIDES 'PERVERT' SYSTEM," "GOV'S AIDES MILK NURSING HOME SYSTEM."

Republicans in the legislature are calling for an investigation, Bacon (a respected policy expert who negotiated the Medicaid reimbursement with health and human services secretary Donna Shalala) is threatening to sue, and the state's political community seems largely to be ignoring the rantings and ravings of a newspaper it long ago learned not to trust.

Yesterday, in the late morning and early afternoon, eighteen hundred New Jerseyans boarded an eighteen-car chartered Amtrak train and went to Washington for the fifty-fifth annual New Jersey Chamber of Commerce dinner there. The train ride is a zoo, a mob scene, a liquored-up political schmooze session on wheels, and a lot of fun if you're not claustrophobic. In gubernatorial years, the train is even more crowded and intense; candidates are expected to make a show on the train. Tradition says they have to walk the entire length of the train, greeting and seeing everyone. Given how packed the cars are with bodies sitting, standing, bending, and leaning, it's a task.

The ride this year, as always, was boisterous and fun. I got on the rear car, number eighteen, and proceeded to walk to car one. It took an hour-and-a-half. Everywhere I went the talk was of Whitman and Edwards and aliens. Someone was handing out stickers that said Hire Me, I'm Legal, and lots of people were wearing them.

Around car eight I encountered Governor Florio. Determined to have an exchange of some sort, I said to him, "You've had a pretty good ten days."

He looked back and said, dryly, "There is a God."

"There's a lot of humorous stuff on the train," I said. "Someone has started calling the Republicans 'Whitless and Careless.'"

"Jon wanted me to say something in my remarks tonight," Florio said, referring to Jon Shure, his communications director, who was standing nearby. "He wanted me to advise the dinner guests that on pay-TV in their hotel rooms tonight they could catch Sigourney Weaver in *Aliens* or —what's the name of that French actor?—in *Green Card*. But common sense has prevailed, right, Jon?"

Shure joined the conversation.

"I think you should do it," I said. "It would make the news."

"Just what I need—news coverage," Florio said acidly, showing his sarcastic streak.

I moved on and eventually encountered Christie Whitman and her entourage in car two. We exchanged pleasantries, and I kept going, to car one, the lead car, where I touched the door leading to the engine, then sat down to relax after my grueling trek. A few minutes later Whitman came by and did the same thing, touched the door.

We chatted again. I told her I would like to photograph her family farm, put it on television and show it to the people. The farm had been in the news this week. Several newspapers had done pieces on how the Whitmans were paying reduced property taxes because much of their 222-acre farm in Oldwick qualified for a farmland assessment. That's the Todd family homestead that Christie grew up on and moved back to a year or two ago after her mother died. The *Star-Ledger* had reported she was also getting a farmland assessment on her prior property in Far Hills. On Tuesday I had called Dave Murray, her campaign manager, and told him I'd like to shoot the farm if the Whitmans would let me.

"I'll have to think about it," Christie said on the train, "but my initial reaction is not negative."

That was a surprise.

I chatted with John Whitman, her forty-nine-year-old invest-ment banker husband, for quite awhile. He's an earnest, pleasant preppie with a few chips on his shoulder over what's being done to his wife by the Democrats and the media. His grandfather was the governor of New York in 1915. Christie's father was the Republican state chairman of New Jersey. They have good Republican lineage, these two, and it shows in how they carry themselves and how they dress. Their style is neither continental nor loud. She wears a gray flannel topcoat, cut very straight and plain. He wears gray flannel slacks and penny-loafers.

I asked John about coming out to the farm with a camera, and he, too, was rather open about it.

"But come in the spring, when there's something going on. Come in April. In June Christie and I even get out there and bale hay. If you were to come now, all you'd see is a field like that," he said, motioning out the window of the train to a vast empty tract of scrub.

Yeah, but the story's hot now, I thought. The video might not be as good, but now would be the time for the tour. John Whitman, I decided, was stalling for time.

Cary Edwards I didn't see on the train. I saw his wife, Lynn, working the train around car fifteen, but somehow I missed Cary. I ran into him at the hotel, however, the Sheraton Washington, as the army from New Jersey was checking in. He gave me a very hearty and hale hello. It felt genuine and warm, if a little forced. We figured out I must have missed him on the train because he got off in Wilmington to dart quickly from car ten to car fifteen. We laughed. It was a good little communication, better than I had had with either Florio or Whitman. Some reporters, perhaps, don't care how they get along with the politicians they cover. I am not one of them. I strive for good chemistry with most of them and am not ashamed to admit it.

Dinner for fourteen hundred at the Sheraton Washington was as you'd expect, with one exception. Bill Clinton came. And it was extraordinary in several respects. First, no off-screen voice bellowed "Ladies and Gentlemen, the president of the United States," as it did when President Bush came to this dinner in 1989 to pay his respects to Tom Kean in Kean's last year as governor. There was no band playing "Hail to the Chief." One minute Clinton wasn't there, and the next minute he was. He spoke for about fifteen minutes, without prepared remarks. After thanking New Jersey for voting for him ("the first time you've voted for a Democrat for president in twenty-eight years"), he gave a moving little talk about how we were all going to have to sacrifice and pull together to get the country out of the mess it's in. It was a preview of the big economic speech he is to deliver on February 17.

The truly extraordinary thing, from a New Jersey perspective, was how, in front of this bipartisan audience, he laid it on about Florio. He said he hoped he could do for the nation what Governor Florio had done for New Jersey—make the tough decisions that would put the economic house in order. "Not so long ago you elected a governor who had to make some of those decisions," he said. "For all the pain suffered by Governor Florio and the legislature, the truth is, your house is in order now. I hope you are proud of him, because I am."

After the speech Clinton came off the large dais and down to the first row of tables, where people gathered five and six deep as he slowly passed from one side of the stage to the other and out the door. Governor Florio and Senator Lautenberg accompanied him. He shook several hundred hands and displayed a remarkable common touch and enormous charisma.

I skipped the parties after the dinner so that I could get a decent night's sleep. I needed to be fresh the next morning for a special one-hour edition of "Reporters' Roundtable" being taped before a live audience at

a breakfast in the hotel sponsored by Coleman and Pellet, a public relations firm. There was a lot of talk about illegal aliens on the show. The
consensus was that Whitman and Edwards are damaged, seriously, though
a third candidate is hard to identify. Senator Bill Gormley was in the
audience. I noticed that after we all predicted Gormley wouldn't run, and
David Blomquist of the Bergen *Record* said he "lacked the fire in the belly,"
Gormley got up and left during a break. I wondered if he was offended.

After the taping I hustled over to James Carville's office with
NJN cameraman Curt Fissell. I had called there earlier in the week to
arrange to come over to do an interview on the subject of the Florio
campaign.

Carville was on the phone talking to his dentist when I arrived.
His office is a very small basement apartment in a brownstone two blocks
from the Capitol. It's messy. There are liquor bottles on the counter in the
kitchen. Carville and Paul Begala have their desks in the front room,
facing each other, amid reams of memorabilia. In a passageway to the kitchen
are desks, phones, and a fax manned by two fresh-out-of-college-aged kids,
Melissa and John. That's the extent of the operation. Out back there's a
little patio. My partner, Curt, noticed cases of unopened champagne bottles
sitting out back, presumably gifts of congratulations for the Clinton victory from friends and admirers. A little gold plate affixed to the wall
outside the front door says THE BAT CAVE beneath an image of a bat
with its wings spread.

Carville wanted to do the interview outside, so we went out
front. I asked him about himself and his role in the Clinton administration, then turned to the gubernatorial race. He didn't say much that was
memorable; he was rushed and seemed to have more important business.
(I later learned he was in the heat of negotiations on his book deal.) He did
say he was pleased that the Republican candidates had acquired illegal-
alien problems, and that Jim Florio has a good story to tell the voters. He
said that he liked Florio very much and that Florio was "my kind of guy,"
meaning a working-class guy and a fighter. He denied sending champagne
to Florio ("Ah don' even know if Guvenuh Flo-rio drinks champagne,
heh, heh, heh"). We spoke maybe seven or eight minutes. While we shot
the set-up and cutaway, he confided that although "people may be feelin'
better about Jim Florio right now, it's a momentary sense of renewal. This
thing is still going to be plenty tough."

The atmosphere is a few degrees less heated this week. On Monday Cary Edwards called a Statehouse news conference for 3:30 to discuss his "domestic help" situation. Why would he call a news conference and keep the story alive? I didn't know, and the Edwards camp wouldn't say until we got there. I thought maybe it was because Christie Whitman had gotten good marks for facing down the Statehouse press corps, and Edwards wanted to show he could handle a similar confrontation.

At 3:40 Edwards walked into a crowded Statehouse anteroom with his wife, Lynn, a few aides, and a lawyer he'd hired in recent weeks. Half a dozen TV cameras and perhaps twenty reporters awaited him. One, Jim Goodman of the Trenton *Times*, chided him for being late. Jim Florio, Goodman said, is never late, and that's true.

Edwards apologized and explained that he'd still been gathering facts together as late as this afternoon. The reason for the news conference was that "after seventeen days I've finally pulled all the records together, and instead of telling you parts of the story, one by one, I want to tell the whole story, to all of you, one time."

He proceeded to explain that his Portuguese housecleaner had paid all her own taxes and social security while she was an illegal alien in his employ. He hadn't known this on January 29, when he paid $3,000 in back taxes to the IRS. Now he would seek to recover a portion of that money. He also said he would pay a fine to the Immigration and Naturalization Service of $1,105, even though he was convinced he was not guilty of even a technical violation. To that effect he produced a letter from one Rosa Soy, an immigration lawyer, stating that she advised Lynn Edwards in 1987 that employing the illegal domestic worker was okay because of the "casual and intermittent" nature of the relationship, and that she still feels that advice was correct. Edwards said he would pay the fine anyway to get on with the race and not get bogged down in a lengthy court battle with the INS.

It was a decent performance. Amazingly, at one point Edwards broke down and nearly cried again. What triggered it was a reference to his late father-in-law, Alfred Cozzolino, who had first employed the alien. "You gotta understand, this was a very close Italian family," he said, and then he lost it. He started cracking up. The pressure of all the criticism, combined with some feeling he must have for his relatives, overcame him. He bit his lip. He fought back tears. He took a breath. Finally he got going again. I looked at Lynn Edwards after a moment, expecting to see empathy etched on her face. Instead, I thought I detected disapproval, as in "Cary, pull yourself together, baby, don't do this again."

In my piece that night I reported it straight. The facts, that is; I left out the crying bit this time. It seemed extraneous to the story, and I didn't want to embarrass Cary for the sake of embarrassing him. The newspapers the next day, however, played up the INS fine. In almost all the papers, the headline, as the *Philadelphia Inquirer* had it, was "Edwards to pay INS penalty." In the *Asbury Park Press* it was "Edwards will pay fine, under protest." If Edwards thought he was going to get a break on the story because of the revelation that his maid had paid her own taxes, he calculated wrong.

After the Edwards news conference, Jeff Michaels, the campaign manager, who's becoming one of my favorite foils in this story, was out in a hallway near me, and we fell into conversation. With the expression of a coach who's just watched his athlete run a successful marathon, Michaels exhaled dramatically and said, "What a way to end the story, don't you think, Michael?"

"It ain't over yet, Jeff," I said.

"Ah, c'mon, give us a break," he said.

The next day Governor Florio delivered his annual Budget Message to the legislature. NJN was there in full force, to broadcast the speech live, provide analysis, news coverage, and legislative reaction. This speech was bland and ponderous. I suppose those of us who continually hear Florio extol his own virtues and defend his policies cannot possibly be moved by a speech that wraps it all into one big package. The budget itself, however, is a good election-year budget. It of course has no new taxes in it (for the third year in a row). It hikes spending by 7 percent, thanks to an optimistic revenue forecast, the $412 million Medicaid windfall, the recent bond refinancing and borrowing package, and some one-time revenues from prior year gimmicks. It shows a surplus. It spreads money around—to the schools, to crime fighting, to construction programs. It also calls for another four-thousand-employee reduction in the state workforce through attrition and early retirement. It will be a tough budget to run against.

The best line in the speech was an anecdote about growing up in Brooklyn. "My uncle, my uncle Tom, Tom Florio gave me one of my first jobs—shoveling up after the horses at Prospect Park," Florio said, stretching it out in a studied manner. "At the time, I thought I was lucky to have a little pocket money. I never imagined it would be such a good apprenticeship for being governor." Another swipe at the Kean administration for leaving him a budget deficit in 1990.

After the speech Christie Whitman was out in the hallway between the senate and assembly chambers giving interviews. Cary Edwards showed up about fifteen minutes later. They both trashed the budget. Whitman said it was bloated and held the hidden promise of a tax hike next year or the year after. The governor must cut spending, she said. Edwards said it was "philosophically misguided." Instead of using the Medicaid windfall and other new revenue for public works job creation, Edwards said, Florio should be giving the private sector investment tax credits and research tax credits so they can create permanent jobs and more fully stimulate New Jersey's economy. "We're ranked forty-ninth in expected economic growth for '93. That's a disgrace!" Edwards whined over-animatedly.

On this same day, former state senator James Wallwork came out of the woodwork, announcing that on March 2nd he will formally declare his candidacy for the Republican nomination. A piece in the *Atlantic City Press* says the Republican State Committee took a private poll which showed that Bill Gormley would be the strongest of eight potential "third" Republicans inquired about, but it's Wallwork, not Gormley, who is jumping in. The Wallwork story did not get front-page play in any of today's papers, a sign that I am not alone in deeming Wallwork a has-been.

The whole country, meanwhile, is still gripped by questions about the rightness of employing illegals and the wrongness of failing to pay taxes on occasional housecleaners and baby-sitters. Federal judge Kimba Wood was dropped by the White House last week as Clinton's new choice for attorney general even though her illegal alien had been hired before 1986, when it was still legal to do so, and Wood had paid all taxes on the worker. Ron Brown, the commerce secretary, and Federico Pena, the transportation secretary, have admitted they never withheld taxes for their household help and have paid back the IRS. And while many are still condemning Clinton for what he "did" to Kimba Wood, dropping her out of fear of talk-radio criticism, a new wrinkle has been put on that transaction. It seems Judge Wood did not come clean with the president when he personally asked her if she had a "Zoe Baird" problem. She gave him a legalistic answer, of the sort *he* was a master of giving during the campaign. He was furious when he learned she had withheld the full story from him and "lost confidence" in her. Viewed that way, he had good reason to dump her.

★ Friday, February 19 ★

The race settled down some more this week. Christie Whitman found a couple of new issues. Cary Edwards talked economics. President Clinton dominated the week with his State of the Union message and the announcement of his economic plan. And, irony of ironies, one of Governor Florio's three closest aides turns out to have an illegal-alien problem.

Brenda Bacon is the governor's chief of management and planning, a woman in her early forties who has been part of Florio's inner sanctum since his early days as a congressman from Camden County. On Wednesday it came out that for two years she had employed a woman from Barbados who had no green card. The story was front-page news, and it was a two-day story. That is to say, on the first day, the bare facts came out with Bacon saying she'd followed the advice of attorneys and accountants and had paid all the appropriate taxes, but refusing to say when. The next day, more was pulled out of her. The $7,000 in back taxes had been paid in one lump sum about one month ago, *after* the Zoe Baird story broke. Several papers pointed out that Bacon had specifically denied having a Zoe Baird problem when asked in January. The dates of the woman's employment also changed from day one to day two of the story: instead of leaving Bacon's employ in June of 1992, it became the end of December of 1992.

Governor Florio is expert at deflecting questions he doesn't want to answer, particularly questions about scandal. I first saw this talent on display in 1988, after the Camden *Courier-Post*'s famous "King James" series about the influence-peddling empire built by the cronies of James Florio in Camden County. When I asked then-congressman Florio about it at a Statehouse news conference he had called on another subject, he completely ignored the question and gave a rambling, nonresponsive answer, no matter how often I tried. He's good at that, and although it's maddening, and not among his admirable qualities, it serves his interests. Which is why he did it again. Asked by reporters whether Brenda Bacon has the same problem as Whitman and Edwards, Florio would say only that she has his full confidence, she thought she was complying with the law, and the state owes her a debt of gratitude for putting aside her duties as a mother to serve the public.

It's lucky for Florio that he hadn't explicitly criticized Whitman and Edwards on this question; otherwise, those words would come back to haunt him now. (Or maybe he refrained because he knew Bacon had a problem.) Not so fortunate is state Democratic chairman Ray Lesniak, who called Whitman the "Leona Helmsley" of New Jersey for evading taxes and called on both Republicans to withdraw from the race. He's now reduced to drawing distinctions between candidates for office and *aides* to candidates for office. His Republican counterpart, Ginny Littell, is trying to make Lesniak eat crow, putting out a statement suggesting that maybe now he will stop criticizing people for their child-care arrangements in a time when good child care is so hard to find.

The Bacon revelation—however trivial it actually is, and in my view it is trivial—should go a long way toward neutralizing the issue for the remainder of 1993. Already there are signs that Whitman and Edwards are managing to put the issue behind them.

The two Republicans were able to change the subject somewhat this week. Whitman had press events on Monday and Wednesday at which she scored some substantive points. On Monday she stood outside the Meadowlands Sports Complex, New Jersey's crown jewel of sports and entertainment, and blasted the authority that runs it for inflating salaries and creating jobs for political cronies of the governor. She also blasted the governor for going along with the Sports and Exposition Authority's debt refinancing scheme last year, which shifted the debt burden from the Sports Authority to the state budget for the first time

ever. It's a good point. There is a perception of arrogance about the way
the Sports Authority operates in the state and gets its way with the
political leaders, and Whitman is tapping into a vein of genuine resentment.

On Wednesday Whitman went to the Statehouse and blasted
Florio for creating patronage jobs for political cronies. A day earlier, the
Asbury Park Press had run an excellent piece, later picked up by the
Associated Press and widely disseminated, that the Florio administration
had hired eight thousand new state workers in 1991 and '92 despite a
self-imposed hiring freeze. There were plausible reasons for most of the
new hires—ranging from new prison beds needing staffing to people
leaving their jobs and needing to be replaced. But the headline still looked
bad. Whitman rode the wave of that story and promised that, if elected,
she would not create a single job for a politically connected person. She
didn't say she'd ban patronage altogether; she would still reward the loyal
and the trustworthy. She just wouldn't create new jobs. As an issue, it
seems to have some appeal.

Cary Edwards, meanwhile, drew less attention this week. His
one big news story was a meeting with the legislative leaders, Haytaian
and DiFrancesco, billed by the Edwards campaign as a "summit." They
discussed the state budget and Edwards's notion that instead of cutting
spending, the state should give tax breaks to business to stimulate the
economy and create permanent private-sector jobs (as opposed to temporary public-works jobs). It's a sensible proposal, but not terribly grabby.

Part of the battle going on between the Republicans is geographi-
cal and territorial. On Thursday Whitman picked up the endorsement of
most of the top Republicans in Middlesex County, a swing county between her and Edwards. Tomorrow Edwards will go to Essex County,
where he is stronger, and display his endorsements from that populous
and high-profile county. The Republican nomination can be won on the
strength of organizational support in enough counties, and so far Whitman seems out in front on that part of the struggle.

A new wild card in the race is Clinton's economic plan. Whitman's
press secretary, Dave Marziale, was quite enthusiastic about its prospects
for reopening the Florio tax issue. If Clinton raises taxes and the public
comes to resent it, the link between Florio and Clinton could serve to
further remind voters how much they resented Florio's tax hikes three

years ago. Both men ran on loose pledges against new taxes, then hiked taxes by record amounts in their first months in office (assuming the Clinton plan passes Congress). The parallels are so obvious that Florio was on "The Today Show" last Monday being asked what advice he'd give to Clinton.

This is the Republican hope, that Florio and Clinton will both blow up in an explosion of public revulsion against high taxes. But as of now, the public is behind Clinton three to one, even four to one in some polls.

★ Sunday, February 28 ★

The poll that everyone's been waiting for is out today. It's the *Star-Ledger/ Eagleton* poll on Governor Florio's "popularity," done by the Eagleton Institute of Politics at Rutgers University, the state's most official polling outfit. The last such poll was in September of '92, when Florio measured a 29 percent approval rating. That is to say, 29 percent of the sample thought he was doing either an "excellent" or "good" job—the remaining 65 percent rated him "fair" or "poor." Florio's numbers have been climb-ing steadily, but very slowly, since he registered 18 percent approval in October of 1990, in the first sampling after his record-breaking tax hike.

Now, under a front-page *Star-Ledger* headline saying "Jerseyans see Florio in more favorable light," the newest poll of 801 registered voters shows Florio's approval rating up 7 percentage points, to 36 per-cent: 6 percent "excellent," 30 percent "good," 41 percent "fair," 19 percent "poor," and 4 percent "don't know." That's the good news. The bad news for Florio is that, when asked whether the governor should be re-elected, 51 percent say "no," 38 percent say "yes," and 11 percent "don't know" or say "it depends." Even among those who say they voted for Florio in 1989, 31 percent say he should not be re-elected. Among registered Democrats, 33 percent say he should not be re-elected. Among independents, who are the group that usually decides elections in this state, 34 percent said he deserves re-election, 55 percent said he does not.

So these are mixed results for the governor. But the trend is up, and the poll showed increases in the proportion of New Jerseyans who feel things are "going in the right direction" in New Jersey. These results dovetail with a private poll, done by the Democratic State Committee and partially leaked to reporters last week, showing Florio with a 20-point lead over Whitman and an 18-point lead over Edwards in head-to-head match-ups. Democrats were said to be ecstatic over that poll, though reporters who wrote about it were quick to point out it had been taken at the height of the Republicans' Nannygate problems.

Another fortuitous circumstance has broken Jim Florio's way. On Thursday of this past week, totally out of the blue, the Republican-controlled state assembly voted 54 to 23 to override the governor's veto of a bill that weakens his original ban on assault weapons. Suddenly an issue that works in the governor's favor was back on page one. Florio and the legislature have been jockeying over military-style semi-automatic "assault weapons" for two years. The governor banned them. The National Rifle Association and its New Jersey affiliate, the Coalition of New Jersey Sportsmen, then worked to defeat Democratic legislators who had supported the governor. Their argument: that by banning all such weapons now in existence Florio was "confiscating private property" and making "criminals" out of otherwise decent and law-abiding sportsmen and gun collectors. The gun lobby helped usher in the veto-proof Republican-controlled legislature in the 1991 legislative election, largely by climbing on board the antitax, anti–school-funding shift bandwagon.

An Eagleton poll once showed 73 percent of New Jerseyans support Florio's efforts to rid the state of assault weapons, and the governor has used the issue shamelessly to try to build bonds with the public. He has acted, of course, both out of principle and out of a desire to rescue himself politically. Every time the issue comes to a head, Florio goes around the state holding press conferences at which he is normally flanked by uniformed police officers, who listen as he lambastes the Republicans for caving in to the gun lobby. He even carries a prop with him, a blue and gold felt banner with a semi-automatic machine gun sewn into it and the words "WHO OWNS NEW JERSEY?" He seems to relish the fight, this former boxer, especially because he perceives himself on not only the right but the *popular* side this time. The Republicans had been threatening for six months to override the most recent veto in the ongoing battle, but they had never put it to a vote, and most observers felt the votes weren't there. Thursday, after the surprise vote in the assembly, Florio interrupted his prepared remarks at an event in Morristown to say that he was "outraged" by this "sneak attack on sanity."

The gun issue now moves to the senate. If the senators go along with their assembly colleagues, assault weapons will once again be legal in New Jersey. The lineup in the senate is close; serious head counting is going on. Either way, Governor Florio will continue his crusade to outlaw these "weapons of war." He has already scheduled another press event on the subject for this Tuesday and undoubtedly will hold more. As long as the issue is hot, conventional wisdom says that he benefits from it. Whitman and Edwards are on the sidelines on this one. Whitman is urging a compromise position that would continue the ban but uphold a "grandfather clause" allowing current owners (an estimated 100,000 people) to keep their weapons. Edwards, in an odd stance, is refusing to take a position on the issue, saying he "refuses to let Jim Florio set the agenda on crime fighting." Pressed by reporters to declare himself on the assault weapons ban, he just repeats his disdain for Florio's approach.

On another front, Whitman held a Statehouse news conference on Wednesday in the hallway outside the state treasurer's office. At her side was a cartoon of Jim Florio, blown up and pasted on posterboard, with bags of money and bloated budgets. The prop didn't work, and the news conference was a somewhat strained attempt at criticizing the fiscal record of the Florio administration. Whitman unveiled a four-point plan for strengthening the state's fiscal management—such things as a constitutional amendment requiring the state to balance the budget using only "recurring" revenues (i.e., no one-shot gimmicks). She was pretty sharp in her criticism of the administration for its recent debt-refinancing package, which in fact resulted in $900 million worth of new debt that state taxpayers will have to pay off between 1995 and 2013 at a rate of $87 million per year.

I was struck by the fact that Whitman's brother, Dan Todd, was at this little gathering. He is a Montana rancher, who came in for her announcement speech last month. Here he was again with his Stetson-style hat in his hand, a nice-looking man of fifty-three, half Wall Street banker, half cowboy. I struck up a conversation with him, as I had once before. He said he planned to be on the campaign trail with his sister through much of 1993. "I got some cowboys who can handle the cattle probably better without me," he said. I was impressed that a brother would take time out to support a sister's run for office, and said something to that effect. "A family affair," said the low-key Montana cowboy who once served in the New Jersey assembly and whose father ran the state Republican party for many years.

★ Tuesday, March 2 ★

In the 1992 presidential race, it was Ross Perot who came out of oblivion to shake up the race and leave a profound imprint on the American electorate and the political establishment. The Ross Perot of the 1993 New Jersey governor's race just could be James Wallwork, who formally declared his candidacy for the Republican nomination at the Statehouse today.

Wallwork is sixty-two, a retired distributor of refrigeration, heating, and air-conditioning equipment (i.e, a "businessman"), and a former legislator. He served for sixteen years, until 1981, when he ran for governor and finished fourth in a crowded field of Republicans. Since then, he hasn't been heard from until a few weeks ago, when out of the loins of Nannygate he sprang, a would-be candidate saying his phone was "ringing off the hook" with well-wishers urging him to run and rescue the Republican party from its ignominious standard-bearers.

I must say, I was pleasantly surprised today. For weeks, people have been joking about Wallwork, saying he was coming out of the woodwork, calling him, as Wayne King of the *New York Times* did on "Reporters' Roundtable" last weekend, "Mr. Wal-mart" and "Mr. Woodwork." But the man who stood before the Statehouse press corps today, next to a big sign sporting a "1-800-801-VOTE" campaign hotline number, was the genuine article—a conservative, with convictions, and ideas, and a forceful manner. He reminded me not only of Perot but of Ronald Reagan in his slightly less polished General Electric days, a raw conservative just itchin' to get his hands on government so he can do nothing with it.

Wallwork's big pitch was to roll back the Florio tax hikes. "I pledge to you that in my first four years we'll repeal every dime of the taxes that Florio and the liberals increased—every dime!" he intoned. Beyond that he offered what's becoming the standard populist stew: term limits, initiative and referendum, less government, less regulation. When pressed to explain how he'd cut spending by $2.2 billion after he rolled back the taxes, he said he'd "look in every nook and cranny of the government" for political patronage jobs and waste. He'd check the heating, the lighting, "the rugs on the floor" in state offices (naturally, from a former heating and air-conditioning man). That answer didn't really wash with the reporters, but it was delivered well.

The scene was a small caucus room across the hall from the senate. About a dozen-and-a-half Wallwork supporters walked in with the candidate, a bunch of people who, by their average age and style, looked as if they'd stepped off of a *Saturday Evening Post* cover. Wallwork himself is physically imposing, perhaps six-foot-two, with a chiseled face vaguely reminiscent of Burt Lancaster, and a cowlick-curlicue in his salt-and-pepper pompadour.

What impressed me most were some of his other ideas that came out spontaneously in the question-and-answer session. For example, he said we should get rid of the oxygenated gasoline the Department of Environmental Protection and Energy recently mandated for winter-driving clean air purposes, because it was cutting gas mileage in New Jerseyans' cars by 15 percent, while only contributing 3 or 4 percent to improvement in carbon monoxide emissions. (Just this morning I had noticed I've been getting less mileage in my van; I hadn't figured out the reason until Wallwork helped me.) He proposed that assault weapons be used only on certain firing ranges, where sportsmen who wanted to shoot them could rent them. And he promised to crack down on tractor trailers, perhaps force them to drive in the right lane only. "Every morning I hear on the radio of a traffic tie-up because of a jackknifed tractor trailer," he said, and he's right. They're involved in too many accidents, and they're dangerous.

Plain talk. It's what got Harry Truman elected. It's what Ross Perot specialized in. And now it's what Jim Wallwork (it's "Jim" now for the campaign) has suddenly brought to the Republican primary sweepstakes.

How far he'll go is hard to say. He has just two paid staffers. But he has hired a New York political consulting firm, Arthur Finkelstein and Co., which handled Senator Al D'Amato's recent victory and counts among its clients Jesse Helms and other notable conservatives. One of the paid staffers, a young Finkelstein associate, was very eager at today's event to show the TV commercial his firm has done for Wallwork. It's a good spot, and it ends with this line: "Jim Wallwork for governor. Finally, a Republican we can be proud of." The way the announcer says it, he might as well have added, "Not like those other two Republicans who hired undocumented foreigners and failed to pay taxes on them."

Meanwhile, television people are an awfully disrespectful lot. Back at the station, I was putting my piece together, and needed to retrieve a tape I had loaned to an associate producer, who had borrowed it to make a freeze-frame for what's called the anchor box, the graphic element that sits above the anchor person's shoulder. I found her in the tape room, searching through the tape of Wallwork's press conference. "Did you do a head with him?" she asked, meaning did I interview him. I explained that I hadn't, that the only shots of Wallwork were at the podium. "There's no close-up of the geek?" she asked incredulously.

If Wallwork and his wife could have heard that, they'd either have been furious or laughed their heads off. His wife's name, by the way, is Lark. And their daughter's name is Lyric. Lark and Lyric Wallwork.

★ Monday, March 8 ★

One of the things that makes this race interesting is that it involves a likely match-up between two nationally known political consultants, James Carville for the Democrats, and Ed Rollins for Christie Whitman. Rollins was in the state today for a luncheon briefing of the state's political reporters. The location was a meeting room in a rather dingy-looking Ramada Inn right off the Garden State Parkway in Clark, a stone's throw from the Whitman headquarters. To my surprise, Rollins walked in with Lyn Nofziger, another well-known Republican operative; I've seen the two of them on Ted Koppel's "Nightline" many times, and here they were in New Jersey.

About a dozen reporters showed up. Rollins and Nofziger sat at the head of a long table along with Dan Todd, Christie's brother, whose presence there signalled a larger role in the campaign than I had thought.

Rollins did most of the talking. He is an interesting man to listen to. He was press secretary in Ronald Reagan's 1980 presidential campaign, managed the '84 campaign, and was co-chairman with Hamilton Jordan of Ross Perot's '92 campaign until a serious falling-out caused him to quit after forty-five days. Perot withdrew from the race the next day, only to jump back in two months later. Nofziger is another old Reagan hand, who's helping Whitman out as an unpaid advisor and probably as a favor to his friend Rollins.

As Rollins explained it, Christie Whitman is positioning herself as an unconventional politician and outsider. He called her "a new kind of candidate, a different kind of a governor, not tied to the old-boy network in Trenton . . . a nontraditional candidate unbeholden to anyone but the voters." He said that although she's presenting herself as an alternative to Florio, "we're focused on Edwards now." Edwards, he said, is a good candidate—"he's run before, he's been attorney general, he's known, he has a good campaign team, but he has vulnerabilities." Pressed to name some, he said Edwards had greatly increased the size of the attorney general's staff and had recommended clemencies for prisoners to Governor Kean. These are previews of the kinds of charges Whitman may throw at Edwards, although Rollins promised a clean race and a no-first-strike policy on negative ads.

"We want to take a high-road campaign, but I promise you, we're not going to be patsies," he warned.

He spoke admiringly of Jim Florio as a politician, calling him "tough," but less admiringly of him as governor, saying Florio, too, has vulnerabilities and "numbers that are still extremely weak for an incumbent." It's clear that Whitman will try to link Florio and Edwards as two similar types of politicians. Rollins pointed out that Edwards's law firm has done bond work with the state, and he called Edwards a "bond salesman" for the Florio administration.

"Cary Edwards and Jim Florio," Rollins said. "If you ask me there's not a dime's bit of difference between 'em."

The most newsworthy thing Rollins said—and the element I led my piece with tonight—was that Whitman is leading Edwards 2 to 1 in her poll, his poll, and a state Republican party poll. I hadn't heard that before. Another interesting revelation was his fee. I asked if it was public information. He said, sure, he's earning $10,000 a month doing this campaign, and it's the only one he's doing this year. "That's less than Carville. He's getting $15,000 a month from the Democratic State Committee and maybe some more from the Florio campaign," Rollins said. He also spoke admiringly of Carville but dismissed the idea that a Whitman-Florio race would be a shoot-out between two top guns. "A political consultant is like a jockey," he said. "He's only as good as the horse he's riding, and if he's got a good horse he wins."

He also said that he warned the Whitman campaign staff not to become overconfident. "'Any time you're feeling cocky,' I've told them, 'take a look at the Brendan Byrne Arena,'" he said, a reference to former Democratic governor Brendan Byrne's record-low 17 percent approval rating in 1977 before he went on to win re-election that same year.

To Rollins the election will be about the business climate in New Jersey, and jobs, and who can manage the state's fiscal affairs. Someone asked if Whitman's wealth would be a liability. Rollins said he was sure the rival campaigns would use it in some fashion, but he pointed to New Jersey's one very rich U.S. senator (Frank Lautenberg), its other pretty rich U.S. senator (Bill Bradley), and its rich and popular former governor (Tom Kean) and said, "The issue is, does the person understand working people? The people of New Jersey are looking not at background, but at who can be the most effective leader." And then he cited the most obvious example of a candidate whose wealth the populace was willing to overlook, his boss for forty-five days, Ross Perot. "Money didn't hurt him," he said. "It gave him his independence. It gives her independence."

All in all, Rollins was pretty upbeat about Whitman's chances to be the next governor, though not so foolish as to telegraph it. "We have to run a perfect campaign to win this race. And they have to make mistakes for us to win this race," he said.

As the session began to ebb, Rollins said he hoped we could do it again and to call him anytime. "One thing I'll never do is bullshit you."

"That sounds like BS to me," said David Wald of the *Star-Ledger*, and everyone laughed, including Rollins.

For the past several weeks, one issue has dominated political life and political discourse in New Jersey: assault weapons. Even though there have been two major disasters in this period, the terrorist bombing of the World Trade Center that killed 6 and injured 1,000, and the Blizzard of '93, which was credited with taking 219 lives nationally and 3 in New Jersey, political talk in this state has been trained on the state senate, where the override of Governor Florio's veto of a bill weakening his assault weapons ban headed after the assembly accomplished the override on February 25.

Ever since then, Governor Florio has been out virtually every weekday staging a media event designed to rally support for his position and, indirectly, for himself. The governor has been riding the issue for all it's worth. Phones have been ringing off the hook in the offices of state senators, so much so that sometimes they can't even call their own offices. (This incessant phone calling is a relatively new phenomenon, part of the post–Ross Perot, talk-radio, direct-democracy trend.) The NRA (National Rifle Association), with 85,000 New Jersey members, has been trying to hold its ground but has been failing, as Republican senator after Republican senator has caved in to public pressure and sided with the governor.

Today the senate voted. It was a stunning defeat for the NRA. Beware the ides of March, a gun lobbyist joked this morning, and he had no idea how bad it would be. Instead of the twenty-seven votes needed to override the governor, instead of the eighteen votes the NRA still counted after all the Republican defections in recent days, the veto override attempt got not one single vote.

Republican senators apparently calculated that they were killing themselves by appearing to be in the hip pocket of the NRA. Seeing that they were going to lose anyway, Republican supporters of the override abstained or voted no in order to heal some of the divisiveness the issue has caused within their party and also to try to take the issue away from Jim Florio a little bit, or at least stop him from grandstanding on it.

What it means for the governor's race is that another issue is off the table, and that Florio continues to play a winning hand in 1993. This issue has been great for the governor. He looks sensible and courageous fighting the gun lobby. New Jerseyans, like people all across America, are horrified at the rising tide of violent crime, and the idea that a governor is trying to do something about it—however marginal the thing itself, and it is marginal—appeals to many people. The position of the NRA and many Republicans, that the private property of law-abiding gun owners is being confiscated without compensation, is being lost in a sea of imagery and rhetoric about drug-dealers, terrorists, and fanatics. The fact that the debate has played out at a time when a religious cult called the Branch Davidians, armed with semi-automatics, is locked in a sixteen-day stand-off with authorities in Waco, Texas, after assassinating four federal agents, only adds to the morality-tale quality of the showdown between Florio and the gun lobby. U.S. attorney general Janet Reno called Florio this afternoon, after the senate vote, to congratulate him, and former Reagan press secretary James Brady, the ultimate symbol of handgun madness, was at the Statehouse with Florio last week.

★ Thursday, March 18 ★

Christie Whitman took a hit today. How serious remains to be seen.

John Rooney is a Bergen County assemblyman, chairman of the assembly energy committee, and a supporter of fellow Bergen Republican Cary Edwards. He called a rare Statehouse news conference to accuse Christie Whitman of having had state employees do some personal work for her when she was president of the Board of Public Utilities (BPU). Rooney handed reporters copies of two memos indicating that BPU staffers had helped Whitman investigate the possibility in 1989 and 1990 of installing a satellite dish on her Far Hills estate.

Rooney described the extent of the help as "massive and continuous." He called it "the tip of the iceberg" on Whitman's irregularities. He said he was sure the Florio administration had this and other information it would use against Whitman if she becomes the nominee. "I don't relish what I have to do here today," he said, but went on that he felt duty-bound as a Republican to warn his party of Whitman's vulnerability on the matter, so party members could rally around Edwards instead.

It was a classic hatchet job, delivered by a big burly double-chinned Republican who is generally likeable and keeps a low profile. Rooney and an Edwards aide both swore that Rooney was on his own here, not carrying out an assignment.

As in Nannygate, the Whitman camp was forced into a defensive mode. It took about three hours to get my phone call returned and a written response faxed out. From that statement and several interviews, a picture emerged of a few staffers in the BPU's Office of Cable Television trying to butter up the boss by helping her learn about satellite dishes and arranging for a survey of her property, for which she paid $135. The dish was never purchased. The help does not seem "massive and continuous." Nevertheless, a minor infraction was committed that enables a charge to be levelled—a charge that plays into the idea of Whitman as a rich aristocrat somehow above the problems of normal people. The irony is that she was investigating satellite dishes because her Far Hills home was in an area where the houses are so far apart that cable TV had never come to the neighborhood. Her press secretary says she still doesn't have cable, or a dish, on the family homestead in Hunterdon County where she now lives.

★ Sunday, March 21 ★

The three top contenders—Whitman, Edwards, and Florio—made their first back-to-back appearances of the year on Friday morning before a gathering of the New Jersey Press Association in Morristown. A taping kept me in Trenton, but I got to see much of it on videotape, which was fed down to me from Newark so that I could put together a small report for the evening newscast.

Each candidate was given an hour. Whitman went first. She was cool, crisp, and in control. An audience of about a hundred newspaper reporters, editors, and executives listened as she held up a booklet and described her new sixteen-point "Blueprint for Economic Revival." The points she discussed I had heard before: multiyear budgeting and the "goal" of rolling back the Florio tax increases. When she said that government should start really examining what it's spending its dollars on, and that under her it would, her rhetoric went dead. Every politician in Trenton has been claiming to do just that since I can remember.

Edwards followed, and he spoke of a five-point plan for the economy. Again, familiar ideas. Edwards is big on tax cuts and credits to stimulate business, and his pet idea has become tourism promotion. He argues, persuasively, that every million dollars spent on tourism advertising brings back seventy million in business and nine million in tax revenues. Whitman was not there to hear Edwards; she reportedly was led out one stairwell while Edwards was led in through another, so they wouldn't have to encounter one another (not that they couldn't handle it).

In the question-and-answer session, Edwards became particularly intense on the subject of assault weapons. He declared that he is against them but blasted Florio for turning the ban into a major symbol of the war on crime. Florio is an ineffective crime fighter, Edwards said, and the assault weapons ban is "a charade." It was a forceful and impressive performance.

In her Q&A session, Whitman adroitly handled a question about her wealth and, therefore, her inability to relate to average people by saying it's not where you come from, but what you believe and what you do. She cited Tom Kean, JFK, and FDR as examples of people of privilege who were able to empathize with and help common folk. Asked about the satellite-dish revelations of the day before, Whitman repeated her explanation and dismissed the charge as political mischief.

When Jim Florio took the floor, the dynamics changed. Florio, as sitting governor, commands a natural respect by virtue of the office he holds. People are one degree more awestruck by being in the presence of this man whose picture is in the paper every day. At the same time, they have heard his rhetoric many many times before. There's no novelty in listening to him defend his record, which is largely what he does whenever he speaks in public.

Florio started off by dropping the name of Bill Clinton (something he's been doing a lot lately) and recounting a discussion they had had recently. "He said just as he likes to hear himself described as the 'comeback kid,' he thinks of me as 'the resurrection kid,'" Florio said. "I know it's near the Easter season, but I'm not sure I'm in that class." The character-istically self-deprecating line drew a nice laugh.

Florio was the only one of the three to mention that he had read a book lately. The book was *Coming to Public Judgment,* by the pollster Daniel Yankelovich, and Florio used it to make the point that public policy is about choices and options, not about what's good and bad in the ab-stract. He was saying indirectly that Whitman and Edwards have to do more than just criticize his tax and education policies.

Later that day, Florio was the guest of honor at a roast at the Trump Taj Mahal in Atlantic City thrown by the Camden County Demo-cratic party. This was a big night for Camden party boss George Norcross, a young comer who has been feuding with Florio but managed to convince the governor to be the roastee at this $650 per person fund-raiser. Ini-tially, Florio was resistant to the idea, but his chief of staff, Joe Salema, and chief counsel, Bob DeCotiis, convinced him to go along with it. It would heal the rift between Florio and the Camden faction for at least the remainder of this year and would send a strong signal of Democratic unity to the state's political community.

The roast was something of a bust. Instead of twelve hundred people, there were more like eight hundred. Instead of Ted Kennedy, James Carville, and Donald Trump, all names that had been bandied about, the list of roasters was limited to former governor Brendan Byrne, Congressman Rob Andrews, and comedian Joe Piscopo. But there was one sterling moment. Piscopo coerced a reluctant Florio to don a pair of shades, hold a toy saxophone, and join Piscopo in a sax duet, as piped-in sax music lent the illusion that they were wailing on their instruments. Florio good-naturedly got into it, rocking back and forth. People who know him—who know how stiff and serious his normal demeanor is—could barely contain their delight. The still photographers went wild (no TV cameras, unfortunately, were there). And it did for Florio just what it did for Bill Clinton. He looked great!

Governor Florio officially became the front-runner today. The Bergen *Record* put out a poll showing Florio ahead of Whitman in a head-to-head match-up, 39 percent to 30 percent, with 31 percent undecided. Against Edwards, Florio was ahead 40 percent to 25 percent with 35 percent undecided.

Somehow I wasn't surprised by this, although the *Record* ran a big banner headline saying "FLORIO AHEAD," as if a tide had turned. I've been sensing since January that Florio is on the rise.

Still, it's early. Whitman was in our studio this evening to appear on NJN's nightly call-in show. I sat with her in the green room for about ten minutes. She attributed Florio's good showing to all the positive press he's gotten on the gun issue, plus a generally positive press of late, plus Clinton's popularity. She said she and Edwards were hurt by "all the negatives," which was obviously a reference to Nannygate and, now, satellite dishes. Today's *Record* had a cartoon of Whitman as an elephant with two big satellite dishes for ears; the caption read, "Dumbo."

It's not all bad for Whitman. The poll had her ahead of Edwards by 28 to 8 among Republicans and Republican-leaning independents, with Wallwork at 2, and a fourth candidate, Patrick Gilligan, at 1 (no one I know has seen him yet). A whopping 61 percent of those voters are undecided still, meaning Edwards has a prayer. Most important for the Republicans, when the entire sample was asked if Florio deserved re-election, 39 percent said yes, and 45 percent said no. In other words, Florio does better against the actual Republican candidates than against a phantom fill-in-the-blank dream candidate called "someone else."

★ Wednesday, March 31 ★

"I hear Cary's thinking about getting out," a veteran lobbyist said to me at the Statehouse on Monday. It's apparently not true, but the fact that he said it, and that I found it plausible, is a sign of the trouble Cary Edwards is in.

After garnering 8 percent among Republicans in the Bergen *Record* poll, Edwards lost the Middlesex County Republican convention to Christie Whitman last Saturday by 610 to 91. Only a handful of counties have a convention, and it's arguable how much any of them means, but Middlesex is one of the few that has symbolic importance this year. A corridor county in the center of the state, Middlesex has a blue-collar, meat-and-potatoes component to it, and Edwards is trying to be the candidate with the working-class roots. And yet he wasn't able to develop much organizational strength here. The county Republican chairman, Sam Thompson, declared for Whitman weeks ago, and Edwards couldn't reverse the momentum. Middlesex went for the blueblood.

Key aides to Edwards deny it, but there is also rumored to be disarray and in-fighting in his campaign—"turmoil," as Florio's campaign manager, Jamie Fox, put it on the phone today. The Edwards campaign manager, Jeff Michaels, seems to have been supplanted by campaign "director" Pete McDonough as the top in-house day-to-day strategist. Last week the campaign announced that Greg Stevens, former communications director for Governor Kean and partner with legendary Republican image-maker Roger Ailes in Arlington, Virginia, was signing on as a consultant. This was seen as a slap in the face to Jay Smith, the campaign's initial consultant, though Smith said he welcomed the extra help. The campaign also brought in Wayne Haselbagh, a former Edwards lieutenant in the attorney general days, as a full-time organizer. "Too many chiefs," says a Whitman person, noting that Bill Palatucci and Larry Purpuro (both of whom worked for Whitman in 1990) are also advising Edwards.

The Edwards camp, of course, has a positive spin for all the latest developments. The *Record* poll had only 277 in the Republican sample. Middlesex was a county they had conceded weeks earlier. They also *won* county endorsements in Atlantic, Cumberland, and Cape May, bringing their county total almost up to Whitman's, 7 to 9. The organizational shuffle, they say, is but a mirror of Edwards's management "style," which derives from Tom Kean's: namely, surround yourself with as many strong-minded people as possible. These answers are satisfactory without being terribly convincing. Edwards may not be thinking of dropping out and "cutting a deal" with Whitman, as the lobbyist said he'd heard. But his campaign is on the defensive.

Cary Edwards is digging in his heels and trying not to panic. He held a Statehouse news conference to unveil his anticrime package last week and another one this week on education. Whitman, by contrast, has not met the press in any formal way yet this month. She is talking to Republican groups and lying low. Her campaign does not put out a daily schedule, as the other two Republicans do. Hazel Gluck told me yesterday a good friend of Whitman's is critically ill in London, and Christie will fly there for a visit this weekend. Gluck expressed a slight embarrassment that Whitman can afford a quick flight to England, which shows how sensitive Whitmanites have become to the wealth issue.

The tone of the primary is becoming more shrill. Edwards has put out his first radio spot. It seizes on a statement Whitman's campaign issued the day of his crime presentation. She said, "the economy is the issue," implying that crime is less so. The Edwards radio spot has an announcer saying, "Maybe crime isn't an issue around Whitman's estate, but it sure is throughout most of New Jersey." The Whitman camp cried foul. The Edwards camp said, in effect, stop whining.

Whitman's radio ads are all geared to the economy and state fiscal policy. They're positive and straightforward, except for one that begins, "Did you know the Office of the First Lady costs a million dollars?" That hit a nerve. "WHITMAN RAPS FLORIO'S WIFE" read a headline in the *New Jersey Herald* of Sussex County. An argument ensued over how much the Office of First Lady in fact costs. Lucinda Florio, who goes around the state spreading good cheer and doing good works (or at least praising those who do) is nonsalaried but has a staff of five. The governor's office says they cost $177,000 a year, hardly a million. The Whitman camp says that figure doesn't include ancillary expenses such as security, transportation, and speech-writing. Jeff Michaels, of the Edwards camp, called me to cluck over this huge "tactical blunder" on Whitman's part. Republicans like to say Lucinda is Florio's strongest asset, and an attack on her could be seen as a mistake. "In the repertoire of things they can use, to go after Lucinda?" Michaels moaned. "The one positive *about* Jim Florio is Lucinda!"

By and large, Whitman is taking the high road and staying fo-cused. She's aiming at Florio. She won another county convention this week in Mercer County, by 70 percent to 30 for Edwards. She is running "a front-runner's campaign," as one of the reporters put it on my show this week. The Edwards campaign, in its eagerness to alter the dynamics, is taking comments by Whitman or her staff and "stretching their mean-ing," as an AP story put it.

Edwards has something to say when he talks about crime. His ten-point plan includes putting four thousand more police on the streets, appointing judges who believe in the death penalty, and creating "gun-free school zones" to mirror the drug-free school zone program with its mandatory prison term for violators that he instituted as attorney gen-eral. He is less convincing when he talks about education, where his basic thrust is to let local districts get "creative" and stop following mandates from Trenton. At his crime press conference, Edwards also attacked Whitman's longstanding membership in the National Council on Crime and Delinquency (NCCD), which he called "a San Francisco–based lib-eral think tank that believes in legalizing prostitution, drugs, public and disorderly drunkenness, opposes the death penalty, and opposes manda-tory sentences." The NCCD is not as leftish as Edwards portrays it, and, except for mandatory sentences, Whitman doesn't agree with any of the positions Edwards imputes to it.

After the crime press conference, I talked to Greg Stevens, the new consultant for Edwards, who has a reputation as the guru who guided Tom Kean's rise to popularity, though people tend to forget he also worked for Pete Dawkins and Jim Courter. "She couldn't do this," Stevens said, referring to Whitman and to the session we'd just sat through. "She couldn't talk substance for an hour about one of the fundamental issues of the state." He said Edwards "understands how government works" and "Florio will eat her alive" if she wins and has to demonstrate knowledge. Did he think Edwards could pull it out? "I wouldn't be here if there wasn't a great opportunity to win," he said. I had heard that he was working with Edwards on "personal presentation" and how to phrase things. "He's got plenty of beef," said Stevens, in his slightly cocky way. "I'm supplying the gravy."

Jim Wallwork, meanwhile, is proving to be a slasher. To get any traction at all, he has to attack, and he's doing it with gusto. On the same day the other two unveiled radio ads, he stood outside Christie Whitman's campaign headquarters in Clark and demanded that she and Edwards release their tax returns, as he has done. Two photographers and no reporters showed up, which is a sign of Wallwork's low status, but thanks to the fax machine he got fairly good press play. He also filed $218,988 in contributions, entitling him to his first allotment of public matching funds, a sign that he is kindling some interest, however small.

There is talk that John Budzash, a cofounder of the antitax group Hands Across New Jersey, might enter the Republican primary before the April 15 filing deadline. That would probably hurt Wallwork. Budzash is a colorful troglodyte, a forty-two-year-old postal employee who talks fast, is full of energy, and embodies the wisdom and values of the common man. He would add spice and possibly alter the field.

★ Monday, April 12 ★

"This is wonderful!" Jim Florio intoned tonight as he looked out over a crowd of about eight hundred at the Meadowlands Hilton. It was the evening rally before tomorrow's campaign kickoff speech. The crowd was a mixture of politicos and normal people who must have been coaxed heavily into attending. The free hot dogs and cash bar were not the draw.

Florio was at the podium surrounded by HUD secretary Henry Cisneros, representing President Clinton; Kathleen Kennedy Townsend, the daughter of Robert Kennedy; Congressman Bob Torricelli; former heavyweight boxing champ Joe Frazier; and Lucinda Florio. The first three gave testimonial speeches, and there was a lot of talk about courage, and candor, and truth. Kennedy Townsend thanked Florio for standing up to the NRA. "Maybe someone else won't lose their father because of what you've done," she said, looking at the governor.

By the time Torricelli uttered the words "truth, courage . . . ," a cameraman on the media platform in the rear of the ballroom said, "It's Superman!" and got a laugh. I was there having done a live shot from the scene. Earlier in the day I'd stopped at Florio headquarters in Edison and

Whitman headquarters in Clark to get sound bites for a piece to go with the live shot. Now we were covering the evening rally, even though none of it is likely to make the air. We don't have another newscast until tomorrow evening, and tomorrow's speech will be far more important than anything said tonight. This is one of those occasions when you shoot tape only in the event something wild gets said—and with Jim Florio it rarely does; he's too controlled for that.

A band played the theme from *Rocky* as Florio entered the room and again when he ended his remarks. Around the room were posters with the new Florio campaign logo on them—a signature-script Jim Florio in red against a blue background and below it in white his name and title: Jim Florio. Governor. It's a hip, bold design. The music was trite, but, then again, he was a boxer, and this is a comeback.

Florio spoke about the importance of "responsibility" and "excellence." He told the crowd that the election of '92 "was very inspiring to me" because people voted for "active leadership. They rejected passive leadership. That's what we've been about—active leadership." He said his administration's aim was to "stay ahead of the curve, stay ahead of the problems," and he quoted hockey star Wayne Gretzky on the importance of being not where the puck is but where it's gonna be, which carried echoes of Bill Bradley's "a sense of where you are," which became the title of John McPhee's biography of Bradley.

Floriocrats I spoke to today—campaign manager Jamie Fox, lawyer-lobbyist Frank Capece, Cherry Hill mayor Susan Bass Levin, state chairman Ray Lesniak—are pleased with their positioning as the campaign formally begins. An *Asbury Park Press* poll this weekend showed Florio behind all three Republicans in head-to-head match-ups, but the Democrats don't believe that poll and say its methodology is screwy. Lesniak says their own polling shows Florio with double-digit leads over all Republicans. "We've at least levelled the playing field, and whoever thought we could do that?" said one.

"Carville told us last year that we'd be behind in the polls all the way until election day," Lesniak said gleefully, noting they were already ahead of that timetable.

Notably absent tonight and, I'm told, again tomorrow: Carville. An article in the magazine *New Jersey Reporter* says there are rivalries in the Florio camp and bad chemistry between Florio and Carville. Trying to check that out today, I got little in the way of corroboration, other than a comment that there is some "resentment" at Carville's "notoriety." Officially, Carville's absence is explained by his work on the Los Angeles mayor's race, which happens soon.

Meanwhile, Mark Magyar, of the *Asbury Park Press*, had a piece on the front page today saying the Republican primary "is Christine Todd Whitman's to lose—and both she and her opponents know it." He was the first to state so baldly this obvious fact.

★   Tuesday, April 13   ★

There was earnestness and calculation to the way Jim Florio announced his candidacy for re-election today, but not much excitement. The setting was a place called the Minnie B. Veal Community Center, a new building tucked away in a residential section of north Edison. I thought I'd been most everywhere in New Jersey, but this spot was so deep in the nexus of the suburban heartland of middle-class Middlesex County that I had never even been near it.

I counted nineteen TV cameras in the hall, a remarkable number for a state political event. Most belonged to New York and Philadelphia stations, but two of them were mine, so that NJN could air the announcement speech as a special tonight at eleven. About two or three hundred Florio supporters filled the hall, and the stage was filled with preteen children in Jim Florio t-shirts, half in red, half in blue.

After the obligatory chant of "four more years," the noontime event was given over to testimonials from seven ordinary people who had been helped by Florio programs, such as the first-time home-buyer program, the tuition assistance program, the welfare reform act, and the small business loan program. As the people read their words of praise for the governor, who was seated with his wife a few feet away, the crowd grew restless, especially the reporters on deadline. "This is ponderous," I wrote to myself in my notebook. As a half hour stretched toward forty-five minutes, reporters began commiserating with one another and criticizing the campaign. Doug Berman, the former state treasurer and campaign manager from 1989, was out in the hallway with many others who had lost interest.

And yet, there was merit to what the people were saying. And squeezed into news pieces, the desired effect would be achieved. "You have to remind people he did more than just raise taxes," Florio's spokesman Jon Shure would say later. Like Bill Clinton inviting fifty ordinary people to his inaugural, Jim Florio celebrated the common man and demonstrated his link to them. Let Whitman, Edwards, and Wallwork announce at the Statehouse; Florio will do it in a nondescript suburb surrounded by real people.

His remarks were good. They had a logic to them, and were not just a laundry list. He began by acknowledging the tax hikes that have defined his governorship, calling them "difficult decisions, many of which I hated to make" and challenging his opponents to say "what they'd have done differently and what they would change now." He painted a picture of the New Jersey he wants to lead voters into—a high-tech state with good jobs in science-based industries. And turning to the children behind him, he said, "The theme of my campaign is simple. The future. It's right here behind us. The children." As themes go, "the future" is grossly unimaginative, but taken as a whole the speech worked. It ended with a call to join "our program of action" and a pledge to continue to make the "tough decisions."

I was surprised at the number of key Florio people not present: Carville, Begala, Joe Salema, lobbyist Harold Hodes, finance chairman Lewis Katz, the cabinet. I guess they had more important things to do than hear another speech many of them had read in advance and approved. In the case of the cabinet, they'd have had to take a half-day off to attend or else cheat the taxpayers. I'm told Carville purposely stayed away because he's become so famous now that he would draw attention from Florio. Carville has become a victim of his own fame. He can't lurk in the back of the room at his candidates' announcements anymore.

While I covered Florio, my colleague Larry Stuelpnagel gathered anti-Florio remarks from Whitman, Edwards, and Wallwork, and wrapped them into a package with a Statehouse news conference called by GOP state chairman Ginny Littell, who blasted Florio and called him

"Governor Kevorkian" for "assisting the suicide of New Jersey's economy." She promised to send a Republican "truth squad" around the state tomorrow to correct Jim Florio's lies about his record.

The candidate filing deadline is two days away, and still no word from antitax activist John Budzash. Jim Florio chose the 13th for his announcement, showing he's not superstitious (the 15th, tax day, it's said, might be more of a jinx in his case).

Former House Speaker Tip O'Neill tells a story about a politician not getting someone's vote, inquiring as to why, and being told, "Because you never asked." A fatalist might note that, however tight his remarks were today, Jim Florio never explicitly declared his candidacy and never asked his listeners to give him their votes again.

★ Wednesday, April 14 ★

The third and final day of the Florio campaign kickoff took me and my crew to a catering hall in the little borough of Almonesson in Gloucester County at 8:30 in the morning. That's where about five hundred people gave their old congressman a big welcome. This was the South Jersey leg of the triad. Democratic national chairman David Wilhelm read a speech and inadvertently insulted Florio, who was standing next to him, by saying, "No one ever accused him of being popular." The line didn't go over well.

After the rally, Florio held his first formal news conference as a candidate and handled questions for about forty-five minutes. NJN was there again with two cameras for another eleven o'clock special. Florio was reasonable, self-assured, evasive at times, as he answered questions about taxes, the state of the economy, education, and his vision for the state. "The vision thing has never been one of my problems," he joked.

Although I got my third lead story in a row out of the Florio kickoff, the real news today was that John Budzash has decided to switch parties and enter the Democratic primary against Florio. This morning's *Asbury Park Press* said he might. Around three this afternoon I left a message on his home answering machine. The former tax-revolt leader called me back while I was in an editing room and confirmed that if he can get enough signatures by tomorrow at four—the filing deadline—he'll run as a Democrat. He said he'd quit his job as a postman yesterday. I recut the last voice track in my piece to reflect the news. When asked this morning about the possibility of a Budzash challenge, Florio's response was, "They say being governor involves making hard decisions—fundamental ones are like which party one belongs to." Florio smiled, but a Budzash challenge might annoy him.

★ Sunday, April 18 ★

My cameraman and I were set up and waiting in the governor's cabinet room around midday Friday. I could hear the governor in his private office being prepped by press secretary Jon Shure, who always asks in advance what you want to talk to the governor about. I was there to do an interview scheduled weeks ago about welfare reform, for a news series on the subject, but the topic of the day was Budzash, and I had asked Shure if I could squeeze in a Budzash question. I couldn't make out what they were saying. Then Florio walked in.

"Interesting week you've given us," I said.

He weighed my words for a second, then said, "That's my job. To keep you from being bored."

The day before, John Budzash—having shaved his mustache, donned a tie, and gotten his first professional haircut in fourteen years—had rushed in to the Division of Elections office five minutes after the 4:00 p.m. deadline and had filed petitions to run in the Democratic primary. Now, the Democratic state chairman, Ray Lesniak, was planning to challenge the validity of the petitions.

In our interview Florio questioned his new opponent's commitment to the Democratic party. "It's like me suddenly becoming a Republican and running in the Republican primary," he said. I asked if he had suspicions that someone had put Budzash up to it. "Not on camera," he said, nodding in the affirmative while the camera rolled.

Florio allies are convinced the NRA is behind Budzash, or perhaps the Republicans. But Budzash denied both when I asked him on the news Friday night. He was our lead story. I did what we call a "live-on-tape" interview with him at four. He was standing in a wooded area near his home in Howell Township. I was in our Trenton studio. Parts of the interview would air at six. Budzash said he was running to give "the people" a voice, and he had one very good line. All week long, in counterpoint to Florio's self-justifications, the Republicans had been saying that Jim Florio didn't make the "tough" choices, he made the "wrong" choices. Budzash had his own variation on that theme. Florio, he said, made "the easy choice. The people of New Jersey made the tough choice of whether to stay in the state and get clobbered or leave."

The Whitman camp chose Friday, while Budzash was dominating the news, to release Whitman's income tax information. She and her husband earned $3.7 million in 1992, on which they preliminarily paid over $1 million in federal taxes and $255,000 in state taxes. The details of how they earned such a fantastic sum may become clear in August. They said they needed extra time to complete their '92 return and had to file for an extension, but will release the information in August if Whitman is still a candidate.

★ Wednesday, April 21 ★

The short, happy life of John Budzash as a Democratic challenger appears over tonight. The taxpayer-crusader's petitions were ruled invalid by an administrative law judge this afternoon. State Democratic chairman Ray Lesniak had pressed a legal challenge to the petitions. Two print reporters and I sat all morning in a small hearing room in the office of the Ocean County Board of Elections as two lawyers representing Lesniak showed the judge that most of the 1,034 signatures on the petitions belonged to unregistered people, or unaffiliated voters, or Republicans—instead of Democrats.

Budzash says he'll run as a write-in candidate. He's angry at being taken out of the race by the big-money political establishment. But write-ins just don't cut it. Budzash blew it by deciding too late to enter the Democratic primary and trying to get all the requisite signatures in two days. He is an articulate, forceful, and strident expounder of antigovernment sentiment, and he could have made Florio's life miserable for the next eight weeks. He still might try.

Money should not be a critical factor in a New Jersey governor's race. Primary spending is capped at $2.6 million for candidates who take public financing, and all three Republicans plus Florio are taking it. In the general election, it's $5.9 million.

But how quickly the money gets raised, and how quickly it gets spent, can be revealing. Whitman is the only Republican to have raised the full $850,000 necessary to qualify for $1.6 million in primary matching funds. Edwards is close, at about $700,000. Wallwork is in the $250,000 range. And yet Wallwork is spending the most right now, running TV and radio spots designed to boost his minimal name recognition so he can raise more funds. Edwards just spent between $150,000 and $200,000 on a nine-minute video that was mailed to the homes of more than 100,000 Republicans. Whitman is hoarding her funds, saving as much as possible for the final three weeks. As the front-runner, she can afford to sit back and let her opponents shoot their wads. Dave Murray, Whitman's campaign manager, told me, "The whole thrust of this campaign is directed toward back-end spending. We've only spent 16 percent of the $2.6 so far."

Whitman is big on "blueprints." Last week, to go along with her "Blueprint for Economic Revival" she unveiled her "Blueprint for a Better Education." It called for a statewide core curriculum, tighter monitoring of schools, and the same freeing-up of local initiative that is at the heart of Edwards's plan. She had it all printed up in a nice booklet, but the ideas had a warmed-over quality about them. She was for "choice" within a public school district, and vouchers for private-school students in one city on a pilot basis. It was all serviceable stuff, served up by a candidate who sends her two children to private school at $9,000 each per year.

Edwards also held a Statehouse event, to reiterate the positions he's taken so far and tie them all together in a bundle. He, too, has a booklet called "Back to Basics," which focuses on the economy, crime, and government reform. There's a sense of urgency driving Edwards now. He seems to know he's in trouble. You can sense a quiet desperation in his voice as he asserts that he's the only candidate in the race with "a vision" for New Jersey's future and "the demonstrated skill to make that vision a reality." Jim Florio, he said, has a "Big Brother" vision in which government knows what's best for people. Christie Whitman has "no vision," he said in one of his baldest attack-lines yet.

Edwards keeps asserting he has vision but not demonstrating it. He speaks as if it's as plain as the nose on your face that his "Back to Basics" white paper is the real thing, while Whitman's "blueprints" are pap, when in fact they read pretty much the same. His only vision seems to be that he *has* vision.

Edwards lasted half an hour before reporters tired of him; the normal length for his news conferences has been one hour. Whitman, by contrast, held her news conference outdoors on the Statehouse steps with no podium or lectern, a set-up designed to keep things short. (Radio and TV reporters have to hold their microphones; print reporters have to hold their notebooks as they write.) Whitman's new press secretary, Joe Justin, even tried to cut off the questioning after ten minutes, but several of us in the press corps told this young up-start from out of state to let us finish. Justin is a prematurely balding, wisecracking spokesman in his late twenties, brought in to replace Dave Marziale, who may have fallen out of favor. Marziale has been moved over to a writing job and insists that's the role he wanted all along. Others suspect he was kicked upstairs.

Jim Wallwork, meanwhile, is attacking Jim Florio for riding around in $635-a-month leased Cadillacs (three of them are assigned to the governor and his wife by the State Police). This is real slasher stuff—entertaining, mildly provocative, but not terribly relevant to the future of the state. To Wallwork it is symbolic of government excess. But even a Chevy Caprice would cost $450 a month, and some would say the governor of a first-rate state should not drive around in a second-rate car.

Whitman is beginning to show a pattern of carelessness. The newest item of high gossip, just out today, involves the school board election in her town of Oldwick (actually Tewksbury Township). Seems the vote on the local school budget there on April 20th ended in a 207 to 207 tie, thus sending the budget to defeat. Whitman didn't vote. It just so happens that day she was in Trenton presenting her education plan, which includes an earnest call for more "citizen involvement" in the education process.

A Florio loyalist called me this afternoon cackling over this development. He talked about the "quirk factor" that haunts every gubernatorial election, the little detail that looms much bigger than it should. In 1981, it was Brendan Byrne's name on the Meadowlands Arena, he said. In '89 it was the barrels of toxic waste on Jim Courter's property. He was convinced this would be it for Whitman: her failure to vote in the school board election dooming her local school budget. "When it ends in a 207 to 207 tie, that's divine intervention," he chirped.

Roger Bodman, the Republican lobbyist who was in our studio tonight for what's become a weekly chat on the news with Democrat Jim McQueeny about the governor's race, was carrying a list Cary Edwards had given him over the phone of Whitman mistakes. Not checking the box on her 1991 tax return that donates $1 to the gubernatorial campaign fund, then taking public financing. Having to pull the radio ad that accused Lucinda Florio of costing the taxpayers a million dollars. Allowing BPU workers to survey her property for a satellite dish. Saying, in answer to a reporter's question about the homestead rebate program, "Funny as it seems, $500 is a lot of money to some people." Filing for an income tax extension, after promising to "set a new standard for disclosure" in this race. Taking advantage of the farmland assessment program to "evade" property taxes on her two "estates." And, of course, employing illegal aliens, though that was not on Edwards's list.

None of these is fatal, but the cumulative effect is beginning to show. Edwards aides are telling reporters that Whitman has a "credibility" problem. They also continue to push the theme that she has no substance. James Carville, who came to New Jersey on Wednesday and held his first press conference at Florio campaign headquarters, is pursuing a similar line. "Trying to get positions out of Whitman is like trying to nail jello to the wall" was the most heavily quoted of his made-for-media *bon mots* of the day.

The other quirk of the week was the failure of any of the Republicans to attack an anti-Semitic questioner who phoned in a question to a radio "debate" that took place Wednesday night at WKXW, New Jersey 101.5, in Ewing Township. Whitman, Edwards, and Wallwork had come through a very tepid sixty-minute session when the final caller asked if they would give half their cabinet positions to Jews "like in the Clinton administration." Each of them answered the question earnestly, denying that ethnicity would play a factor, without any reference to the repugnance of the question. It was like Dukakis giving a technical answer to the question about his wife being raped and murdered, and Democratic partisans like Ray Lesniak immediately seized on it as a sign of the Republicans' insensitivity.

I missed the radio debate and the Carville press conference, because I was doing a piece that day on Take Our Daughters to Work Day, assisted by one of my daughters (who got to interview Gloria Steinem). But we sent a camera to the debate, and I watched the tape and did a piece the next day. Edwards, I thought, outperformed the other two, though not by enough to make noise about. Whitman is forthright and appealing, but she doesn't have quite the range and depth of Edwards on issues. Wallwork failed to break out of the mold of "accidental third candidate" and came across, I thought, as slightly cranky.

★ Tuesday, May 4 ★

Whitman is getting hammered over her failure to vote in the school board election. It's been in the newspapers five days in a row, and yesterday she told the Bergen *Record* she has *never* voted in a school board election.

Today was my first shot at the story. I covered a forum in Atlantic City at which Whitman, Edwards, and Wallwork appeared together.

When Whitman saw me in the hallway she said, "You're the man who's going to control my life for the next few weeks," a reference to the two televised debates I'll be moderating in May. Of the governor's race, she said wryly that she'd been "keeping it interesting."

"How are you holding up?" I asked her a few minutes later as we stood sipping coffee with a few other people in a meeting room of Caesar's Boardwalk Regency.

"Surviving," she said. "I kick myself around the table two or three times a day . . . for stupidity."

It was a candid admission by a candidate who's taken some licks lately. The Edwards camp, meanwhile, finally has something to crow about. And Edwards is blasting Whitman for the missed school board vote, calling it part of a pattern of arrogance, mistakes, and double standards.

When Cary walked into the Caesar's dining room and saw Christie, he walked up to her and they kissed. It was a genuine show of at least respect, and maybe affection. "Two things I like about this election," Edwards said boisterously to the handful of us within earshot. "I get to kiss her a lot. And she has to wear make-up every day—I don't." A strange remark, but everyone laughed at it.

In the forum, before about two hundred people from the New Jersey Business and Industry Association, Edwards was charged up. He spoke with great passion and conviction about being the best person for the job and how this was his time. "A man of destiny," I wrote in my notebook, although I spelled it "density," a Freudian slip perhaps, since there is a thickness about the way Edwards speaks. Whitman, by comparison, was tepid. Steady and interesting, but uninspiring. (A reporter from the *Courier-Post* of Cherry Hill, Rita Manno, told me Whitman had been before the paper's editorial board yesterday, and the editors had been unimpressed. They like her "clean" style, but she didn't answer the questions, Rita said.) Wallwork is not resonating with me these days. He's got many issue positions. He is substantive. But he is running as an antigovernment conservative businessman, and much of his patter about term limits and ending political patronage jobs sounds clichéd.

After the forum I interviewed Whitman and Edwards extensively on the school board flap. They lit into each other pretty good, these two kissy-birds. Edwards said, "Can you imagine when Jim Florio and

Jim Carvel [*sic*] get their hands on this particular track record? They're gonna eat her alive!"

Whitman explained that she tried to vote in this year's school board election in Tewksbury, but got to the polls eight minutes late. She said she never voted in her old town of Far Hills because her kids were in private school, and Far Hills sends its public school students to neighboring Bernardsville. "I just decided not to tell the districts how to run their schools because I didn't have kids in them," she said. And she attacked Edwards for attacking her over filing for an extension on her 1992 tax return after promising a new "standard for disclosure" by saying "Cary's had extensions three of the last four years and has paid penalties four of the last four. If there's culpability there, it's on both sides."

Joe Justin, Whitman's spokesman, called me later in the day from a car phone and offered to fax me proof to back up that statement. Part of my afternoon in our South Jersey bureau at Stockton State College was spent going back and forth by phone between the two campaigns to check the veracity of the charge, which looks to be about half-true and will probably be forgotten very quickly.

The big story, however, is that Joe Salema, Governor Florio's chief of staff, has been subpoenaed by the U.S. attorney in Manhattan in a probe of a $2.9 billion bond sale by the New Jersey Turnpike Authority. The story has been building for five days, and today the *New York Times* put it on page one, above the fold. The Jersey papers had big headlines. The focus seems to be on Nick Rudi, a former Florio ally and Salema's business partner until Salema came into state government in 1990. There's no smoking gun yet, and it's remarkable that this much about a federal criminal probe has leaked out to the press. Florio does not need a scandal involving Salema and Rudi. The ethics of these two former aides of his were an issue in his 1989 election, and he kept them out of his organization and well out of sight.

"This week has been a double whammy for Florio," said NJN's State-house correspondent, Larry Stuelpnagel, as he walked into his cubicle next to mine Friday afternoon. He had just gotten in from doing a story on the new unemployment numbers out that day. They showed nearly a one-point jump in New Jersey's unemployment rate, to 9.1 percent, while New York's and Pennsylvania's were unchanged. "New Jersey Unemploy-ment Surges To Worst Among Industrial States," read the headline on page one of the Saturday *New York Times*. Since all three Republican candidates are building their campaigns around the failed economic lead-ership of the governor, the new numbers lend some factual weight to their rhetoric.

But the unemployment number seems less serious than the bur-geoning scandal surrounding Joe Salema. There is still no smoking gun, no indictment, not even a clear allegation. But it appears that Salema has profited handsomely while serving as chief of staff, and the newspapers, including the *New York Times* and *Wall Street Journal*, have been raking the records of the municipal bond business looking for instances in which Salema, Nick Rudi, and others connected to Florio have reaped substantial gains.

Salema is forty-five, short, intense, quiet, and has been at Florio's side for twenty years. Journalists are fond of saying he got his start as Florio's driver. Salema and Rudi were banished from the '89 campaign after the famous "King James" series in the *Courier-Post* of Cherry Hill laid out how the two had traded on Florio's name and their own govern-ment connections to make money as financial consultants to various gov-ernment agencies in Camden County and beyond. They also gave Florio a piece of a real estate deal involving a bank that netted the then-congress-man about $50,000 and became the one stain on Florio's reputation; he eventually donated $25,000 of the profits to his alma mater, Trenton State College.

After the tax debacle six months into his governorship, Florio turned to his old advisor Salema to help rescue the enterprise. Florio sent his first chief of staff, Steven Perskie, to the Casino Control Commission and brought in Salema, who had a better political "feel" than Perskie.

The rehabilitation of Jim Florio's image has been Salema's main goal these past two-and-a-half years, and he has done it with common sense, compromise, and pragmatism. Personally he has shunned the limelight. He and I have had two private lunches, at an Italian restaurant in Chambersburg, that have been very helpful to me in understanding his role and the game plan, but he resisted my early attempts to let me profile him on TV, and after a while I stopped asking. Self-aggrandizement wasn't his thing, he explained, and, besides, the boss might not like it.

Now, Salema is at the center of "Salemagate," as I found myself spontaneously calling it the other day. It seems that around the time Salema joined the administration, he and Nick Rudi formed a company called Armacon, a brokerage firm that would deal in municipal bonds. Salema eventually put his half of Armacon into a blind trust, but Rudi has operated the business, and it has done remarkably well, rising in assets from about $8,000 in 1990 to $500,000 today, by doing bond work in places like Hudson County, where the Hudson County executive, Robert Janiszewski, just happens to be a close Florio ally. Meanwhile, their other firm, Consolidated Financial Management, of which Salema sold his half to Rudi when he entered the administration, has become the number-one financial consulting firm on municipal bond issues in the state, all in the past couple of years.

I don't know the world of high finance very well, so this scandal has been an education for me, as I imagine it has for a number of the Statehouse reporters following it. In essence, what the U.S. attorney in New York and the Securities and Exchange Commission are both looking at is whether Merrill Lynch got the lead underwriter's role on the sale of $1.6 billion in New Jersey Turnpike bonds based on some tie to Armacon. News reports suggest Armacon may have received some benefit for steering the bond work to Merrill Lynch. Three high-level Merrill Lynch municipal bond executives have been suspended by the company and are cooperating with investigators. Salema has said nothing, but his attorney in New York has put out a statement saying they've been assured that Salema is not a target of the investigation and that Joe has had nothing to do with Armacon since putting his half into a blind trust.

The problem, as I see it, is that even if Salema scrupulously avoided Armacon and any decisions involving it, his net worth has soared while his partner built up the business presumably by trading on his connection to Salema and the governor. The excuse that it's in a blind trust is only good if there's a chance the trustee might sell it. If there's an implicit understanding that the trustee will sit on it until Joe leaves government, it's "blind" with one eye that sees.

This is what the newspapers are digging around in. And they are doing a good job. Like Watergate, new details keep emerging and making the story bigger. The *Star-Ledger* reported on Friday that the committee at the Turnpike Authority that decided on Merrill Lynch as the lead underwriter consisted of five people, one of whom was Clay Constantinou, the big Democratic fund-raiser who is also a Turnpike Authority commissioner. He is someone who would have an open pipeline to Salema and vice versa. Then the *Asbury Park Press* reported today that Harold Hodes, the superlobbyist with very close ties to Florio, was Merrill Lynch's lobbyist in New Jersey and has also been subpoenaed by the U.S. attorney to appear before the grand jury. Hodes, too, is closely wired into both Salema and Constantinou. (Hodes subsequently said he was questioned but not subpoenaed.) Finally, the Bergen *Record*'s lead story today was on how the former law firm of Robert DeCotiis, Florio's other top aide as chief counsel, has also done a whopping business as counsel to bond underwriting firms since DeCotiis joined the administration last year. The firm has stayed away from state work, but it has done a booming business in municipal and utility authority work, and although DeCotiis sold his share of the firm to his brother Al, his son Michael reportedly works there. Al DeCotiis was probably second to Clay Constantinou in fund-raising for Clinton in New Jersey last year and is tightly tied in to the network of top Democrats.

All these men are people I have come to know professionally, and like, and have enjoyed the company of. To me they are not sleazebags, to use the vernacular. Favoritism is the depth we're plumbing here. Cronyism is another name it goes by. Feeding at the public trough is yet another phrase for it. The sums of money that can be made doing it are in the hundreds of thousands—perhaps millions—of dollars. It's not illegal. And when I think of the life that goes with it—the steady stream of lunches to build relationships, the contributions, the networking to get your small piece of the Big Action—it doesn't sound all that rewarding except in the bank account.

Governor Florio, who is not a rich man and who is even said by one advisor to have been slightly embarrassed during the '89 campaign at his relatively paltry fortune for a lawyer turning fifty, is in a serious quandary. The big question is, how long will he stay with Joe Salema? A related question is, can he function well *without* Joe Salema? The *Star-Ledger* editorialized this week that Salema should consider taking a leave of absence until this cloud is lifted from his head. Christie Whitman suggested the same, and Cary Edwards immediately jumped on her for leaping to rash conclusions before all the facts are known just to score a political point. (Edwards's law firm, Mudge, Rose, was involved in the bond sale as counsel to one of the underwriters other than Merrill Lynch. Edwards has to hope the bond business as a whole doesn't get a bad name.)

A new Bergen *Record* poll is out today showing Whitman way out ahead of Edwards, 41 percent to 14 percent, with 8 percent for Wallwork and 37 percent undecided. This confirms all the worst things that have been said about Edwards's standing on "Reporters' Roundtable" in recent weeks. The first televised debate is Tuesday night, and I've got the questions on little pieces of notebook paper folded up in my wallet.

★ **Wednesday, May 12** ★

Little beads of sweat were forming on Cary Edwards's face. We were seated on stage at the Birchwood Manor in Whippany, he, Whitman, Wallwork, and I, waiting for last night's debate to begin, and the television lights were getting hot. Cary had the chair closest to mine. He looked ashen-faced, either from make-up or nerves. And he was sweating heavily.

I suggested he might like to wipe his brow with a handkerchief or paper towel. It was five minutes to air time. I asked the producer to try to get more air-conditioning. I warned Wallwork and Whitman that they, too, might want to have a handkerchief or paper towel handy. Wallwork indicated he had something. Christie, who was seated farthest away from me, shook her head and said she wouldn't need one. This showed a certain devil-may-care, take-me-as-I-am quality, and a coolness that she would exhibit in the debate as well.

The Birchwood Manor has been the scene of many New Jersey political debates. Traditionally, it's where the state Chamber of Commerce hosts the debates it sponsors, this one included. I had been on the panel when Whitman debated Bill Bradley in this room in 1990. Now, before an audience of about five hundred people seated at dinner tables, the four of us on stage were the after-dinner entertainment.

The format was pretty loose, as I explained to the television audience once the broadcast got underway. The candidates would have opening and closing statements, but in between they were free to talk to one another and interject comments as I posed questions and refereed. The questions I conceived fell into four big categories—taxes and fiscal policy, education, crime, and electability—followed by three smaller categories—environment versus jobs, reforming the bond business, and top priorities. I wanted to get at the differences between the candidates, but more than that I wanted sparks to fly, and I felt certain the "electability" section two-thirds through the debate would be the likeliest place for that to happen and the right time for a climax.

Although the candidates had the most to gain or lose, and it was their debate, I think I felt as much pressure as they did. I had begun my preparations on Monday by going over the notes I had been storing and adding to in my wallet, by reviewing files I keep on the candidates, by getting on the phone and calling half a dozen politicos in both parties ("making your rounds," as lobbyist Harold Hodes calls this practice of political reporters, many of whom call him), and by spending an hour trying out questions on my boss, the news director, Bill Jobes. He convinced me, for example, not to test Whitman's out-of-touch quotient by asking her if she knows how much it costs to buy a pound of butter. "Too nasty," he said. "And what if she knows?"

Monday night and much of Tuesday were spent at home, refining questions and sifting through campaign position papers. For the first time, I actually read Whitman's "Blueprint for Economic Revival" and much of Edwards's "Back to Basics" plan. They read well, especially Whitman's.

Now, on stage, I was adhering to my game plan, and the candidates were using me to make points and spar with one another. Conventional wisdom said that Edwards would have to go after Whitman seriously tonight, and he did. He said she didn't know what she was talking about. He mocked her "goal" of rolling back the rest of the Florio tax hikes. He chided her for flip-flopping on school vouchers, which she now favors, and stressed that his commitment was to the *public* schools. On crime he said she should "come down from the hills of Far Hills and see what it's like on the streets, where I'm from."

Prior to the debate, Hazel Gluck, the co-chair of Whitman's campaign, had complained to me privately that it's very hard to convince Christie to fight back. "She believes in the Eleventh Commandment. Her father taught it to her. Thou shalt not attack fellow Republicans," said Hazel, somewhat frustratedly. (Whitman's father, Webster Todd, had been a confidante of President Eisenhower's and an occasional visitor at Ike's farm in Gettysburg. He made his money as the engineering contractor who built Rockefeller Center. Her mother, Eleanor Schley Todd, had been a Republican national committeewoman.)

But Whitman proved far spunkier in the debate than was expected by those who thought it made strategic sense for her to try to stay above the fray. She defended herself *and* attacked back. When Edwards sniped at her for not voting in the school board election, she accused him of not voting in primary and general elections (he denied it). She challenged his vaunted reputation as a crime fighter by stating that violent crime actually rose 9 percent when Edwards was attorney general, and that the murder rate shot up in his final year by more than in any of the previous eight years. When Wallwork accused her of raising taxes during her years on the Somerset County freeholder board (1983–1988), she accused him of voting for six tax increases in the legislature in 1973 and '74.

The "electability" question produced sharp tensions, if not quite the slugfest I had envisioned. Wallwork didn't take the bait when I offered him a chance to criticize the two employers of illegal aliens. And while Edwards accused Whitman of making more missteps in four months than Jim Courter had made in the entire '89 campaign, he held back from arguing that her wealth meant she was out of touch with common people. It was her "background" and life experiences that made her ill-prepared to challenge Jim Florio and govern, not her wealth. "Tom Kean was wealthy," he said, and then delivered the one canned sound bite I detected all night. "I knew Tom Kean, I worked with Tom Kean, and Christie Whitman is no Tom Kean." That play on Lloyd Bentsen's famous line to Dan Quayle eventually produced Whitman's best line of the night. "It's not what's in your bank account," she said. "It's what you've done with your life."

Wallwork offered a lot of original ideas in the debate, like doing away with the Violent Crimes Compensation Board and cutting back on the number of public relations officers at the Division of Consumer Affairs. But his style was so old-fashioned, and he repeated the words "businessman" and "conservative businessman" so many times that by the end the audience was laughing at him. He is trying to appeal to the remnants of the taxpayer revolt, and he exudes decency and a kind of ramrod integrity born of his West Point background. But there is also a wiftiness about him. Early on, as he was speaking, Edwards leaned toward me several times with an expression on his face that said, "Can you believe this shit?"

Edwards was good in the debate—forceful, aggressive, and able to demonstrate both passion and a command of issues. But Whitman was good also—crisp, cool, unflappable. When he accused her of being an "amateur," she simply said part of the problem is we have too many "professional politicians" around. The Edwards persona strikes many people I've spoken to today as "less gubernatorial" than the Whitman persona. One said Whitman was more "accessible" in the TV debate than Edwards. My youngest daughter, who's eleven, said Whitman was the only "normal" one and called Edwards the "neanderthal guy." A Florio fan said Edwards came across as somewhat "abrasive and a bit of a technocrat—in fact, kind of like Jim Florio, which means she's going to look good against him, too."

After the debate ended, I hooked up with a cameraman and did some interviews for an analysis and reaction piece for tonight's news. Edwards supporters were genuinely enthusiastic about Cary's performance. But Pete McDonough, who's the campaign director and generally a straight shooter when talking to journalists, confided to me later that if the numbers in the Bergen *Record* poll are correct, the race is over. He doesn't believe those numbers, however. The Edwards camp put out its own numbers on Monday, to counter the impression left by the *Record*'s. They showed Whitman at 31 percent, Edwards at 19 percent, Wallwork at 13 percent, with 37 percent undecided.

As for the debate, Whitman won—by not losing.

★ **Thursday, May 13** ★

This morning's *New York Times* quotes one of Jim Florio's "closest political strategists" as saying the governor was most impressed with Mrs. Whitman in the debate. "Mrs. Whitman did a good job of parrying the attacks on her," said the Florio ally. The governor watched the debate at his home, Drumthwacket, according to the article, but wouldn't comment on it.

Meanwhile, I just learned from Whitman spokesman Joe Justin that Cary Edwards did not vote in the general election in 1986, nor in the Republican primaries in 1988, 1990, and 1991, and I am going to confront Edwards with that information today. During the debate, when Whitman charged him with failing to vote in general and primary elections, he said, "I do, I do."

★ **Sunday, May 16** ★

With less than four weeks to go, the two men are howling at Whitman. They're howling at her for skipping a debate last night hosted by United We Stand, America, the Ross Perot group, in Westhampton, Burlington County. They're howling at her for missing the school board vote, for flip-flopping on vouchers, for telling several seemingly different stories about her missed school board vote. Edwards is on her for filing for an extension on her income tax this year after promising to set a "new standard for disclosure," and for "guesstimating" in a radio commercial that Lucinda Florio's budget was a million dollars when it's more like $175,000. Wallwork is on her for paying only $47 in property taxes on fifty acres "around her estate," as his radio ad puts it.

To examine Whitman's property tax situation, I paid a visit to her farm Friday morning with NJN cameraman Ron Wagner. I had asked the day before if it would be okay, and to my surprise the answer had been yes. So here I was, on my forty-seventh birthday, walking with Whitman and her brother into a barn full of animals and watching her go absolutely nuts over two calves, rubbing their necks and cooing to them by name. She's a farm woman! This was Pontefract, the 222-acre spread she grew up on. The big white house dated back to the eighteenth century. The pool, the tennis court, and one of the two big barns were more modern, as was the downstairs interior of the house, which had a look of elegant clutter amid slightly Santa Fe-style decor.

Whitman and her husband, John, paid $20,674.26 in property taxes on the house and the surrounding farm buildings in 1992. But on the remaining 218 acres, they paid only $1,050.52. That's because of New Jersey's farmland assessment program, which offers enormous property tax breaks to working farmland. The Whitman farm is a hay farm and earned $12,291.94 in 1992 from hay, pigs, sheep, and wool. On their other residence, which they lived in since 1974 until Eleanor Schley Todd died in 1991 and Christie and John moved into the family estate, the Whitmans paid $9,310.56 in taxes on the house and immediate grounds in 1992 but paid only $47.27 on the remaining fifty acres. It, too, qualifies as a farm, because the Whitmans harvest wood there. Every four or five years they cut trees for lumber, and the average income from the wood and a few head of cattle is about $1,500 a year. Wallwork, in particular, has been critical of the Whitmans for taking advantage of a law intended to help working farmers, not multimillionaire dilettantes.

But Whitman convinced me very quickly that at least the family farm is a real farm. We saw cows, pigs, sheep, chickens, and large hayfields being fertilized by the full-time farmer the Whitmans employ, a Minnesotan named Rubin. As Rubin dropped manure from his tractor onto the foot-high green grasses that would become hay, Dan Todd, Christie's brother, observed, "There's been so much manure spread in the campaign, we thought we'd show you the real thing."

Webster B. (Dan) Todd, Jr., is a magnetic character, a rare blend of East Coast breeding and Wild West speech and mannerisms, with a face cut out of a Marlboro cigarette ad. He is spending the campaign in New Jersey, living in the attic of the house he grew up in, right alongside his sister and brother-in-law. He once served two years in the New Jersey assembly, and when the Republicans took back the White House in 1968 he landed a position in the Nixon administration (deputy director of the Civil Aeronautics Board; later, chairman of the National Transportation Safety Board), but now he's a Montana rancher with about 750 head of cattle, a divorce, and three grown children.

Todd showed us around the farm after Whitman left, which was after we did a quick interview in the barn on whether she's taking unfair advantage of the farmland assessment program. She made a strong case that she is not. In the forty minutes we spent together, I saw her connectedness to this land, to farming, to New Jersey, and to old-money Republicanism. She wore jeans, a sweatshirt that said BUNG's Bar & Grill, and moccasins and looked thoroughly natural. Her brother was dressed like a cowboy and chewed on a wooden matchstick all morning, the tip end sticking out.

If they were putting on a show for the camera, the two youngest of Webster and Eleanor Todd's four children did a pretty good job of it, as Joe Justin hovered around and kept his distance. I had come there hoping to do a tough story on the farmland assessment, to balance the story I had done the night before on Cary Edwards. I had basically caught Edwards in a lie, and he didn't look good trying to scramble out of it. He had told me on camera the week before that Whitman was wrong when she said he had filed for income tax extensions in three of the last four years and paid IRS penalties in all four. Now, he said, it didn't matter what he had done in prior years—the point was that she had filed for an extension in 1993 after promising a "new standard of disclosure." It didn't wash. Neither did he look good when I showed him on camera a copy of his voting record (faxed to me by Joe Justin) showing missed elections in the 1988, '90, and '91 Republican primaries and the 1986 general. Could he still criticize Whitman for missing school board elections? "Absolutely! She never voted in one in her lifetime!" he bellowed, but it came off as a hypocritical whine. (The 1986 entry later turned out to be an error.)

So I was looking to even things up by examining Whitman's farm-land assessment. Unfortunately, everything looks to be on the up-and-up, even at her Far Hills residence, which my cameraman and I shot from the road later that day (Whitman wouldn't allow us onto the property because it's leased to tenants now). Some may resent that she pays only $47 on fifty acres that only technically qualify as a "tree farm," but I called the New Jersey Farm Bureau and the mayor of Far Hills looking for disgruntled condemnation, and both defended her. I'll put the story together for tomorrow night's news, and the visuals from the farm will probably make it a plus for Whitman, not a minus.

★ Saturday, May 22 ★

A week has gone by with no change in the dynamic of the Republican primary. It's not even generating much news. The newspapers go a day here and there without mentioning it. I was surprised that at last week's debate not one TV news crew other than NJN's bothered to show up. Is the Republican gubernatorial primary such a low-interest affair?

If the polls are accurate, it's to Whitman's advantage to lie low. Wallwork and Edwards have to make something happen, and neither has. All three candidates crisscrossed the state this week, going from Rotary luncheon to Republican club to trade association meeting. But none of that makes news. Wallwork's press secretary, Cristyne Lategano, an alumna of the Bush '92 New Jersey campaign, is sending out a blizzard of faxes lately—most of them aimed at engaging Whitman in a debate about her record as a Somerset County freeholder. Wallwork says she hiked taxes twenty-eight times and doubled spending. The Whitman camp replies that Wallwork is counting votes on bond issues as tax hikes and that bonding for senior citizen centers and homeless shelters is nothing to be ashamed of. Edwards has been less aggressive this week, except on television, where his new commercials are all-out assaults on Whitman. They attack her double-talk on tax rollbacks, her missed school board vote, her farmland assessment. They end with the tag line "Christine Todd Whitman—Can We Afford the Risk?" Tough stuff.

I did only one piece on the Republicans this week, and it was the Whitman farm piece. It ran as our "Closer Look" on Monday night, and it was long: five minutes fifty-two seconds. "When Christie Whitman comes home from a day of campaigning, she comes home to the restored eighteenth-century farmhouse she grew up in," it began, and from there it was part farm tour, part exposé on her taxes, and part pissing match between her and her two rivals, who were each in the piece twice. After skewering Edwards last week in a piece that caught him in a lie, I didn't want to be accused of favoring Whitman. The producer I work closest with, Retha Sherrod, saw the video of Christie and me wandering among the animals on her farm and feared I might produce a puff piece. With her help I didn't, and the piece got a fair amount of comment. Some thought I was a little soft on Whitman, some thought I "got" her. Most thought she answered the questions well, but most also thought it a scam that she pays only $47 on fifty acres of land in Far Hills.

Also working to Whitman's advantage is the bond scandal that continues to envelop Jim Florio. Not only does it level the playing field looking toward November, it's keeping the Republican primary off the front pages. Thursday, for example, I was going to do a piece involving Whitman that would have forced her to address why one of her key supporters, Senator John Dorsey, is blocking the reappointment of an Hispanic woman judge, Judge Marianne Espinosa Murphy, the wife of Morris County prosecutor Michael Murphy. Dorsey is being widely criticized for using an informal custom known as senatorial courtesy to blackball a woman family-court judge with a reputation for being tough on "deadbeat dads," and Governor Florio is trying to turn the issue into a crusade to get rid of senatorial courtesy (similar to his crusade against the NRA). So far, Whitman has tried to duck the issue. But instead of forcing her to say something about it, I ended up doing a story about the bond investigation because the *New York Times* had a page-one story Thursday saying that Armacon, Joe Salema's and Nick Rudi's firm, had made more than a million dollars in two years, in some cases without even doing much work!

Reporters flocked to the governor's outer office on Thursday for a news event on senatorial courtesy so that they could ask about the *Times* story. Florio at first gave very quick, soft-spoken answers to the questions. But he soon launched into a vigorous defense of his embattled chief of staff and almost pleaded with the media to stop going wild over the story. "I mean, c'mon guys, there's got be some minimal level of fairness here," he said at one point, and the "c'mon guys" was a touch out of character, a touch too real. As his two closest aides besides Salema looked on, communications director Jon Shure and management and planning chief Brenda Bacon, Florio handled the moment of crisis rather well. He argued that even the *Times* story itself said what Salema and Rudi had done was standard practice on Wall Street. He said that neither he nor we really knew what we were talking about (how true! none of us would begin to know how you make a million bucks dealing bonds! though Florio meant we didn't have all the facts).

The governor's comments were our lead story on "NJN News" that night. The next day the *Wall Street Journal* had yet another front-page story on New Jersey's bond business, this one about how an investment banker with the firm Lazard Freres named Richard Poirier had used political connections to build that firm's business up to number one in the state. Again, the link was to Salema, at least in the story. There's a Watergate-like aspect to the way this story keeps unfolding. Nobody has been accused of illegality yet, but it looks bad, and most people think it's only a matter of time before Salema has to leave. Some Democratic insiders are saying Salema wants to leave, but Florio won't let him because it would be seen as an admission of wrongdoing. Instead of Florio being loyal to Salema, as it appears, what's really happening, according to this theory, is that Salema is once again being loyal to Florio. He sat out the '89 campaign out of loyalty. He came back in '90 not because he wanted to but because his friend needed him. And now he's enduring trial by national media for Florio.

"Armacon had the Wall Street equivalent of a no-show job," said David Blomquist of the *Record* on my show this weekend, and he said somebody's going to have to go to Jim Florio and tell him the cancer has to be excised. Florio's and Salema's offices are each right next to the other, with a common secretarial outer office. What a drama must be going on behind those closed doors.

Last night the Republicans held their second televised debate, this one on WABC-TV in New York and WPVI in Philadelphia. I watched at home and found it a tepid affair, though this morning's papers make it sound at least as spirited as the debate I moderated.

Debate reaction must be highly subjective, because one paper today said Edwards won, and I thought he was the least effective of the three. He kept saying "I have a plan" for this, that, and the other thing, but he didn't lay out any more specifics than anyone else. It's as if having a plan is enough—it doesn't matter what's in the plan.

Wallwork sounded slightly less crackpot and more mainstream than usual. He looked into the camera effectively. He has become convincing as someone who belongs on the same stage as the other two. I can envision him beating Edwards now, if conservatives and antigovernment types come out in force and don't go for Whitman.

Whitman did okay in the debate, which was all she had to do. She was better prepared than either of the other two and got off the night's best zinger, aimed at Wallwork. When he complained about her raising taxes in Somerset County, she came back with a little story about a house she knew that was bought for $260,000 in her first year as a freeholder, 1983. The taxes on it were $6,900. In her last full year as a freeholder, 1987, the house's value had shot up to $600,000, but the taxes were actually less, only $6,200. "You oughta know it's true, Jim, because that was your house," she said. *Zing!* A good research job unearthed that nugget, and later I learned it was Whitman's husband, John, who had done the research.

Whitman also had a prepared closing statement, obviously memorized, whereas Wallwork and Edwards were winging it and losing cohesion. Edwards kept saying "my children and your children and my grandchildren" in a kind of litany of future-orientedness that bordered on babble.

Short of a Nobel Prize, it's hard to imagine a better award a politician could win than the John F. Kennedy Profiles in Courage Award. Today, Jim Florio became the 1993 recipient at a ceremony at the JFK Library in Boston.

I flew up last night with a cameraman. Most major New Jersey news organizations were represented, as well as Channels 3 from Philadelphia and 7 from New York. Florio won the award for his stand on gun control and his progressive income tax hike in the name of providing more equitable school funding.

Caroline Kennedy Schlossberg was the front-person for the family on this one, although Jackie Onassis, Ethel Kennedy, John Jr., and Senator Ted Kennedy were also on hand. We each got five minutes with Caroline Kennedy and Jim Florio an hour or two before the ceremony. (Earlier, they and John Jr. did the "Today" show and "CBS This Morning.")

All morning long, journalist after journalist asked the same two questions: why Jim Florio, and is this some kind of put-up job to help him win re-election. Caroline had a good answer for the second one. The award, established in 1989, is meant to go to an *elected* official who demonstrates political courage. "If we only gave it to people who weren't running, we'd have to disqualify half the politicians in America every year," she told me and every other reporter who asked.

For the record, the committee that selects the winner is made up of fifteen people, chaired by the president of Nike, Inc., and includes business people, academics, Caroline, John Jr., and others with ties to the Kennedy family.

Connecticut governor Lowell Weicker won the award last year for his crusade to pass an income tax in the state. Now Florio, another Northeast governor known for his tax hike. "It's not popular to raise taxes. Unfortunately, it sometimes needs to be done, and it takes personal responsibility to do it," said Caroline Kennedy Schlossberg, who was very charming and seemed slightly bemused by all the Jersey tax-angle questions.

Several dozen of Florio's closest friends and supporters made the trip to see him honored. To them, and especially to his wife, Lucinda, this was a sweet vindication of the policies for which he's been so criticized and abused at home. The governor was appropriately modest throughout the morning interviews and the ceremony with the Kennedy family, but he was also stiff and, with hometown reporters, a bit testier than the occasion called for. Later we would learn that as Florio was accepting his award, Joe Salema was leaving the Statehouse for good.

The award, as I see it, goes partway toward offsetting the bond mess that's surrounding Florio. "It's a shot in the arm in a week when we needed a shot in the arm," said fund-raiser Karen Kessler, one of the Floriocrats who made the trip. "It's like a shot of adrenalin in the middle of a storm," said Lewis Katz, the governor's friend and chief financial backer, "and it links him with a Democrat that Democrats feel good about [JFK]."

I asked lawyer Carl Poplar, another old friend of Florio's, if the bond mess was eating Joe Salema up alive. "It's eating Jim Florio alive," he said. "They're good friends."

The award is a silver lantern designed by Caroline's husband, Ed Schlossberg, plus $25,000. Florio said he was giving the money to Lucinda for her birthday. "Nice present," I said during our interview. "She's a nice wife," he shot back. She says she doesn't know what she'll do with the money. Already I've heard suggestions that they should be giving the money to charity.

I was surprised that the Florio campaign didn't have a film crew at the ceremony, for use in a campaign commercial. Florio's spokesman Jon Shure explained that people aren't impressed by seeing a politician getting an award. This award from this family, however, was supposed to be special, and I think people would be, and are, impressed.

Covering the event reminded me again what a grind and a hustle the TV news profession can be. Fly up Sunday night, cab to hotel, grab a midnight meal, up at seven, no breakfast, MTA to the Kennedy Library by 8:45 lugging suitcases and TV equipment, cover the event 'til noon, cab to the airport, no lunch, catch a one o'clock flight to Newark, wait for shuttle bus, shuttle to parking area, drive to NJN Newark bureau, write and edit a three-and-a-half-minute piece by six o'clock. We were in Boston a total of fifteen hours and glimpsed the city from the window of a cab.

★ Tuesday, May 25 ★

To no one's great surprise, Joe Salema resigned today. Only the timing was a surprise, coming in almost the same news cycle as Governor Florio's receipt of the Profiles in Courage Award. Either it was timed to slide in under the courage award, or it wasn't timed at all—Salema just couldn't take it anymore. I was supposed to have the day off to attend the funeral of my ninety-year-old great-uncle, but the news was sufficiently big that I was asked to come in at four in the afternoon and put together a quick "essay" on who Salema was and what his departure might mean.

My gut tells me it means the diminution by half of the news coverage of future developments in the bond story. Like the illegal-alien story, it will sit in the back of people's minds but cease being topic A unless and until an opponent revives it in a campaign commercial. Even then it might not count for much. I don't believe we in the media were out to scalp Joe Salema, but now that his scalp has been taken, the juiciness of the story just isn't as great. Unless, of course, there are bigger revelations.

Salema gave no interviews and apparently just cleaned out his desk yesterday morning and left, while Florio was in Boston. Today the governor was in Jersey City, leading other governors on a welfare reform tour, and wouldn't comment on Salema. Late in the day his office put out a statement saying he accepted the resignation "with deep regret" and that it was motivated by a desire not to let political opponents "take the focus off the main issues that affect the people of New Jersey." The statement noted that Salema and his family "have had to endure a very stressful period, and I wish them well."

★ Sunday, May 30 ★

The week just past will be remembered as the Week of the Shake-Up. This was the second time Governor Florio has shaken up his staff. The first was when Joe Salema arrived, in late summer 1990, and Florio dispatched his then-chief of staff Steven Perskie to the Casino Control Commission. Now Joe Salema has gone.

The day before it happened, Florio had invited Rick Wright over to Drumthwacket. Wright, who lives in Princeton, is a fifty-year-old government manager who for the last three-and-a-half years has been an associate state treasurer. He was a fairly quiet presence at the Statehouse, inconspicuous despite his six-foot-five-inch frame. He worked on economic development projects in Camden and other cities, and he thought Florio was inviting him to Drumthwacket to discuss a project. Instead, the governor offered him the chief of staff job. Wright played basketball with Bill Bradley at Princeton and was brought in to the Florio transition staff in late '89 by Doug Berman, who had managed Bradley's 1984 re-election campaign.

So when Florio and Jon Shure were in Boston on Monday, they knew Salema was leaving but didn't let on. The plan was to announce Salema's resignation and Wright's selection simultaneously on Wednesday. But Salema couldn't play along for the extra two days. Apparently he was just too distraught about the mess he was in to be a good soldier for two more days. He came in very early Monday morning, cleaned out his desk, took himself off the payroll, and left before most people had even come to work. The Statehouse press corps—those who hadn't gone to Boston thinking *they* had the hot story of the day—got wind of it and printed it, spoiling Florio's award coverage, or at least relegating it to a less prime spot in the newspapers.

The selection of Wright sent a signal through the Statehouse that former state treasurer Doug Berman was again playing an influential role in the governor's decisions. Berman is highly controversial. A lot of people blamed him for pushing the $2.8 billion tax increase on Florio. Others blamed him for the headstrong attitude of the early Florio administration. When Salema came in, it was said, Berman's influence began to wane, and Berman resigned as state treasurer in January of '92, returning to his family's garment business. But he and the governor never stopped talking. Florio values the forty-one-year-old Yale graduate for his ability to develop political strategy, his understanding of how to use communications to create a message, and his coolness under fire.

Berman and Salema were like Florio's yin and yang, one appealing to the governor's desire to make a difference, the other trying to hold him back from unpopular moves. With Salema gone, the idea that Berman is back sends a shudder through some Democratic quarters. Berman and

Jon Shure both insisted to me on the phone this week that it's overblown. "He never really left," said Shure. Although several newspapers have reported Berman is getting $1,000 per day as a consultant to the campaign, he told me he has not even set foot in the Edison campaign headquarters (and declined to confirm the per diem rate).

Still, two other key members of Florio's inner circle—Secretary of State Dan Dalton and Chief Counsel Bob DeCotiis—were so upset by the week's developments that, according to Jim Goodman in the Trenton *Times*, the governor personally had to talk them into staying. Both were said to be fed up with how shabbily Salema had been treated by the world in general and the media in particular. Dalton, a former legislator, was also especially irked that Berman, who antagonized some legislators, had resurfaced. There is a lot of anger at the press within the Florio circle over the Salema affair. "I have seen a level of sloppiness in these stories that just amazes me," Jon Shure said to me, citing examples. Berman complained to me that the *Asbury Park Press* and NJN had reported that he had been subpoenaed by the U.S. attorney, when in fact he'd only had one casual inquiry by the FBI. I corrected us on the air that night.

Someone was quoted in an article this week to the effect that Doug Berman is the political equivalent of "root canal," meaning something dreaded and unwelcome. The phrase stuck and was repeated back to me by two of the many Democratic insiders I tried to reach out to in this week of the shake-up. There is an enormous amount of resentment against Berman, most of it unearned, in my estimation. Berman, himself, at the time he resigned as treasurer, privately chalked some of it up to Statehouse anti-Semitism, which also strikes me as a misplaced thought. He can be overbearing in discussion. It takes him ten minutes sometimes to make a point that others could make in thirty seconds. He likes to elaborate and explain things in a way that demonstrates how he thinks or how much he knows. But he is smart, thoughtful, and always aware of the Big Picture. He is a humanist, a liberal, and, like Jim Florio, someone interested in government for what it can do for people, not just for the power itself. Joe Salema was successful because he didn't care much about policy ends— he just wanted to keep everybody happy, and make Jim Florio popular, and find what was politically acceptable and do it. And he was quite good at that. Berman was less successful in Trenton because he wanted to help Jim Florio redistribute income and send more school aid to the poor children in New Jersey's thirty "special needs" districts, where half the children in the state go to school—and because he was convinced he was right.

In addition to the Wright-for-Salema switch, the governor changed campaign managers this week, bringing Jamie Fox back to the Statehouse as deputy chief of staff, and installing a non-New Jerseyan, thirty-seven-year-old Jim Andrews, who worked in New Jersey for six weeks during the Clinton campaign and apparently impressed the Democrats here. His background in politics is in Illinois, where they play the game as rough as we do here.

Andrews was on "NJN News" the night he was named, being interviewed by one of my colleagues. He is short and intense, with bulging eyes. He handled the questions like a pro, and when he said Jim Florio's election would hinge, not on any bond scandal, but on the fact that he's tough and courageous and has a vision, I thought that if you closed your eyes and changed the accent, it could have been James Carville speaking. Some people are saying that Andrews is a Carville protégé, but I'm told that is not the case.

On Friday Rick Wright met the Statehouse press corps for the first time, although he had given an earlier interview to the *New York Times* (which can sometimes get preferential treatment). Here's a guy who's been in the Statehouse for three-and-half years, and he had to ask the reporters to identify themselves. To me, that bespeaks a certain un-awareness. (He knew me because I had made a point of speaking to him during the Berman era and because our children have gone to school together in Princeton.) Wright is modest, unassuming, laid back, and seemingly more concerned with the economic problems of the world than with his new boss's poll ratings. His selection surprised many in the Statehouse. Perhaps with unemployment the real albatross around Florio's neck—not bonds—the governor is turning to someone who knows something about public-sector projects that create jobs. Still, on the surface it's an odd choice. I have trouble envisioning Florio and Wright in a room together alone having a free-flowing exchange that hits on all cylinders. The two have no particular history together, and both are reserved types. One imagined Salema functioning as almost a brother, like RFK to Florio's JFK. "Not having Joe there is a personal loss for Jim Florio," Democratic consultant Steve DeMicco told me, "a loss of comfort level."

In the midst of the shake-up and partly drowned out by it, the third and final live televised debate among the Republican gubernatorial candidates took place Wednesday night. Again, I moderated, except this time the format was town-meeting style; the audience asked the questions. The debate was held in the Robert B. Meyner Reception Center at the Garden State Arts Center in Holmdel. It was cosponsored by the New Jersey Association of Women Business Owners (NJAWBO or "ne-jaw-bo") and NJN, so a majority of the audience of three to four hundred was women entrepreneurs.

Before the debate, cocktails and fancy finger-food were served on an outdoor patio, with two musicians adding a little atmosphere. At the last debate, I was wrapped too tight to eat and had to go off in a quiet room and be alone with my questions. This time, I was looser because my role would be easier. I brought my wife, Carolyn, and introduced her to the candidates and members of their staffs as they worked the patio.

Dan Todd gave me a nice greeting, joking that since I had put him on TV in the piece about farmland assessments, he had gotten offers to become an anchorman back in Montana. I asked him what their polling was showing. He said it was still showing Whitman around thirty-nine, Edwards in the mid-to-high teens, and Wallwork back down to single digits now that his TV ads were no longer on the air. He insisted that Edwards's negative ads against his sister were causing a backlash and hurting Edwards as well as Whitman.

Jim Wallwork and I chatted on the patio for about ten minutes, mainly about how much in property taxes he had paid on his home in Somerset County. He tried to explain why his taxes had gone down, as Whitman had revealed in the last debate. It all had to do with reassessments and revaluations. He tried three times, and I still didn't get it. He also assured me that, contrary to what his opponents were saying about his being out of money, he would have $450,000 on hand for television advertising in the final week of the campaign.

The debate itself went more or less according to form. Edwards sniped continuously at Whitman about her flip-flops, her unfamiliarity with the public school system, and her lack of life experience ("at least I've *had* a job," he said, after Whitman said his answer to an unemployed questioner sounded like he was offering the young woman a job). Wallwork gave his best performance to date, answering the questions more directly and taking more definitive stands on sensitive questions than either of his more "political" rivals. For example, when someone asked about managed health care, Edwards said he was for accessibility, affordability, quality, and choice—in other words, the moon; Whitman showed she knew that the state was about to mandate that all health insurance policies for individuals and small groups come in one of five uniform packages, and then added for good measure that some form of managed care is "probably inevitable"; Wallwork simply said he is against managed care, because giving medical decision-making power to third-party providers and government bureaucrats would reduce the quality of the health care New Jersyans receive. It may not have been the progressive answer, but it was definitive and strong and maybe right!

Wallwork has a kind of goofy integrity. Edwards is passionate and emotional. He comes across as the "hot" ethnic next to Whitman the "cool" WASP (even if he's Scotch-Irish-French). Since television is a cool medium, she probably wins more admirers than he in these debates. On stage, I sensed about her a slight detachment, as if the debate were something she had to endure and would tolerate, but it was no big deal.

Whitman again scored the best debating point of the night. In the last debate, it was Wallwork's property taxes going down. In this one, she waited for just the right moment to spring a planned attack on Edwards. After he chided her for never holding a "job," she said it was an offensive remark and went on to demand an apology from Edwards for having said last weekend in New York at a taping of a WPIX-TV interview program that he "was a little resentful having to run against a woman." She called the remark "offensive to all thinking people" and wondered aloud how he could possibly govern a state made up of men *and* women if he harbored such resentment of women candidates. As Whitman scolded him, Edwards looked down sheepishly and, uncharacteristically, held off return fire.

After the debate Edwards told reporters that the remark had been taken out of context, that he had been talking about what a good record he had on women's issues and had said he was a little resentful having to run against a woman with less experience than he had in actually delivering to women some of the things they need, like day care and flex time.

Before leaving, I introduced my wife to Edwards, and he introduced us to his twenty-one-year-old daughter, Kari Lynn. I was glad
Carolyn got to meet him, because he came on with all the exuberance and
charm that has won over many Trenton insiders through the years and
which I had unsuccessfully tried to describe to her. It gets lost on television.

The next day when I got to work, it was suggested at the 11:30
news meeting that I do a piece about the gender issue. I had planned on
simply summarizing the debate and running a few post-debate reaction
bites from the candidates and members of the audience. But two key
colleagues—news director Bill Jobes and anchor Steve Highsmith—
thought that the Edwards remark about women deserved a piece all its
own. They had already asked the assignment desk to put in a call to WPIX
for a copy of the tape.

I tried to talk them out of it. I argued that Edwards's words *had*
been taken out of context and that he was hardly a sexist. If that's so, said
Highsmith, then we should point out the lengths Whitman is going to in
an effort to stir up this pot. Jobes and Highsmith both said Whitman's
demand for an apology had been the centerpiece of the debate, and that
from that point on Edwards had never really recovered from the body-blow.

At the next meeting, at 1:30, after looking again at what Edwards
actually said and calling the two campaign offices and hearing from my
colleagues one more time their arguments for pursuing it, I reluctantly
agreed to attempt a story on it. The only place to interview Whitman and
Edwards before six o'clock would be at the *Asbury Park Press*, where
each was going in the late afternoon to meet the editorial board. It was too
far for me to be able to get there and back and still edit a story by six. So
we took a junior reporter off the story he was working on and sent him
from Newark to Asbury Park with questions I hastily composed and
messaged to him via computer. Then we ordered our one "live" truck to
leave Upper Montclair, where it had been sent to enable sports anchor Pat
Scanlon to do a live shot from a seniors pro golf tournament, and sent it to
Neptune and the *Press* so it could microwave back to me in Trenton the
interviews reporter Eric Luskin would do with Whitman and Edwards.
Pat Scanlon, I figured, would not be pleased, but at NJN politics takes prece-
dence over sports.

The interviews were microwaved in to Trenton at 5:15. I had

already written and edited the back end of my story on other aspects of the debate. Now, watching Edwards and Whitman spar anew over gender, I quickly picked out the good sound bites, wrote a lead and a script, sat with the editor who stitches it all together, and went out on the set without make-up (no time) to "tag" the story on camera.

Whitman said Edwards has displayed a pattern of insensitive remarks during the campaign, and while she had ignored the earlier ones she just couldn't let it go any longer. She's playing the wounded damsel. Edwards admitted he could have phrased what he said on WPIX a little better, but he insisted he is no sexist, has a record on women's issues second to no one's, grew up in a single-parent household and saw sex discrimination against his mother firsthand, and that Whitman is using the gender issue to distract attention away from the real issues.

I got a good story out of this confrontation. My piece ran 3 minutes 58 seconds, long for a news story. The next day the *New York Times* and *Philadelphia Inquirer* did stories on the gender issue. The day after that, David Wald in the *Star-Ledger* caught up to us. I still don't think Edwards's remark was very important, but I appreciate my colleagues' news judgment and was reminded again of why I often defer to it.

★   **Wednesday, June 2**   ★

With six days to go before the primary, it's difficult to predict the outcome. It's easy to imagine Whitman walking away with it, as has been the expectation for months. It's possible to imagine Wallwork finishing second and Edwards third. But I can also envision a scenario in which Edwards wins.

In the absence of polls, one has to rely on feelings and signs to gauge a race, and I sense a little burst of momentum for Edwards. Last weekend he got the endorsement of the *Philadelphia Inquirer.* Word is going around that his own polling shows him seven to nine points down and closing (although I thought they weren't spending money on formal polling). I'm starting to see more lawn signs around the state for Edwards, an admittedly unscientific index of support and one that has misled me in the past.

Most revealing, however, is that Whitman has begun to attack Edwards in a direct-mail piece and a television commercial. It has always been understood, and suggested by the Whitman campaign, that Whitman would stay positive as long as she could and only go negative if she had to. Now, in a four-page direct-mail piece, page four is devoted to a mockery of Edwards's record on crime ("Cary Edwards says if he can't reduce crime he doesn't deserve to be governor—he's right."). The TV commercial says Cary Edwards has raised taxes, like Jim Florio, has increased state spending, like Jim Florio, and ends with images of the two men side by side and the tag line "Jim Florio and Cary Edwards—not a dime's worth of difference" (a line Ed Rollins was using three months ago).

"That's a fundamental reversal of campaign strategy seven days out," Edwards's campaign manager, Jeff Michaels, said to me on the phone today, sounding delighted. "It confirms what we've been saying all along. The race would tighten, and is tightening. You don't go negative for the hell of it."

Yesterday I saw Whitman, Edwards, and Jim Florio give back-to-back speeches at the New Jersey Narcotics Enforcement Officers Association convention in Atlantic City. This was only the second time all year, I believe, that Florio shared a podium with his chief rivals, and so we went, and since the issue was crime, we were able to turn the presentations into a lead story. (In the '80s, Trenton insiders began to refer to the top issues in state elections as "the three Es," meaning the economy, education, and the environment. In '93, it's two Es and a C.) They staked out positions on various drug and criminal-justice questions, agreeing in the main, disagreeing on many of the shadings. What struck me was their demeanors. Whitman was complacent, although she spoke well and without notes. Florio was stronger, but he read from a prepared text and dwelt on his record perhaps a bit more than the audience of narcs and prosecutors needed to hear. And Edwards was on fire—shouting, lecturing, preaching, almost hectoring this audience of fellow members of the law-enforcement brotherhood that included some of his protégés from his attorney general days. He came closest to speaking their language, and he was the only speaker to criticize the other two by name, taking issue with Whitman's positions and Florio's "commitment" to the war on drugs. But it was hard to know whether his shouting energized listeners or alienated them, whether they found it endearing or off-putting.

The picture that didn't materialize in Atlantic City was Florio and Whitman bumping into each other in a lobby. That's always a great shot for television—it's often such an awkward encounter, and the body language can be revealing.

Edwards said one pretty ridiculous thing on NJN last night. We're running profiles of the three Republicans this week, followed by live anchor interviews with each. Last night it was Edwards's turn, and Larry Stuelpnagel's six-minute profile piece ended with Edwards, seated in the living room of his Bergen County home in front of a wall of photos of his kids, responding to a question about why he wants to be governor. "Governing the state of New Jersey would be an incredible honor for me personally, but an incredible opportunity to, uh, achieve, uh, uh, an amount of personal satisfaction that I can't get doing anything else in life," he said. In other words, I'm doing it for me and for me. (Edwards sometimes misspeaks. I'm sure he would revise this statement if he could.)

Tonight was Wallwork's turn on NJN, and his foible was that he got stuck in traffic on the New Jersey Turnpike and couldn't make it to our suburban Trenton studio by 6:15 when the profile was supposed to run. He wanted to just turn around and go home or to his next stop, but by car phone he was told by an NJN staffer, "Senator, we've already promo'd that you'll be here later in the broadcast." He came.

The closing days are often a time for wild, last-minute charges. Wallwork tried accusing Whitman of being anti-Israel last week, but no one covering this race about state issues seemed to care. Two news stories, however, have put Whitman on the defensive. Chris Mondics of the Bergen *Record* disclosed that one of Whitman's final acts as BPU president in 1990 was to approve a sale by the Hackensack Water Company of watershed land around a reservoir, a sale that Whitman had previously opposed. The circumstances of the approval and the apparent switch in Whitman's position have the appearance of a back-door deal, and the sale was later overruled by a state appeals court. Edwards jumped on the story and held a news conference in Hackensack with Bergen County officials who opposed the sale and hold Whitman responsible.

Then, today, Jim Goodman in the Trenton *Times* reported that in 1989, the year after Whitman became BPU president, she set up a blind trust at the Somerset Trust Company. Her uncle Reeve Schley, Jr., is the bank chairman. Her cousin Reeve Schley III is on the board of directors. She herself is on the board. And, according to Goodman (who probably got the story spoon-fed to him by the Florio campaign), she arranged government appointments for seven of the bank's managers and advisors when she was a Somerset County freeholder. None of which adds up to a hill of beans, except that she criticized Joe Salema's blind trust last month for not really being "blind." Now her own trustee turns out to be an institution she is awfully cozy with. Within hours, senate minority leader John Lynch had a press release out blasting Whitman's "hypocrisy" and "self-righteous" attitude toward Salema.

So with six days to go and no new public polls, it's possible that Whitman has been damaged and bruised to the point where she's slipping. Tomorrow morning I interview her for the profile piece I have to have ready by six o'clock.

★ Thursday, June 3 ★

The mood at Whitman headquarters was hardly one of panic. I arrived at 10:30, and Christie was in a hallway near the receptionist. As she shook my hand, she looked me square in the eyes. An NJN cameraman was already set up in a big back room in an empty wing of offices that the Whitman camp will expand into if they win the primary.

In the interview, Whitman told me that she still had a double-digit lead on Edwards. She said the reason she had gone negative against him was that, first, she just "couldn't stand being a punching bag anymore," and second, to show the Florio campaign that if attacked in the fall she is willing to attack back. She conceded that all the negative ads of Edwards and Wallwork had damaged and bruised her. "To think there would be no impact would be naïve. And I am not naïve," she said emphatically. She complained about the tone the campaign had sunk into and said she was sure voters wanted to hear more about issues. She conceded she had made a number of mistakes and misstatements through the primary but not an inordinate amount. "When you're the perceived front-runner everybody looks very closely at everything, and some of the things that are called mistakes are really not heinous offenses," she suggested.

I sensed from her protestations that the most damaging or upsetting attack has been the one that focuses on her $47 farmland assessment on fifty acres in Far Hills. John Whitman had said to me at the last debate that in hindsight he never would have released that information to the press in early February. Now Christie was complaining about the frustration she has felt trying to get the message out that she and John pay a total of $30,000 in property taxes on their two homes.

Another interesting comment came in answer to a question about whether the daughter of Webster Todd could really lay claim to the label of "outsider." She acknowledged she was really more an "outside-insider" who knew this state quite well. "I know how it works, and I watch politics. I saw more knives in my father's back from friends than I ever did from enemies. I know how it works in this state."

Nuggets of truth stand out amid the rhetorical fog when you interview politicians. The trained ear picks them up. I wondered who'd stabbed Webster and who might be stabbing Christie, but there wasn't time to ask. I had a piece to pull together back in Trenton. Jeannie Moos of CNN was in the lobby with a crew waiting for an eleven o'clock interview. And Whitman wouldn't have told me anyway.

On my way out, and without a camera, I poked my head in on Ed Rollins, who was sitting in an ordinary staff cubicle typing a script of some sort on a laptop. After telling me that the race was right where he expected it to be—"I always assumed it would be a 10-point race"—I asked how he could be so confident in the numbers. He explained their polling operation, how GOP pollster Richard Wirthlin in Washington arranges for one hundred and fifty New Jersey homes to be called in a night, and then each morning he and Wirthlin look at two nights' worth of results together on a conference call.

"I've read polls for thirty-two years," Rollins said. "I've been in this situation [the last days of a campaign] probably two hundred times."

Whitman, he said, was at about 40 percent, Edwards had moved up to "below 30," and Wallwork was not showing up well at all because he's got little money. "It's the commercials that drive the reaction," he said, adding that he could tell just by looking at poll results who had been putting what kind of commercials on television.

"It's not an exact art form, but it's close," said this voice of experience, and he had a believer in me.

He told me he's been trying to keep a low profile in the campaign, but agreed to give me a live interview next Tuesday at Whitman's election-night headquarters, where I'll be stationed.

Tacked to the wall at the entrance to his cubicle was a memo on campaign letterhead offering three reasons why the Whitman camp had decided to go negative on Cary Edwards. Presumably all relevant staffers had copies of the memo and were to follow it if asked.

Two other visuals caught my eye. One was a large blown-up color photo, perched on a piece of furniture in some staffer's office, of John and Christie Whitman posed like the farmers in Grant Wood's famous *American Gothic*, standing in front of their barn with him clutching an upright pitchfork. Across the barn roof is a huge white sheet with a big "$19,866" painted or stencilled all the way across it. I noticed it while walking with Whitman, and she explained that in March she and John had put the amount of their Tewksbury property tax payment on the roof after hearing that either Edwards, or Florio, or both planned to fly over the property and shoot pictures for an ad attacking their farmland assessment. On my way out, another item caught my eye, a simple black-on-white sign in the reception area that said "Florio—the new F word."

★ Saturday, June 5 ★

Yesterday I made a point of visiting Edwards headquarters. It might not be there after Tuesday, and I wanted to see it, so I designed a piece around it on "where the race stands four days out."

The headquarters is in a low-slung office-industrial park off Route 1 near the Princeton Junction train station. Campaign director Pete McDonough showed me around. Phone lines were being put in so that volunteers could make twenty thousand phone calls between last night and election day. The Edwards camp had four other locations around the state where phoning would be done on this magnitude. McDonough showed me the field plan as outlined in a very official-looking loose-leaf binder. He had touted it to me on the phone last week, calling it "Cary's idea" to assemble a get-out-the-vote effort unlike anything a Republican statewide candidate had ever done before. Now here it was, built around three thousand volunteers, one in each of the top half of the state's fifty-nine hundred voting districts. "The best army the state has ever had," McDonough called it.

Pete was genuinely upbeat. The Trenton *Times* endorsed Edwards Friday. Tom Kean was said to be miffed at Whitman's ad criticizing the taxing and spending of "Edwards" during the Kean years, and had given permission to Edwards to repackage a 1989 testimonial sound bite in a radio ad this weekend.

While I was there, a call came in from Edwards's car after a taping at WCBS-TV in New York, where the candidates met. Three reporters interviewed afterward on the program apparently said the race had gotten too close to call, and that if the election were postponed a week or two Edwards would probably win. McDonough was elated.

It is possible to imagine Edwards winning. If I were Whitman I would be nervous. But I still think she will win.

★ Tuesday, June 8 ★

Election day, and the headline on page one of the Trenton *Times* says "Whitman Lead Over Edwards Weakens." With just a few hours left before the votes are counted, Christie Whitman is in the same position Bill Bradley was in when she challenged him in 1990—hanging on for dear life (except that Bradley didn't realize it until the votes started to be counted).

The Whitman camp's tracking polls are down to a six-point margin between her and Edwards. We know this because, surprisingly, the Whitman campaign told everyone who asked yesterday instead of guarding the number closely. They say they did it to counter a Sunday *Asbury Park Press* poll that showed Edwards faring slightly better against Florio (40 to 43) than does Whitman (37 to 43).

I stopped in at Edwards headquarters on my way into work around noon, to gauge the mood. There is real optimism there. Jeff Michaels and Pete McDonough are already explaining how they pulled off a coup. Michaels said a "sea change" had taken place in the electorate the past four days. McDonough spoke passionately of the Whitman campaign's "collapse." They pointed out all the mechanical mistakes they thought their counterparts in the Whitman camp had made, such as not responding to the *Asbury Park Press* poll on Saturday night or Sunday, but waiting until Monday when the damage had been done. They gloated over the fact that Michaels and his wife, who live in Somerset County and are exactly the type of voters one would expect to be targeted for direct mail and phone-banking in a Republican primary, had not received one mail piece or phone call from the Whitman campaign.

At my office, I prepared for my assignment at Whitman headquarters tonight by making calls and reading the papers. Press secretary Joe Justin told me that Christie Whitman was at Pontefract, the family farm, with her husband, brother, and Ed Rollins, making thank-you calls to about forty-five key supporters. I imagine they are quite nervous, although Justin and another staffer I spoke to exuded a certain calm that suggested confidence. A Wallwork aide predicted victory, but I didn't take it seriously, even if she did.

In my newsroom this afternoon, several colleagues predicted an Edwards come-from-behind victory. While that's entirely possible, I'm more inclined to go along with a Republican I spoke to on the phone, who said, "She has just enough gas left in the tank to make it."

★ **Wednesday, June 9** ★

It's over. And it ended more or less as the conventional wisdom always said it would, Whitman over Edwards by seven points, with Wallwork in third. This morning's papers are talking once again about the Whitman "magic." After a brief scare, the phenomenon of Christie Whitman continues.

Within a few hours of my arrival last night at the Brunswick Hilton, Whitman supporters were breathing easier. Whitman led in the early returns, and she kept right on leading all night. I was stationed with the rest of the media in a cordoned-off area in the rear of the room, watching NJN's live coverage on a monitor when I wasn't on myself. Ironically, it was Jim Florio, around 10:25, who was first to declare Whitman the winner. He was at the New Brunswick Hyatt Regency two miles away, at his own "victory" party, and in his speech to the celebrants, carried live on NJN, he congratulated Mrs. Whitman on her apparent victory before any news service had declared her the victor. Shortly thereafter, the Associated Press made it official.

Between nine and midnight, I did five live shots, usually with guests: Ed Rollins, Dan Todd, Hazel Gluck, and one in which I introduced a taped interview with Whitman herself, shot in a holding room where she was giving one-on-ones to TV stations about ten minutes after she knew she'd won. Being ushered into that room—with several print reporters screaming outside about the favoritism being shown to the TV people—I was aware of a heightened reality about the moment. Whitman accepted my congratulations and made a joke about the interview I had done with her brother (which she had watched from her suite on the eleventh floor), but she was in a slight daze, I thought. VIPs, like senate president Don DiFrancesco, were drifting in and out of her immediate airspace, hugging her and conferring secular benedictions upon her. Cameras were flashing and rolling. Anyone in that situation—at the center of a bubble—might be in a slight trance.

The highlight of the night for me was that I got a scoop out on statewide TV. I had learned a few days ago that Dan Todd, Christie's brother, was likely to replace Dave Murray as campaign manager for the general election. I got it confirmed before we went on the air last night and learned as well that Carl Golden, the former press secretary to Governor Kean, would join the Whitman team. Joe Justin was returning to California to get married, and Dave Murray was becoming a consultant for the campaign. With Dan Todd on live, the two of us standing on chairs so the camera could get the stage and a big "People for Whitman" banner in the shot, I asked if indeed these changes at the highest level of the Whitman camp were in the works. He confirmed my information, even complimenting my intelligence-gathering ability on the air. Ironically, Carl Golden was the last of a handful of Republicans I had called in the afternoon just to pick their brains. I hadn't an inkling about what was up, and he was completely poker-faced (if you can be that on the phone). Six hours later I was scooping my colleagues by announcing his appointment on TV.

One of the oddities of American politics is that people can say nasty things about one another in a primary, then overnight start acting as if they never meant it. That's what happened at a unity brunch this morning hosted by the Republican State Committee and the legislative leaders at the Hyatt Regency in Princeton. Edwards and Wallwork gushed over Whitman in a heartwarming show of party unity. The best picture was Edwards and Whitman embracing outside the main ballroom as two dozen cameras rolled and clicked. The best sound bites were Edwards telling seven hundred brunchgoers that Whitman, whom twenty-four hours earlier he was describing in TV ads as a huge risk, was actually one of the finest people he's ever met in his life and God bless her; and Wallwork, whose commercials had just branded her a dreaded liberal, now saying, actually she's a moderate.

John Whitman approached me at one point and said he was upset that in my interview with Christie last night I had asked questions about "her negatives" on what was supposed to be her victory night. "Totally inappropriate," he said. I wasn't sure what he was talking about until he explained that in my questions I had made reference to some of the gaffes and misstatements that, in my view, had come to characterize the campaign. He was also upset with a hostile interview the NJN anchors had done with Whitman last week. "We've given you good access to this campaign, but if you keep bringing up the negatives that'll stop," he warned me. I chalked it up to inexperience, tried to pacify him, and defended my questions, but he remained huffy.

After the brunch, Whitman held a news conference in the hotel, to announce that Tom Kean and two other people were joining the campaign as co-chairs and that Carl Golden was the new communications director. Under questioning, she also disclosed that Dan Todd would be the new campaign manager. After the news conference and after another interview I did with Whitman for tonight's news, Golden pulled me aside and asked somewhat incredulously, "Did John Whitman threaten you?" I hadn't taken it as a threat exactly, but when I recounted the conversation for Golden, I suddenly could see it as a threat. Golden was annoyed and agitated. He apologized and intimated that John Whitman is a "problem" for the campaign. (Someone else had suggested to me that Dan Todd was the problem.) John, he suggested, doesn't really have a job, and besides that has to live with all the attention focused on his wife, and that it causes him to do politically unwise things, such as springing to the defense of his wife's honor over some slight that is better left ignored.

Whitman herself didn't seem upset with me. I had asked Dan Todd directly if he was upset about anything, as John was. "Naaaaah," he said reassuringly. "Dad told us long ago to write five articles in a day. If you can do it, then you have a right to get upset at journalists, but if you can't, keep your mouth shut."

So the battle is joined, as Jim Florio put it today. Florio was in New Brunswick announcing a $42 million Rutgers construction project that held the promise of creating five hundred jobs. Whitman was rallying her party behind her, laying out some of the themes and rhetoric she'll be using in the fall, and calling the Florio record "disastrous" for New Jersey and its economy.

"We'll make New Jersey Florio-free in '93!" she shouted, borrowing the phrase from a bumper sticker commonly seen on pickup trucks.

★　Sunday, June 13　★

The primary ended with Whitman getting 40 percent, Edwards 33 percent, and Wallwork 24 percent. Whitman won fifteen counties, Edwards won five, and Wallwork surprised everyone by winning in Atlantic County. Considering that he got into the race late and spent less than half of what each of his rivals spent, Wallwork acquitted himself well. One in four Republican voters preferred him to the other two, and he comes out of this contest with far more stature than he had going in. He is not a joke today.

In my mind, however, this was always a contest between Whitman and Edwards (in their minds, too). Whitman won because she started off with more name recognition and more political IOUs than Edwards; because she handled Nannygate with more precision than he did; because she didn't get rattled when she made mistakes or suffered attacks; because she took positions slightly to the right of Edwards and, therefore, more in the Republican mainstream; and because she comes across well on television. Edwards tried to paint her as inexperienced and out of touch, but neither charge entirely hits the mark. She has less experience than he, but she is hardly a novice. And she is rich, but she does not speak with an upper-class accent or carry airs. In fact, she projects a certain down-to-earth quality, although it remains to be seen whether she can relate to the really poor in New Jersey's cities.

Edwards tried hard. He hit her hard and always above the belt (though sometimes just above). He campaigned with enthusiasm and occasionally fervor. He assembled a good team. He made no obvious mistakes. What he was offering just didn't have quite as much appeal as what she was offering. Edwards has said on several occasions since his first run in '89 that he thinks of himself as better at government than at running for office, and even some of his supporters agree. Sadly for them and for him, we may never get to see how good a governor Cary Edwards might have been.

The media now are whipping themselves into a bit of a froth over the titanic clash ahead. In editorials this week, the *Philadelphia Inquirer* said, "It should be a wingding of an election." The Bergen *Record* warned of "an all-out attack on Mrs. Whitman (in the next few weeks) in an effort to muddy her up." And the *New York Times* said that with Carville and Rollins involved, "no one expects a pillow fight." Several of the Sunday papers today did features on Carville and Rollins as the sort of dark geniuses who make politics such a deliciously naughty spectacle.

Another strain in the editorials and op-ed columns this week was that Whitman has gotten away with being vague, unspecific, and superficial. It's a charge that rings half-true. Whether by design ("Whenever you take a position, you alienate some people," Cliff Zukin of Rutgers keeps being quoted as saying) or because with Whitman it's not going to get much deeper, we don't know yet. Her "Blueprint for Economic Revival" is the policy centerpiece of her campaign, and it's not bad. But her rhetoric is a little thin. She is good at laying out broad principles, not so good at saying what she will *do*. Columnist Elizabeth Auster in the *Record* warned that Whitman needs a message and a vision—"a vision that amounts to more than vague paeans to a new era of public participation in government." She went on, ". . . in her victory speech, as in the campaign she ran these past several months, she said almost nothing."

The Florio campaign seems to have gone right to work on Whitman. Jim Florio had no opponent for two months (except the fleeting John Budzash), and there seems to be pent-up energy that the Florio campaign is eager to release. Two days after the election the governor shocked almost everyone in Trenton by signing an executive order that does away with blind trusts for people in state government. It was Joe Salema's blind trust that marred Florio's spring. Now the governor was further insulating himself from the bond scandal by outlawing the very mechanism that was supposed to prevent government officials from profiting while in office but which, in the Salema case, had apparently failed.

The announcement caught Whitman off guard. She was at the Statehouse that morning, and I was trailing her at the time. Carl Golden, her new press watchdog, tried to tell me what the governor had done was no big deal and not worth a story. In the meantime, the Florio campaign was faxing out reams of information pertaining to Christie Whitman's blind trust, set up when she went to the BPU and still active, along with a demand that she disclose all her assets.

In the NJN newsroom, they were trying to figure out what to do with the story. A key producer argued there was really nothing "political" about the governor's action.

At that same moment, I was in Jon Shure's office in the Statehouse, getting ready to do an interview with him on the blind-trust executive order because the governor was out of the Statehouse and unavailable for comment, when the phone rang.

I could tell from Shure's voice and the conversation who it was.

"They've just gotten the material we put out, and they're probably still looking through it. . . . Some of them seem to think it's significant. . . . She was here. A few of them asked her about it. . . . I don't know. . . . Yes, it's been engaged."

PART TWO

Summer

Christie Whitman turned toward the hotel ballroom and started walking in.

She saw Jim Florio, whose voice wafted her way.

"I'm not sure they want us to skip or hold hands going down the aisle, but we're supposed to go down together," said Florio, ever the sarcasm-master.

Whitman sidled up next to him.

"Okay, we're supposed to go down together," she said, seemingly at a loss for words.

And so Christie Whitman and Jim Florio came face-to-face for the first time this year. The occasion was a dinner held by the New Jersey Business and Industry Association last Tuesday night at the Princeton Hyatt Regency. The state's business climate is probably the hot issue of this campaign, and about 750 people turned out to hear the candidates give back-to-back speeches to a business audience.

As they stood waiting to enter the ballroom together, cameras clicking and rolling all around them to get this rare informal "two-shot," they made small talk about the high level of interest in the election as registered in the newest Eagleton Poll.

". . . could be a whole lot worse," Whitman could be heard saying to Florio, and then, "No, that's great. People are truly interested, which is good."

Fortunately for them, applause soon rose from inside the ball-room and the need to make forced small talk in the midst of cameras ended. Florio let Whitman go first, then walked in right behind her. As they moved down the aisle in tandem shaking hands with people, they looked like running-mates on the same ticket. But when it came time to speak, they suddenly became two people living in different worlds.

"This state has been driven to the brink of economic ruin by circumstances beyond and *within* its control," Whitman declared from the podium, with Florio seated about six feet away. She painted a picture of a state mired in bankruptcies, mortgage foreclosures, and unemploy-ment, a state over-taxed and over-regulated. "There are those who would blame the national recession entirely for this state of affairs," she said. "That simply is not true. Historically New Jersey's economy has per-formed better than the national average. Now it lags behind the rest of the nation. That dramatic reversal can only be attributed to the current policies in Trenton."

She spoke for eighteen minutes and got standing ovations at the beginning and end from maybe a quarter of the room.

When Florio got up to speak, the reception was a shade cooler. Although some people rose to their feet, I could see most of them were the governor's staff seated at a table close to the dais.

Florio began his remarks with a wry ad lib. "You've just heard how the glass is half empty," he said. "Now let me tell you how it's half full." The audience seemed to appreciate this acknowledgment that they shouldn't take too seriously what either candidate says.

Florio spoke for twenty-three minutes about all he's done to try to create jobs. He talked about making tough decisions based on "values," such as "hard work, persistence, and investing in the future." ("Values" has become a common staple of Florio speeches.) "These past three years haven't been easy," he said. "But I don't come here looking for sympathy, because they've been just as tough on you as they have on me." This was classic Florio: self-effacing, defensive, hurt, proud, and still in tune with the tenor of the times. He touted his enhanced Economic Development Authority (EDA), his worker retraining program, his high-tech initiative, his welfare reform. "As we've grown to know each other over these past three and a half years, we haven't always agreed on everything," he told the businesspeople, plaintively. "But you always knew where I stood. And on matters of principle, if you knew where I stood one day, you knew that's where I'd stand the next day."

Where Whitman spoke of the 1980s as a golden era, Florio spoke of them as a "big party" from which we're now just getting over the "big hangover." Where Whitman promised "multiyear budgeting" and spoke of California as a state that has experimented successfully with it, Florio said New Jersey already does budgets with the out years in mind and anyone who uses California as a model of good budgeting doesn't appreciate what's gone on there recently.

On my way out of the hotel, I chatted with Ginny Littell, the Republican state chairman. "I think she disarms him," Littell said of Whitman and Florio. "He doesn't seem to know how to attack her, whether to attack her. He's not used to a woman." Others saw the evening differently, finding Whitman a bit cowed by Florio and by being in the big leagues.

The first *Star-Ledger*/Eagleton poll of the general election season, released last Sunday, showed Florio ahead of Whitman, 48 percent to 43 percent. This was greeted as great news in the Florio camp. "Who would have expected a year ago that Jim Florio would be where he is right now?" said Harold Hodes, the lobbyist and advisor to Florio, a line that was echoed by other Florio loyalists.

But Whitman supporters found solace in the second-level numbers in the poll. Among independents, Whitman led 47 percent to 40 percent. Florio supporters were more likely to consider switching their vote, 45 percent to 30 percent. "There's a lot that's very encouraging," said Carl Golden. "Despite the negative campaigns that were run against her over the past month, it's basically a dead heat."

That argument could just as easily be turned on its head. Having just come through a high-visibility primary and still wearing the glow of victor, Whitman might have been expected to lead Florio at this point. The poll was better news for Florio, and you could see it in the more excited reaction of his people.

The Florio campaign staff is jabbing away at Whitman every day. While the governor walks the high road, his campaign press secretary, Jo Astrid Glading, sends out a press release a day ridiculing Whitman. The

Florio camp is working intensely to throw Whitman off balance. One day it's her blind trust they go after. The next it's her statement about California as a model of budget-thinking. That press release even contained quotes from a Democratic politician in California "astonished" that someone from New Jersey would hold California up as a model. The day after the business speeches, Florio's personnel commissioner, Anthony "Skip" Cimino, called a news conference to blast Whitman for having said the night before that the state workforce increased under Florio; the administration insists it has been reduced by forty-seven hundred jobs. And the same day, an abortion rights group, N.J. Right to Choose, held a Statehouse news conference to criticize Whitman for having "bankrolled" prolife Republican legislative candidates in 1991 through her political action committee. Both events were backed up by Jo Glading press releases lambasting Whitman. The Florio camp even has a "rapid response" component. The night of the business speeches, as soon as Whitman finished speaking, Glading handed reporters a press release containing an "instant critique" of Whitman's speech ("Again she offered no real ideas for creating jobs. . . . C'mon, Mrs. Whitman, let's give the people something more than phony blueprints and bumper sticker slogans.").

Glading, thirty-four, and Jim Andrews, thirty-seven, are the two key operatives at Florio's campaign headquarters. Glading used to be an Associated Press reporter at the Statehouse. She joined the Florio administration in 1990 as spokesperson for the insurance commissioner, moved to deputy press secretary for the governor while beginning to study law at night, and was then dispatched to the campaign. She is tough and smart. She and Andrews seem delivered by central casting. They smoke cigarettes and curse freely. Andrews managed Harold Washington's second campaign for mayor of Chicago and spent fifteen years in Chicago politics, which he insists are rougher than New Jersey's. He learned how to read polling data while studying for a Ph.D. in statistics at the University of Chicago, and he showed me how Florio's lead in the latest Eagleton poll is not as "soft" as the poll's directors said it was. They misread their own data, he said, but he wasn't about to antagonize them by pointing it out to them.

With these two kamikazes in charge—and Andrews talking to Jim Florio and James Carville at least once a day on the phone— the

Florio camp is trying to repeat what it did to Jim Courter in 1989: un-
nerve the opponent, throw her off balance, put her on the defensive, and
start "defining" her in negative ways for the public before she defines
herself.

Whether it will work against Whitman is unclear. (Courter cooperated by flip-flopping on abortion, uttering a homophobic remark about
teachers, and generally drifting.) The Whitman camp has been less visible
and less aggressive than the Florio camp. But Carl Golden, the new press
secretary, has parried the Florio attacks with skill and effectiveness. For
example, after Jo Glading and N.J. Right to Choose put out the list of pro-
life Republicans Whitman had helped, Golden issued a press release list-
ing all the pro-life *Democratic* legislators Florio had run with, supported
financially, or given jobs to—a list as long as the Whitman list. And when
several newspapers reported that N.J. Right to Choose had gotten research help from the Florio campaign, calling into question the group's
professed independence, the whole thing blew up in the Florio camp's face.

None of this sparring is consequential at this point. It's the equivalent of two fighters feeling each other out in the early rounds. Some
people think it's aimed at the press corps more than at the public. It's
indicative, however, of the Florio camp's early aggressiveness and hardball attitude and the Whitman camp's low-keyed, resolute response posture.

Republicans and Democrats alike are calling the hiring of Carl
Golden a master-stroke by Whitman. "The best thing they have going for
them is Carl Golden," said Harold Hodes.

"Carl Golden will be excellent at coaching her in how to keep
her foot out of her mouth," said Carl Zeits, another Democrat-turned-
PR-man.

Golden, fifty-five, is wiry, nervous, and perpetually in motion.
Personally he favors cowboy boots and country music. Professionally his
style is "in-your-face" politician-protection. Younger reporters he insults
and intimidates. Older ones he challenges and criticizes. It's all aimed at
keeping reporters from writing what Golden doesn't want them to write,
by reminding them that he's reading them closely and they had better
understand his point of view. After guiding Tom Kean's press effort for
eight years, he became spokesman for New Jersey Supreme Court chief
justice Robert Wilentz and the judicial branch of government. He took

the woman he was involved with, Linda Monica, with him to that job as his assistant, and has done the same with the Whitman job. Last year they married. If you want Carl, you take Carl and Linda, as the tabloid *Trentonian* pointed out a few years ago in a front-page banner headline that said "TOP JUDGE PADS PAYROLL WITH LOVE BIRDS."

With Golden on board, and Tom Kean now signed on as a campaign co-chair and even attending the weekly Monday morning strategy meetings, which Hazel Gluck has been running for months, the Whitman campaign takes on the aura of a Kean cabal. One of NJN's weekly analysts, Democrat Jim McQueeny, thinks Jim Florio was crazy recently to criticize Kean. You don't want to "energize" Kean right now, McQueeny says. He claims it's well known that Kean was cool toward Whitman during the primary and secretly wanted Cary Edwards to win. (Others dispute that.) Kean's support for Whitman now can be half-hearted or it can be gung-ho, and if you're Florio you'd rather keep Kean in a laid-back mode. (Kean may be thinking about challenging U.S. senator Frank Lautenberg next year, in which case he'd have a real personal incentive to see Whitman win the governorship.)

The Florio strategy is to portray Jim Florio as a person of vision and courage who made difficult decisions which have left New Jersey better off coming out of the recession than many other states. "The idea is to make it a race between someone preaching the new '90s gospel of responsibility and someone who's a kind of classic fence-sitter," says Jim Andrews. Florio's advisors know they can't get the public to embrace Jim Florio personally as someone warm and wonderful. The game plan is to get the public to accept what he did, reward him for his courage, and see the election as a choice between someone who had the courage of his convictions and someone who has no convictions.

"How are we going to win? By keeping the election a choice. Continually comparing the two of them," says Andrews. "This is not a referendum on Jim Florio. It's a choice. People are gonna have to pick one.

"There's a yearning on the part of people for real leadership. Florio, like Perot and Clinton, said, 'Hey, we gotta be responsible.' This race on a national basis is about whether or not that message works. Governors, mayors, and senators throughout the country are looking at this race."

The effort by the Florio camp to "Courterize" Christie Whitman continued this week, but the Whitman camp emerged from its temporary slumber and fought back.

On Monday the Florio camp faxed out a copy of an article from the *Jersey Journal* of Jersey City describing how Whitman last week, wearing jeans and a t-shirt, had taken an unpublicized tour of Jersey City that ended with a stop at a gun shop, Caso's Gun-a-Rama. According to the article, Whitman told the shop owner that she felt Florio's assault weapon ban "should be cleaned up a bit" and that several weapons on the list "shouldn't be included."

To the Florio camp this was a major flip-flop, since Whitman had said during the primary that she opposed the effort in the legislature to overturn the ban. "As always, Mrs. Whitman's position changes as her audience changes," said Jo Glading's press release.

Two days later, to hammer home the point and get more coverage than the press release had gotten, a Statehouse news conference was held featuring Democratic congressman Robert Torricelli, gun control advocates, and a dozen uniformed law enforcement officers, each holding a picture of an assault weapon. Torricelli, who's a good speaker except for a tendency in every set of remarks to sound as if he's delivering the Gettysburg Address, blasted Whitman for courting the gun lobby and sending "coded messages" to the NRA. "In Mrs. Whitman's neighborhood, these weapons may be used for shooting fox on horseback, but in Jersey City," said Torricelli, moving his hand to his heart as he mentioned the newest part of his congressional district, "they're used to defend the territory of drug dealers."

The Whitman campaign scoffed at all this. Carl Golden accused the Florio campaign of trying to divert attention from the economy, which the latest poll shows is the top concern of 72 percent of the electorate. Of the steady fax-attack coming out of Florio headquarters, Golden was downright contemptuous. "If you could translate truth into nutrition, the Florio campaign would be somewhere between Twinkies and potato chips," he said to me *twice* this week.

By Wednesday, so many reporters were so aware that the Florio camp was attacking while the Whitman camp was doing nothing that the Whitman camp suddenly fought back. A press release challenged Jim Florio to say where he stood on the Clinton budget package, which passed the U.S. Senate last week 50 to 49. The Clinton plan contains tax hikes. New Jersey's Senator Frank Lautenberg, up for re-election next year, voted against it. Whitman's release said the Clinton plan would cost the average New Jerseyan $412 and questioned "the Governor's refusal to speak out on the issue."

While their campaign staffs engage in what one person this week called "petty skirmishing," the candidates move around the state, attending maybe three or four public events per day, and trying to stay positive. Jim Florio uses the power of incumbency to get news coverage. On Tuesday he signed the state budget (in private), then went to South Brunswick to accept a report from the attorney general showing that domestic violence incidents were down last year. On Wednesday, in Union City, he accepted, from the attorney general again, the 1992 Statewide Uniform Crime Report, which showed crime down 6 percent over the year before. On Thursday both Florio and Whitman spoke at the swearing-in of the new Jersey City mayor, a thirty-four-year-old Republican wunderkind named Bret Schundler, but where Whitman wished the new mayor and his city luck, Florio took the opportunity right there to sign a bill that gives Jersey City $3 million and about $70 million to the state's other 566 municipalities. "Take *that!*" you could almost feel him thinking as he signed the law with Whitman seated a few feet away on the dais.

The Whitman camp knows it can't compete with Florio's ability to get media coverage. So it doesn't try. Another fax from Carl Golden this week began, "Rather than spending his time arranging self-congratulatory public events, the Governor should turn his efforts toward explaining the dismal state of New Jersey's economy and what he intends to do about it." Whitman just goes to events, meets people, and attracts a local reporter or two, the way she's been doing for the last two-and-a-half years. Democrats say she's hiding, that her campaign is keeping her "under wraps" for fear she'll say something stupid. That may be half-true or it may just be that news coverage in early July is hard to come by wherever one goes. "We were looking at her schedule," Jo Glading told me, "and Jim Andrews said it looks like she's running for freeholder."

My role in all this is to report what the candidates and campaigns are saying, and to facilitate an over-the-air dialogue. Of the five daily news packages I did this week, four were about the governor's race. I interviewed Florio twice, once at his domestic-violence event, the other time at the Governor's Gala '93, a fund-raising dinner that raised $2 million for the State Democratic Committee and that featured a cameo appearance by Texas governor Ann Richards. Try as he might, Florio just can't resist attacking Whitman. On camera he tries to stay positive and takes only light swipes at her (which may explain why Ann Richards, whose most famous line is that "George Bush was born with a silver foot in his mouth," said nothing about silver-spooned Christine Todd Whitman and only talked about what a great guy Florio is. One got the sense she would have attacked if asked.). Off camera, however, Florio says the same things that are in his campaign's press releases, leading me to believe that at least some of the assaults originate with him.

In South Brunswick he said to me and another reporter, "The idea of someone hunting for votes in Gun-a-Rama . . . ," and on the issue of assault weapons, "she's trying to have it both ways."

"She's rope-a-doping," said the former boxer, an allusion to Muhammad Ali's old phrase for avoiding engagement with a ring opponent. He then talked about the difference between "specificity" (him) and "unspecificity" (her). He thinks the electorate is hungering for specifics and that they're getting them from him but not from her. "It's why Ross Perot has built such a following," Florio explained, revealing again how Perot haunts establishment politicians. "He's out there *giving information.*"

The next night, at the fund-raising dinner, I interviewed Florio in the middle of the ballroom right after he had danced with his wife. The subject was the Clinton tax hikes, which he defended. He chided Whitman for supporting the "Republican approach" to deficit-reduction, with its maintenance of "tax breaks" for the wealthy. Then off camera he said, "Off the record? It's amazing. She ran in '90 against Bradley by running against me [she challenged Bill Bradley to take a stand on the Florio tax hikes]. Now she's running against me by running against Bradley [raising the issue of federal tax hikes, which Bradley supports]." A few moments later he said, "Y'know what someone called her recently? 'Jim Courter with pearls.' " I told him I had heard the line before but that it had been "Tom Kean with pearls." He seemed to like it better his way.

I only interviewed Whitman once this week, the day the crime stats came out and Torricelli attacked her for visiting the gun shop. We sent a crew to Jersey City to show what Gun-a-Rama looked like, and a junior NJN reporter interviewed the owner for me. Whitman wasn't available until 4:30 in Burlington County, where she was attending the dedication of a hydroponic greenhouse on the grounds of the county resource recovery plant. Given the lateness of the hour, I asked my questions about guns quickly. She answered with aplomb. When I asked if she had been sending a "coded message" to the gun lobby, she laughed and explained that she'd been touring Jersey City with a police officer, who had said the gun shop owner was a supporter of hers, and so they had made a quick, impromptu stop. She said she has consistently been for the assault weapons ban except that current owners should be allowed to keep their weapons and certain .22s that are mainly used for target shooting should come off the list.

I was struck by how well she deflected my questions without getting rattled. With Jim Courter in 1989, you got answers but a kind of shiftiness. Whitman projects candor. She has been called a "teflon" candidate by some of her supporters. I feared that in my haste I hadn't been tough enough on her.

Before hustling back to Trenton, I did a quick closing stand-up about the Whitman camp challenging Florio on the Clinton tax hikes. The next day Jon Shure, the governor's communications director, called to say he had liked my piece last night, had enjoyed seeing Whitman waffle on the gun issue (so I *was* tough! good!), but next time they'd appreciate an opportunity to get the last word on a charge like the one that I ended the piece with. I explained that Jo Glading had returned my 2:45 call at 5:15, too late for me to want to alter my piece. He was understanding and almost apologetic. Press secretaries are supposed to return phone calls faster than that. I had been in an NJN van heading back to Trenton at 5:15 when my beeper went off with Glading's number on the display, but we don't have cellular phones in our vans and there was no way I was stopping at a pay phone for another tit-for-tat charge when my stand-up close was already on tape and the news goes on at 6:00.

In addition to amplifying what the candidates are saying and doing and facilitating a dialogue between them, my role as TV reporter is to analyze what's happening and, if possible, force a question onto the agenda. After three straight days of covering the race, on Friday I chose to do an analysis piece instead of following Governor Florio as he stumped the Jersey Shore at the outset of the Fourth of July weekend. I wanted to show how the Florio camp is trying to "Courterize" Whitman and needed interviews with both campaign staffs. I ended up interviewing Jo Glading and Carl Golden at their respective headquarters.

Glading was nervous but said she was doing the interview because Jim Andrews "doesn't like doing TV" and would have been more nervous. She did fine as a kind of New Jersey version of Dee Dee Myers. After the interview and while my cameraman got a shot of her hyperactive fax machine at work, she told me that two people who had worked for Whitman, one in 1990 and one in the primary, had said of Whitman, "She believes there's a mystique about her." That's what enables her sometimes to "ignore the advice she gets." These people had told Glading that Whitman was "refreshing in that she says whatever is on her mind— on the other hand, nobody knew what the f—— she was going to say from day to day, and they sometimes had to backtrack to fill out her statements." I didn't tell her that I had once heard the exact same thing said of Mikhail Gorbachev, by one of his press secretaries.

Whitman headquarters has been moved around and expanded. The candidate now has a big office worthy of her stature, though, from the glance I got at it, it's still under-furnished, slightly ratty, and very eclectic and personal in style. Dan Todd now has a windowless little office directly across the hall from his sister's, and Carl Golden shares a small office next to Whitman's with his deputy, Dave Marziale.

Golden is such a ball-buster. I'm sorry, but there's no other word for it. As we set up the camera in his office, I told him I was doing a piece based on an original thought. He feigned shock and said, "Oh, my God. At least maybe for once you'll be objective!" I said we had seen enough this week of the campaigns' setting the agenda and that I thought I'd try it for a change. "Are you kidding? The media has been setting the agenda for one hundred years!" he snorted, his face twitching as we both laughed. I asked him when Christie Whitman would be releasing her 1992 tax return. "Michael, you know me. It's the Friday before a holiday weekend. We're doing it at five o'clock today." It was 3:30, and I panicked ever so slightly 'til I realized he was just kidding.

In my younger days, Golden's constant needling unnerved me. I've since learned to tolerate it and marvel at it.

"How old are you, Carl?" I asked at one point after the on-camera interview.

"Oh, Michael. I'm a hundred and four," he said. "At least that's how I feel. In my day, 'safe sex' meant padded headboards."

★ **Monday, July 5** ★

A race for governor is composed of internal factors—the candidates' records, positions, statements, performance, character, and whatever mistakes they happen to make—and external factors. The most important external factor in this race is the economy. If it's good in the fall, that's good for Florio. If it's bad, that's good for Whitman.

Since May, when the state unemployment rate spiked up to 9.1 percent and drew ominous headlines, it has dropped precipitously two months in a row. In June it went down to 7.6 percent. Last Friday it went down again to 6.9 percent. Such wild swings make a lot of people suspicious of the numbers (for example, 140,000 of the 400,000 new jobs in America last month were created in New Jersey, according to the Bureau of Labor Statistics, and that seems very unlikely). But they are the only official numbers we have, and so they take on meaning.

The steep drop in unemployment takes the sting out of Republican complaints of all the jobs "lost" on Florio's watch. When a Whitman press release said last week that Florio better start explaining why 325,000 jobs disappeared since he became governor, the cry lacked urgency.

Several other external factors have come out in Florio's favor in the past ten days. McGuire Air Force Base and an advanced communications command at Fort Monmouth were removed from the Pentagon's hit list by the U.S. Base Closure and Realignment Commission, whose chairman, ironically, is Jim Courter. This was cause for celebration in the locales of the bases and a source of great relief to the governor and the state's U.S. senators and key congressmen. Florio doesn't get particular credit for saving the bases, but their closing—especially McGuire—would have contributed to a psychology of gloom about the state's economic picture.

Then came the crime stats. Down 6 percent for 1992. Crime is one of the three acknowledged top issues this year, and had the statistics gone up, Whitman would have been handed fresh ammunition. Instead, the numbers broke Florio's way (one assumes the State Police is nonpartisan in these matters), and Whitman was left having to say what wonderful news that was for New Jersey and that it seems to be part of a "national trend." Funny how reduced crime is part of a national trend, but not job loss.

The only external factors that might be working for Whitman at this moment are named Schundler and Clinton. Bret Schundler is the first Republican elected mayor of Jersey City since 1913, and his victory in this capital of Democratic machine politics has Republicans excited and pundits searching for deeper meaning. (Jack Kemp spoke at the swearing-in last week, George Will wrote about it, and Schundler was on "This Week with David Brinkley" yesterday.) Florio won Hudson County by a 3 to 1 margin in 1989, but his 63,000-vote margin of victory there wasn't crucial, because he won statewide by 500,000 votes. This year's election will be closer. If the Schundler phenomenon cuts into his plurality in Hudson, it might hurt.

Then there is Bill Clinton. Although he bombed Iraq last weekend, and his poll numbers went up twelve points, the Clinton "factor" is another big question mark for the fall. The president has gotten off to a shakier start than anyone imagined six months ago. His tax package is especially sensitive in this tax-traumatized state, enough to prevent Senator Lautenberg and Democratic congressmen Rob Andrews, Frank Pallone, and Herb Klein from voting for it. In the governor's race, Clinton creates a general climate around Democrats and in particular serves to remind voters of Jim Florio's inclination to tax. If Clinton is still floundering this fall, that's good for Whitman. When I asked Congressman Robert Torricelli off-camera last week how things were looking for Florio, his first response was, "The Clinton situation does not help."

★ **Thursday, July 8** ★

The Florio campaign is trying like mad to turn assault weapons into a "wedge" issue. On Monday Christie Whitman, attending a July "5th" parade, told a WABC-TV news reporter the assault weapons ban was a "lousy piece of legislation." That bite appeared on the air, and the next day the Florio campaign took a tape of the newscast to the Statehouse to try to drum up interest in Whitman's statement.

I was in Camden covering Florio, who was there to hand out a check for $600,000 to help fund a new mini-police station in a rundown neighborhood (a neighborhood Florio himself lived in during the late '60s). He was being gubernatorial. But on camera, when I asked him about Whitman and guns, he said he'd seen her on the news last night and was shocked at how "out of touch" she is with the majority of New Jerseyans.

Whitman is straddling the gun issue, trying to have it both ways. She says she supports the ban but just thinks that current owners should be allowed to keep their weapons and that certain .22 rifles on the list of thirty-seven banned weapons don't belong there. The only thing new in her statement on WABC was the use of the word "lousy." One might rightfully ask how she can support a law she thinks is lousy.

But the way the Florio camp has jumped on this bespeaks a certain over-eagerness, if not desperation. The Whitman camp's response is to accuse Florio of "a deliberate strategy to divert attention away from the incumbent's dismal record on the issues which concern New Jerseyans more than any others—the economy, taxes, and jobs," as a Whitman press release put it. Except for my pieces on NJN, in which the candidates themselves are interviewed, the skirmishing is taking place mainly through press releases and spokespersons. The candidates are not staging events in which they raise these points.

Whitman, in fact, is lying so low that the Florio campaign is accusing her of hiding from the public and the press. Tuesday her only public appearance was at a county employee recognition ceremony in her home county of Somerset. Yesterday her only appearance was a radio interview at 7:30 a.m. on a Jewish music program at the Upsala College radio station. Today and tomorrow she is in California at the biannual convention of the National Women's Political Caucus. That bipartisan group pushes for women in elective office, and Whitman will appear with five would-be woman governors in 1994 elections, all of them Democrats.

The Whitman camp also bought radio time on a dozen New Jersey stations this week to run an ad in which Whitman promises a more open style of government. "Listening. It's not a new idea, it's just a common sense idea that Jim Florio seems to have forgotten," she says in the ad.

The idea is to play on the notion that Florio is arrogant and didn't consult the people when he hiked taxes. "Command and control from Trenton doesn't work," Whitman continues. I asked Florio in an interview yesterday whether he thought it was a mistake, as some of his aides do, for Whitman to be spending money this early on broadcast advertising. He declined to get into a discussion of campaign tactics. I asked him about the "command and control" charge. He shot back, "I don't know what that means," and we left it there.

Meanwhile, a new poll by the Bergen *Record* has the race a little tighter than the last *Star Ledger*/Eagleton poll—Florio 39 percent, Whitman 38 percent, and 22 percent undecided. This was welcome news at Whitman headquarters yesterday, where Whitman told an NJN intern for my piece last night that "the independents seem to be breaking our way."

And Governor Florio lost his second top lieutenant in as many months on Tuesday when chief counsel Bob DeCotiis resigned for health reasons. DeCotiis had been upset at the harsh treatment accorded Joe Salema by the media—and he himself had come under press scrutiny in recent weeks over public clients doing business with his old law firm— but I'm told his resignation had nothing to do with any of that. He is a heavy-set man, and his doctor apparently advised him that he needed a change of lifestyle and a heart operation. DeCotiis was in charge of keeping relations with the Republican legislative leaders on a smooth footing, and he did quite well at it and was well liked. His absence, on top of Joe Salema's, is a minor blow to the government side of Jim Florio's responsibilities at the moment. The political side is unscathed, and most of the governor's business with Republican legislators is concluded for this year. Still, Dan Todd of the Whitman campaign compares the loss of Salema and DeCotiis to Richard Nixon's loss of Haldeman and Ehrlichman during Watergate. "It left a big vacuum," says Todd, who was there at the time as an assistant in the White House personnel office.

A month after the primary, while the two staffs hurl barbs at each other, the campaign itself feels as if it hasn't really begun ("RACE? WHAT RACE?" asked a Bergen *Record* headline the other day). A Florio aide thinks Whitman missed a golden opportunity to capitalize on the glow of her June 8 primary win and build momentum. "She went into the woodwork," this aide says, "like Michael Dukakis [after the 1988 Democratic convention]. She should have come out of the box stronger—with something to say. Instead she disappeared off the face of the map. It is *the* major blunder of the campaign. When all is said and done, if you look back at this first month you'll see that's where she lost the election."

I tried this theory out today on Carl Golden, who scoffed at it. "If we missed an opportunity, why is it a dead heat in the polls?" he replied. He called the observation "nitpicking" and said, "One thing I've learned over the years: there is never a shortage of second- and third-guessers in this business."

Confirming Golden's point, Dan Todd would later tell me, "I get five hundred calls a week from well-meaning Republicans who say, 'why don't you do this,' 'why don't you do that.' "

But a Whitman aide informs me that a campaign strategy document, drafted by five top advisors, called for a number of things to be done in the weeks after the primary that were not done. The aide implies that an opportunity *has* been missed. "Why didn't we do these things?" the aide asked, anticipating my question. "Because Dan Todd moves in mysterious ways."

Todd says, "We have only two finite resources in this campaign—capped dollars and my sister's time. My job is to preserve them. Time is a vital part of this. Her time is prioritized four ways. The first is *personal*, because tired candidates do dumb things. . . ." The others are time for fund-raising, for "insider" objectives like keeping Republicans happy, and for external objectives like meeting the public. "Every decision has to be weighed on that basis. And besides, you can only talk to people when they're ready to listen. There's the question of timing."

It will be interesting to see whether assault weapons become a major issue in this campaign or turn out to have been a June-July stab.

★ **Saturday, July 10** ★

The Florio campaign may be overdoing its criticism of Whitman's gun position, but the tactic is working. Yesterday at our taping of "Reporters' Roundtable" we spent the first several minutes of the program assessing the seriousness of Whitman's mistake in visiting Gun-a-Rama and whether her position on assault weapons is tenable. Then on "NJN News" last night two pundits, Roger Bodman and Steve DeMicco, raked the same ground. The inside crowd is talking about what the Florio campaign wants us talking about. Gun-a-Rama is becoming one of those words people like to say and write, like Nannygate.

One can differ on whether Whitman is consciously courting the gun lobby or has made a couple of inadvertent moves. You can argue about whether her position on assault weapons is logical and politically acceptable. Either way, journalists covering a governor's race need to fill space and air time, and we're doing it with material pushed onto the stage by the Florio campaign.

★ Tuesday, July 13 ★

Picking up on a little-noticed article in last Saturday's *Asbury Park Press*, I did a piece today on the split inside the New Jersey chapter of the National Organization for Women over a gubernatorial endorsement. Some of the leaders of the 12,000-member group are passionate about endorsing a woman. Others are just as passionate about not endorsing a Republican who supported Clarence Thomas for the U.S. Supreme Court over a Democrat who has been a friend of the "choice" lobby, and they want the organization to stay neutral.

This was one of those days when I set my own agenda. Florio is doing "a hit a day," as one person called it; his event today was a ceremony in Camden honoring the one-year anniversary of the Family Development Program, Florio's welfare reform law. The governor was in Washington yesterday touting the program as a potential model for the nation.

Instead of covering his event, I let another reporter cover it and used its relation to women as a springboard for a long piece on who should get the NOW endorsement. NOW's president, Myra Terry, is clearly pushing Whitman—which is a surprise, since she was formerly executive director of the Religious Coalition for Abortion Rights and gave Florio that group's man-of-the-year award in 1992.

Liberal groups like NOW don't like the welfare reform law because it deprives poor women of additional benefits for additional children. But Whitman supports the law, so that's not the key issue driving the endorsement question. Terry told me Florio's record on appointing women to high positions is "abysmal." That's the driving issue. But the governor's office gave me statistics this morning that show Florio appointing slightly more women cabinet officers, judges, and prosecutors in three and a half years than Tom Kean appointed in eight years!

I interviewed Florio in Trenton outside the West State Street office of CTN, a cable television network, where the governor had done an interview program. He defended his record on "women's issues" and said it was "as good as anyone who's ever held this office." He even segued into the assault weapons issue, saying he finds that women particularly are interested in the issue because they're worried about the safety of their families. It was a good bite, and I used it, prompting my news director to send me a computer message on how Florio is beginning to "caricature" himself by bringing up assault weapons at every turn. After the interview, while my cameraman was shooting the set-up and cutaway shots we need for editing purposes, I asked Florio how important the NOW endorsement was.

"They're all important," he said, but it was clear he doesn't think this one is terribly crucial. NOW didn't endorse Florio in '89 or Whitman in '90, staying neutral both times, and the Florio camp would be happy with that outcome this time.

"Some are less important than others," I observed, goading the governor ever so slightly.

Turning to Jon Shure, he said, "Get his list." He smiled and walked back across the street to the Statehouse.

The heart of my piece tonight would be the information about Florio's appointments of women. The rest would be a rehash of NOW's situation and posturing by the candidates and Myra Terry. Whitman had a two o'clock event at the Shore. She was appearing with Republican legislators who sponsored a bill creating a shore protection research center. I called Carl Golden to half-warn him that I'd be asking his candidate about women's issues in a few hours, to see if he had different facts from Florio's, and to make sure I could interview Whitman before the event rather than after for the sake of my deadline. (Florio got a forewarning also, though only a five-minute one. These things I improvise and try to keep even.)

Whitman helicoptered to Spring Lake from Manhattan, where she'd accepted an impromptu invitation to attend a luncheon with Republican national chairman Haley Barbour. She then rode in her car, a modest, aquamarine Mercury Sable, to the beachfront event, where I and several dozen other people were awaiting her, including about a half dozen reporters. (Whitman hasn't been out much lately. The press is getting anxious to see her and poke at her.)

Aware of my request, she did the interview right away, and before I could even bring up Jim Florio's record on the appointments of women, she was criticizing it and comparing it unfavorably to Tom Kean's. She was playing right into my hands. When I told her Florio actually had a better record than Kean, she scrambled a bit and sought refuge in the fact that Florio has never had more than four women in his cabinet at a time, out of nineteen positions. How many would she have? I asked. She wouldn't specify, except to say it would reflect the population. "Does that mean your cabinet will be half women?" I asked. "I'm not talking any numbers," she said. "That's not the way you do things. That's not the way you promote good policy."

There was something Courteresque this time about the way she slipped and slid under persistent questioning. But she pulled it off better than Courter.

I got a four-minute, fifty-two-second piece out of it, one that I was pleased with because it broke new ground. Only at NJN could you let a daily news piece run that long.

As I was crunching at 4:15 in the afternoon ("crunching" means racing to pull a piece together), Carl Golden called from Whitman headquarters to say he'd been informed that out in the field I had asked Whitman about Florio having a better record on women than Kean. He challenged that. I gave him the numbers and reminded him I'd offered him a chance earlier in the day to provide his own numbers, which he didn't have. He complained about the way the governor's office was presenting the numbers and accused me of "falling for" their trickery, but I told him Whitman would be given plenty of time in the piece for rebuttal and there were months left in the campaign for him to raise his objection.

The race is becoming a tug of war between the economy and assault weapons. Whitman today held her first real press event in a month—a news conference at the Newark Airport Marriott—to unveil an economic braintrust she has put together which she calls with some fanfare the Council on Economic Recovery. Its co-chairs are Malcolm S. (Steve) Forbes, Jr., the editor-in-chief of *Forbes* magazine, and Lawrence Kudlow of the investment firm Bear, Stearns in New York who writes for the *Wall Street Journal* and pops up on television shows like "The McLaughlin Group" as a starchy conservative economist.

The council has seven task forces that will hold public meetings and make recommendations. Several of the task force leaders were at the news conference. John McMullen, owner of the New Jersey Devils hockey team, couldn't make it, but he heads the sports and tourism task force.

This gambit adds intellectual heft to Whitman's campaign and, if the process is run properly, could actually produce some fresh ideas for job creation in the state. It also buys time for Whitman, though she was questioned pointedly about using this as a way of forestalling real proposals. Asked when the council would report to her, she first said "before the election," then, when pounced upon for that answer, changed it to "sometime after Labor Day." David Wald of the *Star-Ledger* asked if she were running for governor on a "secret plan" to fix the economy, which she of course denied, and a Florio press release ridiculed her. ("This is the best she can do? [She] has been running for governor for three years on the issues of taxes and the economy. Now, sixteen weeks before the election, she forms a commission to *study* those issues?")

Jim Florio was in Camden again today, sealing a $30 million Camden Initiative to revitalize that desperate city (and solidifying his geographical base). This was a governmental event. Tomorrow he holds his first "campaign" event in many weeks, at a firing range. Whitman wants to talk taxes, Florio wants to talk guns.

For half an hour at the Marriott, eight reporters and members of the Whitman camp listened as Whitman, Forbes, and Kudlow blasted the Florio tax hikes of 1990, blaming them for everything from the flight of business to the South to the collapse of the construction industry and a $70 decline in real per capita income in the state. If it wasn't clear before that Whitman is running against the Florio tax hikes, it is now. That is the essence of her candidacy at this point. Republicans like Dave Murray, her direct-mail consultant, have been designing campaigns around the Florio taxes three years in a row now, and know how it's done. In '90 it almost capsized Bill Bradley, and it launched Whitman. In '91 it swept in veto-proof Republican legislative majorities. In '92 Bill Clinton barely survived it, but now he's trying to raise taxes, too, possibly setting up Florio and New Jersey Democrats for another fall.

★ Friday, July 16 ★

Weapons and watermelons. That's what the media advisory from the Florio campaign said. At a firing range overlooking the Delaware River in Titusville, twenty minutes north of Trenton, two young State Police weapons experts shot semi-automatic .22s at about a dozen watermelons lined up on benches, while Jim Florio and reporters looked on. Florio wanted to demonstrate the destructive power of the .22-caliber weapons that Whitman has suggested need not be banned.

The .22s only pierced the melons like BBs, but a Colt AR-15, which looks like an Uzi, blew big chunks off the melons, exposing the red pulp and leaving the pink juice pouring onto the ground. I thought of President Kennedy. I couldn't help it.

Florio blasted Whitman for wanting to legalize these weapons. He suggested she visit a hospital emergency room to look at gunshot wounds, as he has done. He suggested she visit Officer Frank Sharkey of Jersey City who was shot with a semi-automatic .22 while breaking up a burglary in Journal Square. Pointing to the AR-15, he asked how "anyone in their right mind could want to legalize one of these."

It was an effective demonstration. Suddenly, assault weapons didn't seem so much like props in a political stunt as like evils that New Jersey citizens obviously want off the streets.

In a question-and-answer session I tried to throw the governor off balance on the gun issue, as I had thrown Whitman off balance a few days earlier on the gender issue. Citing statistics that show 8 deaths from assault weapons over a recent 30-month span and 366 deaths from hand-guns and rifles over a recent 24-month span, I asked why he was focusing so much attention on assault weapons. With just the slightest loss of traction, he replied that it was because this was the one classification of firearms on which there was almost universal agreement on the lack of need for them. Jim Goodman of the Trenton *Times* started pressing him on whether he'll next try to restrict handguns, and after the third or fourth parry by Goodman, an incredulous Florio said, "People are talking about *rolling back* what we've done! And you're asking me why I don't go further?"

The Whitman campaign put out a press release again accusing Florio of grandstanding and ignoring the real issues. "Rather than staging events," it said, "the Governor might make himself available to discuss those underlying causes of crime—joblessness, low quality of education, grinding poverty—which he has ignored for the past three and one-half years."

Florio again told reporters Whitman was using "rope-a-dope" tactics, meaning she is feinting, bobbing, weaving, hanging back, and not engaging the fight. Some think Florio is frustrated and "worried," as Henry Holcomb of the *Philadelphia Inquirer* put it in a piece headlined "Whitman's strategy: Avoid giving specifics." Florio told the reporters Whitman's economic braintrust meant that after three years of being "fixated" on taxes and the economy, she still has no ideas of her own, and he called it "almost Nixonian" that she would now run on some kind of secret plan to fix the economy.

Returning my call after the Florio event, Carl Golden asked if I wanted to join a new group the Republicans were forming—the New Jersey Society for the Preservation of Watermelons.

My piece ended with a close-up shot of blown-apart watermelons dripping juice. Moments after it aired, I passed the NJN front desk where the security guard was hanging up the phone. He saw me and said the call had been from a viewer. "He wants to know why Florio is shooting watermelons when people are starving."

SHE SAID . . . HE SAID. WHITMAN AND FLORIO AT THE SECOND DEBATE.

A GOP PRIMARY DEBATE. I MODERATE, THE AUDIENCE ASKS
THE QUESTIONS.

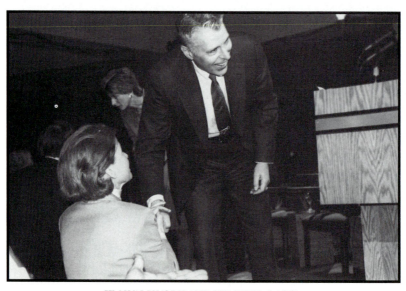

JIM WALLWORK AND HIS WIFE, LARK.

PREDEBATE MINGLING.

CARY, WE HARDLY KNEW YE.
LEFT TO RIGHT: GREG STEVENS, CARY EDWARDS, REPORTER MARK MAGYAR,
ME, UNIDENTIFIED PERSON.

MY FAVORITE CARTOONIST, JIMMY MARGULIES OF *THE RECORD*.
THE DAY AFTER WHITMAN WON THE GOP PRIMARY. REPRINTED BY
PERMISSION.

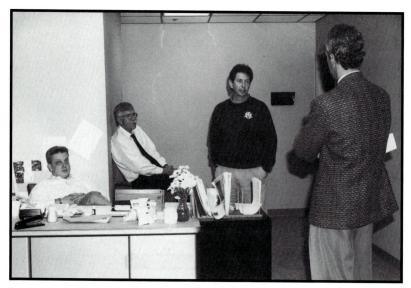

A CHAT WITH FLORIO BRAINTRUST.
LEFT TO RIGHT: JIM ANDREWS, HAROLD HODES, DOUG BERMAN, ME.

JAMES CARVILLE. MAESTRO.

DAN TODD. COWBOY ARISTOCRAT.

ED ROLLINS AND DAN TODD ON THE DAY ROLLINS TOOK OVER
DAY-TO-DAY CONTROL OF THE CAMPAIGN.

BEING SPUN BY CARL GOLDEN, IN-YOUR-FACE PRESS SECRETARY PAR EXCELLENCE.

HAZEL GLUCK.
WHITMAN ADVISOR
AND CONFIDANTE.

BRENDA BACON.
SENIOR FLORIOCRAT ON THE
CAMPAIGN TEAM.

CAMPAIGNING AT THE GARDEN STATE ARTS CENTER.

FLORIO GIVES HIS STUMP SPEECH.

"I ASK YOU, IS THIS A WORKING FARM?" WHITMAN AT PONTEFRACT
WITH CARL GOLDEN AT LEFT.

THE MEDIA MEET THE ANIMALS.

WEAPONS AND WATERMELONS AT THE RIFLE RANGE.

"I SUGGEST MRS. WHITMAN GO VISIT A HOSPITAL
EMERGENCY ROOM." JO ASTRID GLADING TAKES NOTES FOR A
FAX ATTACK AFTER THE RIFLE DEMONSTRATION.

GAZING INTO SPACE BEFORE THE SECOND DEBATE:
"THE VISION THING HAS NEVER BEEN MY PROBLEM."

LEFT TO RIGHT: JON SHURE, DAN WEISSMAN OF THE *STAR-LEDGER,*
FLORIO, JIM GOODMAN OF THE *TRENTON TIMES.*

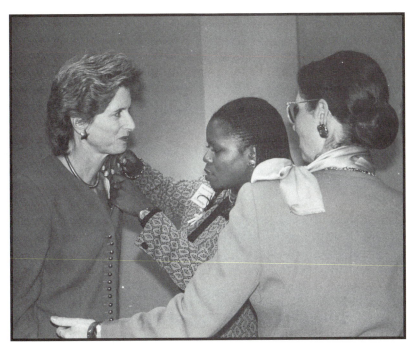

LONNA HOOKS AND GINNY LITTELL PREP THE CANDIDATE FOR A RALLY.

JOHN WHITMAN WITH REPUBLICAN STATE FINANCE CHAIR, CLIFF SOBEL.

HEADING FOR THE HANDSHAKE AT THE FIRST DEBATE.

WHITMAN UNVEILING HER ECONOMIC PLAN.
FORMER GOVERNOR KEAN LOOKS ON.

WHITMAN, WATCHING THE RETURNS ON NJN, SEES SHE HAS WON.
LEFT TO RIGHT: KATE, JOHN, CHRISTIE, TAYLOR.
PHOTO COURTESY OF M. CHESMAN.

FLORIO CONCEDING WITH LUCINDA AT HIS SIDE.

DRUMTHWACKET: EYES ON THE PRIZE.

★ Sunday, July 18 ★

In the propaganda war, the Whitman campaign faxed out material showing that in 1981 the NRA enthusiastically supported Florio in the gubernatorial primary because of his "pro-gun, pro-sportsman" views, while
the Florio campaign faxed out articles about Bear, Stearns becoming New
Jersey's leading bond underwriting firm in the mid-80s after making big
campaign contributions to Tom Kean and state Republicans. Whitman's
new economics guru Lawrence Kudlow is a senior managing director of
Bear, Stearns.

   If the voters aren't paying attention, one might as well go after
the hearts and minds of the reporters.

★ Wednesday, July 21 ★

Add another to the list of dumb Whitman mistakes. Yesterday the campaign announced its new media consultant, Larry McCarthy of Washington. I'd never heard of him. Within an hour, the Florio camp was letting
reporters know that Larry McCarthy created the famous Willie Horton
ad in 1988 while working for well-known GOP image-maker Roger Ailes.
This was rapid response at its best. "They were searching Lexus and
Nexus," says a Democratic insider. And they came up with a *Washington
Post* article linking McCarthy to Willie Horton.

   Willie Horton, in case you've forgotten, was a black Massachusetts convict who, while out of prison on a weekend furlough, terrorized
a white Maryland couple in their home, raping the woman. With its
suggestion that Democrats like Michael Dukakis can't be trusted to
protect white couples from violent black convicts, the Willie Horton ad
was the most notorious political commercial of the past quarter century.
And the Whitman campaign hired its creator. Immediately the campaign
and the candidate were besieged with questions from the media. State
and local NAACP leaders expressed "outrage." And suddenly, this afternoon, Larry McCarthy withdrew, less than twenty-four hours after being

named. As I wrote for our anchors to read at the top of our newscast tonight, "It happened faster than a weekend furlough."

The producer of the Willie Horton commercial has finally paid for his sin. He lost a big client.

I interviewed Whitman twice today, once before the withdrawal and, after it, live on the newscast. She says McCarthy worked for Tom Kean in '85, Governor Pete Wilson of California in '90, and is just a skilled technician who follows the lead of the candidate. No way was he gonna make a racist commercial for her, she insisted. But it's clear that the campaign badly miscalculated. Whitman and Dan Todd had been unhappy with their media consultant in the primary, Russo, Marsh of California. They had felt that Tony Marsh missed the essence of Christie Whitman, that his commercials didn't convey her as a woman of principle, a woman who could think. In deciding whether to hire a new media consultant, they sought the advice of Lyn Nofziger. Somehow they settled on McCarthy.

The flap ranks up there with illegal aliens and missed school board votes, in my estimation. It's the second overt mistake of the general election campaign; the first was Gun-a-Rama, which even her advisors now admit privately was a mistake.

The flap also marred two very good events. Last night about six hundred women attended a $100-a-person Women for Whitman fundraiser at the Brunswick Hilton. The featured guest was former U.S. labor secretary Lynn Martin, whose fiery oratory whipped the women in the room into a lather. Whitman is trying to become the first woman governor in state history. "So *what* if you vote for her because she's a woman! So, yeah, go get it!" Martin shouted in her flat Chicago accent.

Then Whitman spoke, saying the real "women's issues" are unemployment, education, and health care, notably breast cancer and AIDS, and promising to bring to the job of governor "the same common sense women bring to their households and jobs every day."

"This is not women against men," she said. "This is women *and* men. We've enjoyed men for a long time. We just want to be partners in solving the problems."

After the speeches, women lined up to greet Whitman, while a sound system blared "Don't Stop Thinking about Tomorrow," Bill Clinton's signature song. This was the first sense I got that for some New Jersey women, the Whitman candidacy is a cause. John Whitman, viewing the scene, said to me, "Something like this could never have happened in America four years ago," meaning women filling a room for a woman politician. He may have been overstating it, but there was female solidarity in that room.

Then today Whitman gave the lie to those Democrats who have been complaining about her "hiding" from the press and public. She did a whirlwind tour of the 36th legislative district in the Essex-Bergen-Passaic area, making eighteen stops from morning 'til evening. It was a good media event, except that reporters kept asking her about the Willie Horton fiasco. That even brought out two New York TV stations, which usually cover the race only when there's a big controversy or an election a few days away.

Something is wrong in the Whitman camp. I'm told that Carl Golden almost quit yesterday. Apparently he is frustrated by a lack of professionalism. As the most seasoned hand on the staff, he is called upon to do more than just handle the press, and it's getting to him. Ed Rollins talked him into staying.

Jim Florio, meanwhile, keeps signing bills, giving out money, attending events at which job-stimulation is a theme, and getting news coverage. There's a four-page feature about him in *People* magazine this week. The day it came out, by coincidence, the Bergen *Record* cartoonist had two people reading in bed, the woman reading a magazine called *Vague* with Whitman in pearls on the cover. On Monday the governor named a fifth woman to his current cabinet, shifting environmental commissioner Scott Weiner over to be his new chief counsel and elevating Weiner's deputy, Jeanne Fox. When I asked him on camera if he had consciously chosen a woman because he's running against a woman, he answered a different question.

★　Saturday, July 24　★

The Willie Horton fiasco is being laid at the feet of Ed Rollins. Before I even read it in the Thursday papers, a Whitman insider said Rollins and Larry McCarthy, the media consultant, are good friends and told me, "Look, Rollins pushed this guy. He said, 'If Willie Horton comes up, it will be a one-day story.' He persuaded the people he had to persuade that McCarthy is a very talented guy." That meant he persuaded Christie Whitman and Dan Todd. Should we blame them for listening to their veteran consultant and deferring to his professional judgment? "One could argue the decision circle should have been larger," said the insider.

Carl Golden tried to downplay the story when I called him that morning, "The story's over. The guy left," he said. Like Whitman the night before, he wouldn't even admit that hiring him was a miscalculation. "If this is a misstep," he said, "so was hiring Joe Salema." I pointed out that Jim Florio had hired Joe Salema around 1974. "Yeah, but he made him chief of staff in 1990," Golden shot back. He was in a testy mood. He sounded beat. He hinted that had he known about Larry McCarthy, he would have objected.

According to the *Asbury Park Press*, there were two TV commercials in 1988 exploiting the Willie Horton case, one made by Roger Ailes, the other made by his subordinate Larry McCarthy. They were made for a Republican citizens' group supporting George Bush, and Mr. Bush disassociated himself from them. Many people found them racist.

Was it a mistake for Christie Whitman to hire the creator of one of those spots? If you're trying to reach black voters, as the Whitman campaign definitely would like to do, then it probably was. But when you consider that Larry McCarthy was Republican Pete Wilson's media consultant in the 1990 California governor's race and no newspaper there raised a fuss about an ad then only two years old, you can see how Ed Rollins assumed it wouldn't kick up much dust here. He was wrong. A Carl Golden, Hazel Gluck, Tom Kean, or Dick Zimmer (New Jerseyans all) might have seen the pitfall, but they apparently were not part of this decision. Campaign co-chair Lonna Hooks, an African-American woman friend and confidante of Christie Whitman's, might have been able to warn of possible fallout, but she, too, apparently wasn't consulted.

And yet I am bothered about the way Whitman is being tarred in the media over something as extraneous as her political consultant's selection of a media consultant. I participate in it at the same time that I question its relevance. It makes good copy. It's sexy. People will hear about it from my rivals—so they might as well hear about it from me. But does it say anything about Christie Whitman's ability to be a good governor? "Who you hire is a reflection of your judgment," said Jim Florio when I asked him about it. Carl Golden, on the other hand, argues that the media in New Jersey (and perhaps he means this part of the country) are unique. "The press corps here sometimes focuses on a small corner of a big picture," he said, adding, "Every few years in this state, the media has to burn a witch. This year it's Larry McCarthy."

I was shocked to read in the *Asbury Park Press* that as I was interviewing Whitman in the field on Wednesday, McCarthy was there. The article said he "listened stone-faced as Whitman told NJN, 'My understanding is that Roger Ailes was responsible' for the Willie Horton ad more than McCarthy. . . . Then he walked up to Whitman and said quietly he was leaving." I had no shot of McCarthy, not even a newspaper photo, in my piece that night, and could have used one. Now I learn not only had he been standing very near me, I had played some small part in pushing him over the edge!

Added to the other gaffes Whitman has committed, the episode becomes serious. As columnist John McLaughlin pointed out on "Reporters' Roundtable" this weekend, "If it becomes the conventional wisdom among reporters, editorial writers, and columnists that she doesn't know what she's doing, it'll destroy morale within the campaign. It'll feed into the public eventually. It could kill her."

Christie Whitman had no public schedule Thursday, the day after the McCarthy story climaxed. Then yesterday she and her husband and children left the state for a week's vacation. They went mountain-biking in Idaho, something they had done the summer before and enjoyed. (She has indicated on several occasions that being with her children is a priority for her.) It could be dangerous to leave the state in the middle of a campaign. Another politician in her shoes might have chosen to vacation at the Jersey Shore. The fact that she leaves with her tail between her legs, instead of on a high note, doesn't help. But maybe the mountain air will clear her head and recharge her batteries.

Jim Florio, on the other hand, was in fine spirits Thursday on the boardwalk in Long Branch as he signed a bill that provides loan funds for wastewater treatment plant improvements. A bunch of beachgoers gathered at the ceremony and then surrounded him afterwards to shake his hand or take a picture. The weather was gorgeous. Someone asked him to sign a copy of *People* opened to the first page of the article about him. The photo on that page has him in a wing chair in the study at Drumthwacket reading the comics section of a Sunday paper. "I don't know if you saw this month's *People's* magazine," Florio informed those around him, "but they came to my house, and they did a nice story about Lucinda and me. And they got a picture of me reading the funny sheets!" he said, holding up the page. I wondered: Is he that out of it that he thinks it's "People's" and it's a monthly? Is "funny sheets" an old Brooklyn term? Or was this just Jim Florio trying to be folksy?

After the bill-signing, the governor went to one of his favorite sub shops for lunch. The lunch was on his printed schedule, and since it was nearby, we went, too. I thought we'd get a few shots of the governor greeting patrons. But Faccone's sub shop was a hole in the wall, and there were hardly any customers inside except Florio, Jon Shure, and two reporters, Jim Goodman and Mark Magyar, sitting at little tables waiting for their subs. So I decided to stay, too. Cameraman Rafy Rosario put his gear away.

Florio invited me to squeeze in with him and Goodman. The conversation rambled from sports to Congress to the floods that are ravaging the Midwest. Very little about politics, and nothing about Whitman, except that when I asked Florio about his siblings, and he told me one brother had died and the other was a professional diver who lived in South Jersey but commuted to New York, Jon Shure piped up from the next table, "But he's thinking about becoming a campaign manager!" We all laughed.

As we were leaving, the proprietor, Andrew Faccone, a young crewcut red-headed hoagie-maker, who is such a Florio fan that he was one of the testimonial speakers at the governor's campaign kickoff speech in April, tried to pump up the governor's spirits by telling him how good things are, how good business is, and how people are more optimistic than they used to be.

"Anything you need, anytime. You just call," Andrew Faccone said to Florio in a voice that sounded like Sylvester Stallone's.

"Can you cater an inaugural?" Florio replied, and everyone erupted with laughter.

★ **Sunday, July 25** ★

Christie Whitman got killed in the Sunday papers today. The tabloid *Trentonian*'s front-page headline was "Christie's campaign stuttering and stumbling." Across the top of the front page of the Bridgewater *Courier-News* was, "When the going gets tough, Whitman gets going—way out West." The *Asbury Park Press* analysis piece was headlined "Suddenly, a need for damage control" above a picture of Whitman. And the headline on David Wald's Sunday column in the *Star-Ledger* was "A bumbling campaign is bound to cost Whitman sooner or later."

It was a good Sunday to be in Idaho.

Jim and Lucinda Florio attended a fund-raiser in Princeton, then marched in a Peruvian Day parade in Paterson and a Puerto Rican parade in Newark. At the $100-per-person brunch, in the woods behind an enormous Princeton home, Florio stood on a tree stump and gave his stump speech to about seventy-five rapt supporters. After reviewing some of what he's done and how the "tough decisions" are starting to pay off, he launched into his "values" pitch. "This is an election not between two candidates, or two parties, but two value systems," he said. "I've worked hard these past few years to develop a vision that gets back to some old values, like responsibility." Florio expounded on what responsibility means to him, relating it to child-support enforcement, assault weapons, and even abortion rights. He talked about responsibility "not just to ourselves but to our children and our community." Moving on, he said whether he serves four more years or not, "I'm hopeful if there's any word associated with the administration, it's 'opportunity,'" then talked about his own youth as a high school dropout, invoking his immigrant grandfather, shipyard worker father, and Irish mother.

In the July 4 issue of *Parade* magazine, Bill Clinton wrote a piece called "What Today Means to Me," in which he argued, "As we move toward the 21st century we must reaffirm bedrock American values: *opportunity, community,* and *responsibility.*" I think Florio was first, but talk about two politicians on the same wavelength!

The values pitch strikes me as feel-good Democratic cant devoid of real content. You can use those "values" to justify any *policy* you choose. But those in Florio's audience today who spoke to me afterwards found his remarks thoughtful and sincere and found him "warmer" than they remembered him.

★ Wednesday, July 28 ★

While Christie Whitman is away mountain-biking, her campaign back home is sliding downhill. She had another bad day in the newspapers Monday, then yesterday Roger Ailes, the legendary Republican media consultant who worked with Nixon, Reagan, and Bush, faxed a press release to New Jersey political reporters attacking Whitman for linking him to the Willie Horton ad. "Slick Christie," he called her, and he blasted her for dishonesty and disingenuousness. "If Christie Whitman can't get the facts straight, isn't courageous enough to admit when she's in error, tries to sneak her misjudgments past the press corps, and can't tell the truth, she'll end up like Bill Clinton—a joke." What an unlikely source for an attack on Whitman! It's keeping the story alive for at least another two days.

What upset Ailes is that Whitman said it was her "understanding Ailes was responsible" for the Willie Horton commercial (she said it to me, and it was heard and reported by Mark Magyar in the *Asbury Park Press*). According to Ailes, Larry McCarthy stopped working for him in 1986 or '87, well before McCarthy made the Horton spot in '88. He apparently asked the Whitman campaign to issue a clarification, even sending them copies of old newspaper retractions to prove that others had made the same mistake. Why he focused his attack so squarely on Whitman—instead of on her campaign in general or on Ed Rollins—is a mystery. Ailes so far isn't talking. Whitman did speak disparagingly of him last week, saying, in a way that implied he was sleazy, she'd have never hired him to do her media. But that was to me, and I didn't put it on the air. Maybe Larry McCarthy heard it and told Ailes. The Whitman camp at first called Ailes's rantings "the totally preposterous statement of a totally preposterous individual," then today put out a fax apologizing to him for mistakenly attributing the Willie Horton ad to him. What a low-level comedy this affair has become.

With Whitman away—and the Florio campaign sending out faxes ridiculing her for being in "her own private Idaho" and suggesting she stay there another week to figure out what her campaign is all about, and so on—Governor Florio is attending to the substance of being governor. I've covered him each day so far this week. On Monday he was at the largest oil refinery on the East Coast, Bayway in Linden (the one you see from the Turnpike), celebrating its transfer from Exxon to the Tosco Corporation and the preservation of eight hundred jobs. Yesterday he was at a new warehouse in South Brunswick where the Liz Claiborne company will soon be stocking five million pairs of shoes, at a net gain to the state of one or two hundred jobs. At both stops, he was thanked by the executives for his administration's business-friendly service, and at both stops he told the story of his father, Vincenzo Florio, being out of work and the family sometimes eating oatmeal for breakfast and oatmeal again for dinner. That quote is also in the *People* piece. In my piece last night I played him saying it back-to-back Monday and Tuesday, to underscore how this personal experience with unemployment has become a central part of his stump speech. The riff ends, "So if there's one person in New Jersey who doesn't have a job, then my job is not done." I played the governor saying it twice in a row, and there was a discussion in my newsroom today of whether it "worked" or came off as a cheap shot.

Today Florio was the featured speaker at an all-day state AIDS summit. He gave a strong and compassionate speech, but he completely ducked the two hot-button issues in the AIDS debate right now: needle exchanges for IV drug users and condom distribution in the public schools.

Pressed by reporters, he became that quintessentially evasive Florio we see from time to time. He looked bad because of it in my piece tonight, and I perhaps did not give him enough credit for the good words he did say. On the other hand, there's the sentiment of the Act-Up member who got up on stage in the middle of Florio's speech this morning and stood silently for the remainder wearing a sheet that said "ENOUGH TALK. PEOPLE ARE DYING. WE WANT ACTION." Florio's response was to pretend the demonstrator wasn't there and keep right on talking.

I've been at Whitman headquarters twice this week, once to interview Dan Todd, once to get a couple of bites from Carl Golden. I asked for an interview with Ed Rollins, but, although he was in the office Tuesday, he is lying low. (Like Carville, Rollins still spends most of his time in Washington.) I had hoped maybe he'd tell his side of the Larry McCarthy story, but of course he just wants it to go away.

Dan Todd, in our interview, was upbeat, defensive, and seemingly unruffled by the cries of disarray and turmoil aimed his way. He said the campaign was on track and achieving 95 percent of its objectives. When I brought up Larry McCarthy, he admitted "misjudging the breadth and immediacy" of the reaction but quickly shifted the focus to Joe Salema and said of McCarthy "at least he didn't leave with a subpoena in his pocket." Todd almost always now wears a bandanna or kerchief tied around his neck and tucked into the front of his shirt. Monday he wore a blue-and-white striped preppie oxford shirt and a purple bandanna that got an awful lot of comment back at the TV station of the "hey, Dan, lose the ascot" variety. Although it looks western, it comes off as an upper-class affectation.

With the candidate in Idaho, a fellow Republican, Ailes, trying to savage her, the newspapers still writing about Willie Horton, and her brother on television talking tough but looking eccentric, the Whitman campaign is at its lowest ebb since January.

After two people informed me that the governor was not happy about the way I had him repeating lines from his stump speech in my piece the other night, I called Jon Shure yesterday and asked if I could speak to the governor to explain myself. I'd never done that before, but—partly for the sake of this journal that will soon be a book, and probably because I would have done it anyway—I wanted him to understand my intent had not been to ridicule him. I was prepared for a phone exchange, but Shure suggested I come down to the Statehouse.

Florio was at his desk eating Chinese soup-to-go when Shure ushered me into the governor's small back office. I sat down in a chair and sank so low in the cushion that I found myself looking up at the governor (and wondering if the chairs were rigged, or chosen for that reason).

I told him I had heard he didn't like what I had put on TV the other night and I was here to discuss it.

"You're a thoughtful person, and I like you," he said. "So I think I can tell you this. I think there's a real angst inside of you, a kind of Dr. Jekyll and Mr. Hyde."

It took five or ten minutes from there, but we patched things up. (Like the other major players in this story, the governor has known since June I am writing a book about the election.) He explained to me it was Bill Bradley who taught him it takes repetition to hammer home a message. I explained to him I was merely trying to underscore how in his stump speech he plays up his humble roots, and I apologized for not setting it up properly and perhaps making him look foolish.

The conversation turned to Christie Whitman. "Tell me something," he said. "Aren't you in the press frustrated that I seem to be running against Dan Todd?" I said it was alright with me to interview the campaign manager when the candidate is on vacation, but he made the point that Dan Todd and Carl Golden are making *decisions* for her without consulting her, like apologizing to Roger Ailes and enunciating a new position on the senate's practice of allowing one senator to block the reappointment of a sitting judge.

Then, sounding a bit like the acerbic press releases Jo Glading faxes out, he said of Whitman, "I've really come to think there's no *there* there. She has offered absolutely no rationale for her candidacy. No basic concept has been articulated. She's been at this since 1990, and she doesn't have the foggiest notion of what she'd do if she won. It comes across as though she feels she's *entitled* to it somehow."

I asked if he meant she hadn't paid enough dues.

"She's like a kid asking her father for a pony. She doesn't know why she wants it or what she'd do once she gets it. She just wants it."

The governor said Whitman wasn't offering any specifics.

"She should go out and tell people what she stands for. Her strategy seems to be, vote for me 'cause I'm not Jim Florio. I don't think that's going to wash."

He said we reporters should press her on such issues as guns and education.

"She's sliding all over the place," he complained.

I pointed out that she's getting creamed in the press for the very things he's talking about, but he seemed dissatisfied. Even all the flak she's taken over Larry McCarthy and Roger Ailes wasn't enough for him. "She's slipped off the hook," he said, as if the media somehow let her get away. "I can assure you, if they had their choice between being skewered on substance and skewered on tactics, they'd much rather be skewered on tactics."

Florio came across as a man frustrated—at the press for not hounding Whitman, at the New Jersey Education Association for not crying out against her plan to test school vouchers in the parochial schools of Jersey City, at the fact that there are still many Perot voters out there with a very low opinion of practitioners of democracy like himself.

Florio said he was "comfortable" with where the race is, and "comfortable" with what he's been saying consistently over the years about the issues. And at one point he said of the Whitman campaign's apparent wobbliness, "I think there's a discomfort level over there." But all the while, *he* seemed uncomfortable with where the race stands, and more obsessed with it than I had realized.

I asked if, as in February, he still felt himself to be the underdog. "I do. There's a high degree of alienation out there about government. I am the government."

In the lighter moments, Florio recommended a new biography of Woodrow Wilson by August Heckscher ("you'd like it—it's got a lot about Princeton in it"), and pointed out a framed picture on the wall of Wilson seated at the same desk the governor uses today.

I left and went back to the station. An hour later Florio held an impromptu news conference. I missed it, but we had a camera there. When I saw the tape, I was surprised to see him do in public what he had just done with me privately. Even though by all outward appearances he's riding high, Florio can't control his acid tongue—or doesn't want to. Asked if it bothered him that certain decisions this week were made by Whitman operatives without apparent consultation with the candidate, the governor said:

"I don't mind running against Mr. Todd . . . Mr. Todd with the ascot as I saw on TV the other day. No, I'm really going to be talking about my campaign. However they want to manage or mismanage their campaign is clearly up to them. But I guess I am startled to see what it is coming out. Someone is making these major policy decisions at the same time one acknowledges the candidate is not involved or even in communication. Either you do apologize or you do not apologize, but if you don't have anything to do with what it is you're apologizing for because you're backpacking somewhere—you know, that's fine. I don't have any difficulty. Backpackers are nice people."

I thought the bite belonged on our newscast, all fifty-three seconds of it. Others might disagree, but to me when one candidate publicly ridicules the style of dress of a family member of the other candidate, that's something I want to share with my viewers. It is indicative of that candidate's state of mind.

I called Carl Golden to get a response that the anchors could briefly paraphrase. "It's not an ascot," he said. "It's a bandanna that people wear out West. Maybe he ought to take a better look at *GQ*."

"It's classic Jim Florio," Golden added. "Don't talk to me about issues. Just give me a personality I can attack. It's the guy's entire history."

★ Monday, August 2 ★

Jim Florio has been using the power of his incumbency to good advantage. Day in and day out, he is putting on demonstrations of what it means to be gubernatorial.

Since the primary on June 8, Florio, among other things, publicly has:

* dedicated a $42 million redevelopment project in New Brunswick;
* given a $4.5 million job training grant to General Motors in Linden;
* toured a new $48 million state-financed Episcopalian nursing home in Moorestown;
* dedicated Bristol-Myers Squibb's new $115 million building in Plainsboro;
* handed out $5.3 million in federal emergency disaster funds to 183 towns and agencies along the Shore;
* visited the Jersey City waterfront to welcome three new firms bringing 500 jobs;
* unveiled the Camden Initiative, a multimillion-dollar public-private partnership;
* handed out $14 million in Princeton to six performing arts centers;
* announced in New Brunswick a $250 million expansion of the first-time homebuyer assistance program;
* announced in Long Branch $195 million worth of grants to upgrade twenty-one wastewater treatment plants;
* announced in Jersey City $30 million worth of Green Acres open-space grants to thirty-four towns and counties;
* gone to Paterson to award $400,000 to renovate City Hall;
* announced in Newark the launching of a new renovation project, the University Heights Science Park, with $4.2 million in seed money; and
* signed a $1.3 million bill in Atlantic City to expand the county jail by fifty beds.

Aside from passing out checks in a very public way, he has held ceremonies around the state to sign bills that:

* enable victims of bias crime to sue in civil court;
* overhaul and soften the much-hated Environmental Clean-up Responsibility Act (ECRA);
* prohibit furloughs for violent criminals;
* distribute $77 million in utility taxes to New Jersey towns for property tax relief;
* create 1,500 summer jobs for urban kids;
* grant property-tax exempt status to all nonprofit nursing homes;
* enact six tax breaks and tax credits that Republican legislators conceived as a comprehensive business incentive package;
* provide $9 million in bond funds for college construction projects;
* impose a retaliatory income tax on New Yorkers who work in New Jersey;
* establish a special license plate whose proceeds will go toward animal population control;
* overhaul and strengthen the state's twenty-year-old law governing development along the Shore (CAFRA);
* increase the filing fee for divorce by $25, the proceeds to go toward a displaced homemakers program;
* provide loan money to small- and medium-sized export businesses;
* extend the death penalty to cover terrorist murder; and
* grant immunity from civil suit to people who use Mace in self-defense.

The governor also has been out in public:

* taking Continental Airlines' inaugural flight from Newark to Atlantic City;
* battling the Federal Aviation Administration over a persistent aircraft noise problem in North-Central Jersey;
* observing the lowering of the state's first artificial reef into the Atlantic Ocean 250 feet off Avalon;

* visiting the White House three times and testifying in Washington on welfare reform and assault weapons;
* taking part in the successful lobbying effort to save McGuire Air Force Base; and
* giving a major speech on AIDS.

These are all things an activist, hard-working governor like Florio does as a matter of course, but there are more of them this summer, and he is doing them more publicly.

He has also played a role in the state's most diverting political melodrama of the summer (after the governor's race), the effort by Republican state senator John Dorsey to block the re-appointment of Superior Court Judge Marianne Espinosa Murphy. Dorsey is a bright, stubborn conservative who likes to throw his weight around. He is using the unwritten custom known as senatorial courtesy to deny the judge lifetime tenure; it allows a senator to block the nomination of anyone from the senator's home county. Murphy is forty-four, Hispanic-surnamed, and has such a stylish haircut she looks like an actress playing a judge. She is also the wife of the Democratic prosecutor of Morris County, Michael Murphy, whose stepfather was the revered Democratic governor and supreme court chief justice Richard Hughes. Senator Dorsey says Judge Murphy, who sits in family court, lacks judicial temperament. Murphy supporters say she's just tough on "deadbeat dads" in child support cases.

The standoff has brought the state bar association, three former governors, four former attorneys general, New Jersey Chief Justice Robert Wilentz, and Governor Florio charging in to save Judge Murphy from the wicked senator. It has also spilled into the governor's race, because Dorsey is a prominent Whitman supporter and Whitman has taken three different positions on the matter since it erupted in May. First, she said it was a matter for the senate to decide. Then she wrote a letter urging Dorsey to allow the full senate at least to consider the re-appointment and says she followed up the letter with phone calls. Then last week, while Whitman was in Idaho, Dan Todd released a letter stating that Whitman, like Florio and other governors, has always been for doing away with senatorial courtesy.

The issue resonates throughout the political community because it involves a "minority" woman judge and all three branches of government. It pits a woman against a man, a member of a prominent Democratic family against a staunch Republican, and the executive branch against the legislative, which is controlled by Whitman supporters. Democrats and women's groups keep holding press conferences demanding that Whitman show "leadership" and get her party's senators to strip Dorsey of his courtesy privilege, as the senate has done twice before in the past decade. Governor Florio rides the issue, appearing at news conferences with women who have been abandoned by ex-husbands and who demand continuation of "outstanding" judges like Murphy. For Whitman it is another shoal to navigate. The issue must come to a head before September 11, when Murphy's seven-year initial term on the bench expires.

★ Wednesday, August 4 ★

Christie Whitman came back from vacation Monday night, sporting a scraped left arm from a mountain-biking spill. She was met at Newark Airport by Mark Magyar, of the *Asbury Park Press*, and NJN cameraman Tim Stollery, both of whom she told not to worry about her campaign.

Yesterday she had no public schedule.

Today she met the Statehouse press corps inside the Statehouse for the first time formally in a very long time—since January, I believe. It was part of a five-stop day in Mercer County, and enough pressure had built up in recent weeks that I decided to attend, even though I'm on vacation this week and next. The atmosphere was almost like her illegal-alien news conference back in January. *The candidate is in hot water: how is she going to handle it?* The water temperature was just a few degrees lower this time.

Perhaps because she grew up in a home of well-educated, well-bred, well-mannered people, Whitman knows how to keep her poise after someone at her table has spilled the soup. Asked if her campaign is in disarray, she flashes a smile, then says of course not. The smile goes part way toward disarming reporters and puts her on *their* side of the question, as if to say, we all know this is a game and that question is part of the role-playing we both must carry out. A front-page article in Sunday's Trenton *Times* had anonymous GOP "leaders" pointing fingers of blame at her husband and brother, suggesting that John Whitman in particular is a meddling amateur; asked about it today, she dismissed it with a simple: "Am I supposed to divorce my husband?" Magyar, at the airport, had thrown up to her a line of Governor Florio's about her vacationing among the beautiful people. "They were beautiful people," she told him. "On our mountain biking trip, we had an endocrinologist, an assembly line worker from GM, a firefighter from Chicago, a grocery store clerk, two housewives, and a librarian." A perfect response.

Today, she continued to maintain that hiring Larry McCarthy was not a mistake, just "the handling of it." Yes, the campaign should have apologized to Roger Ailes sooner, but she was on vacation and so it was difficult. "At least my errors in judgment have not cost the taxpayers a penny," she said.

I asked if she had seen the terrible press she'd received while she was away and what she thought of it. I wondered if she would take the bait and criticize the media. Wisely, she did not—wisely, because it's a game the politician rarely wins. She had seen the clips and, "While I can't say I enjoyed that kind of coverage, if you know you're on track, you don't worry about it. My message is to the people. The people aren't the ones making those kinds of judgments right now."

She, too, is "comfortable" with where things are, she told us twice. I'm glad both candidates are so comfortable.

The Whitman campaign very much needs to change the subject right now and to show more substance—at least to the media if the public doesn't care yet. So today's news conference featured a surprise guest, Jim Wallwork, and an announcement that her former rival for the GOP nomination would head up another Whitman campaign task force, the Commission on Regulatory Reform and Government Waste. Wallwork looked tired or postoperative; he had red eyes and puffy bags under them that he'd never had in the primary. But he is an obvious choice for this role, both thematically and because 95,728 Republicans voted for him. He deflected the inevitable questions about some of the rougher things he'd said about Whitman in April and May. Asked when the commission would report to the candidate, Whitman and Wallwork did not repeat the mistake of her last task force announcement. The first report of Wallwork's group is due September 1st. There would be no accusations of "secret plans" or "stalling tactics" this day.

You've got to hand it to the Florio campaign. They are sharp and quick. They must have known about the Wallwork task force, because Monday the governor issued an executive order to create the exact same kind of task force under the aegis of Scott Weiner, his new chief counsel. (The Florio campaign says it was a coincidence.) On top of that preemptive move, a teenaged Florio volunteer stationed outside Whitman's event in the Statehouse today was handing out a press release containing seven quotations Wallwork uttered in attacking Whitman this spring for not disclosing her income tax return. Preempt and undermine.

That tax return, Whitman informed us, will be made available to the press and public tomorrow. Some Democrats think it's full of potential minefields for Whitman. In a bow to the importance of perception, her campaign scrapped a plan to make reporters troop to a lawyer's office to see the complicated return, which they would not be able to photocopy. That smacked of game playing and insincerity. Instead, photocopies of the return will be available at her Clark headquarters tomorrow.

John Whitman almost scuttled that change in plan with a last-minute insistence on giving the reporters "nothing." He feels turning over his tax returns is an incredible invasion of his privacy. But his wife and brother-in-law overruled him.

★ Friday, August 6 ★

I missed the strange scene yesterday but saw fleeting pictures of it on NJN: reporters seated around a conference table at Whitman headquarters poring over the candidate's sixty-eight-page tax return. Eight showed up. They stayed about an hour. The candidate was seventy miles away in deep South Jersey, almost as far away as you can get and still be in state. Her husband, John Whitman, the tax expert in the family, was unavailable. The communications deputy Dave Marziale wrote down about thirty questions that the reporters wanted answers to before they left, then he and Carl Golden got the answers from John Whitman and faxed back the information late in the day.

The good news for the Whitman campaign is that there were no big surprises. The Whitmans earned $3.6 million in 1992, six times what they earned the year before. One million eight hundred thousand dollars of it came from selling stocks and bonds, partly in preparation for the gubernatorial run, another $1.5 million from John Whitman's private investment and consulting firm, Broken Bridge, Inc.—English for Pontefract. They paid $1.2 million in state, federal, and New York non-resident taxes. The newspapers played it very straight, and while some put the story on page one, the *Star-Ledger* relegated it to page twenty-four.

The bad news for Whitman is that there are vulnerabilities in the return that the Florio campaign can exploit. The Whitmans declared an operating loss of $60,000 on Pontefract farm and took a deduction for it, at the same time that they were getting a property tax break on the farm because its "income" of $5,500 exceeded the threshold for a farmland assessment. That smacks of using the tax law coming and going. John Whitman reaped enormous gains from small investments in two stocks: Reliance Electric ($1,139,829 over six years on a $30,629 investment) and Dr.Pepper/7-Up ($213,973 over four years on a $1,760 investment), raising questions. The Florio campaign is also pointing out that if the capital gains tax cut that President Bush proposed and Christie Whitman supported had become law, the Whitmans would have saved about $250,000 in taxes.

On the positive side, the Whitman camp can say that the Whitmans paid a higher percentage of their income in taxes than the Florios, and gave a higher percentage to charity. Their charitable giving was $102,867, including $15,545 to the Lamington Presbyterian Church and $10,100 to the United Jewish Federation (which, if known, would probably win a few Jewish votes).

On the negative side, the Whitmans are not revealing their total net worth, and for some reason they will not release their 1990 tax return, although in April they released 1991, and during the 1990 senate campaign they released Christie's separate return for '89. This enables the Florio campaign to keep making accusations that the Whitmans are hiding something.

We'll see what develops out of this welter of data. Several news-papers are having tax experts look it over. The Florio campaign is studying it, too. Campaign manager Jim Andrews spent much of yesterday looking at the tax return and framing the campaign's response.

In the spin battle, Jo Glading is quoted as saying, "What it shows essentially is that she's very, very wealthy and wants to disclose as little as possible about her wealth." But Carl Golden, noting that no campaign law requires a candidate to make public his or her tax returns, had a good response. "The three returns (1989, '91, and '92) disclose more than has ever been disclosed by Bill Bradley or Frank Lautenberg, so I assume the governor would argue those two are hiding something."

★ Monday, August 9 ★

As I head off to New England for five days and let go of the campaign—something Jim Florio hasn't done yet, and something Christie Whitman is being criticized in some quarters for having done—it is time to take stock of where this race stands after nine weeks of a twenty-one-week general election period.

Being on vacation has enabled me to talk to a lot of politicos on the phone (in other words, to work). It's fair to say the election is still a fifty-fifty proposition. Some think Florio will win because, so far, he has done all the winning things and Whitman has stumbled. Some think Whitman will win because she's new, female, good on television, and because Florio is still disliked. "Her newness, plus her persona on TV," says Bill Palatucci, who worked for Cary Edwards in the primary, "those two things can overwhelm all her negatives."

Florio gets high marks for bouncing back from the loss of Joe Salema and Bob DeCotiis, for working hard, attacking, and setting the agenda. George Norcross, the Camden County Democratic chairman and a Florio rival, says the campaign has been "flawless." Everyone is impressed at how the governor is acting gubernatorial and demonstrating the powers of the office. Janice Ballou, who directs the Eagleton Poll, says that Florio is showing "he's in control, he's got an agenda. 'I know how to do this job.'"

Ballou thinks campaign organizations are important in New Jersey elections, because it's difficult to get media messages out in this state. The Florio campaign in 1989 was a well-oiled machine, especially by comparison to the clunker Jim Courter assembled. This year the Florio team looks fast and mean but a little less wieldy. Jim Andrews runs the campaign, and Jo Glading speaks for it. But everything has to be coordinated with the governor's office, and that means Rick Wright, Jamie Fox, Jon Shure, and now Scott Weiner. And none of those names were among the ones reeled off to me by Doug Berman when he praised the "terrific team" around Jim Florio of James Carville, Paul Begala, media consultants Carter Eskew and Tom Donilon, pollster Jeff Garin (all Washington hands), and himself—"as good a group of minds as I can think of that can be brought to a political race." Coordination is said to be good among all these entities, although Republicans say they hear stories about Andrews ruffling a few feathers in the governor's office with his temper and his seeming nonchalance about his own lack of New Jersey experience.

Around that core group are about a dozen helper/advisors: Harold Hodes, Susan Bass Levin, Bob Torricelli, Karen Kessler, Lewis Katz, Frank Capece, Tom Higgins, George Zoffinger, Carl Van Horn, staffers Jon Shure, Brenda Bacon, and David Applebaum, and a young researcher named David Bocian who was brought on by Carville.

There is camaraderie and spirit in the Florio camp. A Democratic lobbyist explains it's partly a function of the opponent: "There's a genuine dislike for this babe, from the top down. That's motivating the staff." It also explains the contemptuous tone of the Florio campaign's fax attack.

"There are three factors out of Jim Florio's control," says PR man Bob Sommer, another Florio insider. "The economy, Clinton, and Salema." The economic news has been good of late—unemployment at 6.8 percent two months in a row, after being at 9.1 in April. Clinton is a mixed bag at this point: his tax and deficit-reduction package passed the Congress last week, and the country seems about evenly divided on it and on him. The wild card is Joe Salema. Florio insiders say he definitely will not be indicted. But Congressman John Dingell of Michigan, a Democratic potentate who chairs the House Energy and Commerce Committee, is threatening to hold a hearing in late September on bond sales and political contributions. One report has him holding the hearing in New Jersey. He and Florio apparently have a longstanding dislike of one another, although Florio denied it when I asked him about it over hoagies two weeks ago. If true, the conflict springs from the days when Florio was running Dingell's environmental subcommittee and trying to slap controls on Dingell's auto-maker constituents in the Dearborn, Michigan, area. If Dingell holds a hearing in the circus atmosphere of an election season and subpoenas Salema and Nick Rudi, he will reopen a wound in Jim Florio's hide that has had all summer to heal.

Republicans believe that Florio is working feverishly through the White House and any other avenue of influence to call off Dingell. Meanwhile, Florio and Salema still talk, according to a member of the inner circle, and Salema is bitter about what's happened to him. He feels that had he stayed on and had Jim Florio gone on to win re-election, he would have earned a small spot in New Jersey political history as the guru who "brought Florio back from the dead." Not only has that opportunity been denied him, his good name has been besmirched.

The Whitman camp is more befuddled and dispirited than the Florio camp. The focus of all the disagreement is Dan Todd. Many think he is simply not up to the job. They complain that he has been out of the state for too long and out of big-time politics for even longer. (He claims to have helped run statewide campaigns from 1958 to 1970; his critics say in terms of political techniques, that might as well have been the paleolithic age.) Newspaper articles are starting to focus on him and John Whitman. The staff at Whitman headquarters all came to work one day last week wearing kerchiefs around their necks, as a practical joke to ease a little of the tension.

The rap on Todd is that he's making too many decisions himself, or in consultation with only Christie and John. Some understand the importance of trust and loyalty in politics, and they don't begrudge the candidate's entrusting her fate to her brother and her husband. But even they say she should "open up the circle" a little more. Ed Rollins, Carl Golden, and Hazel Gluck are all feeling in one way or another frustrated. Republicans less close to the campaign say they want to help but aren't being encouraged to. A contingent of Republicans in Hudson County, the bastion of working-class politics, offered to help and were told to call Whitney Todd, Dan Todd's twenty-five-year-old daughter. "What's Whitney Todd?" they asked one another, not knowing if it was a company or a person, and if a person, what gender.

"A lot of people want to help," says Republican state chairman

Ginny Littell, whose Republican State Committee opened an office next door to the Whitman campaign's and who now talks about "their side of the wall and our side of the wall."

"There's not enough bonding," she says.

Another party regular says, "If people come to your house to help rake the lawn, you've got to give them the rake."

Consensus opinion says Whitman has made three mistakes in the general election so far—she walked into a gun shop, an inadvertent error; she hired Larry McCarthy, a bigger but still understandable miscalculation of press reaction; and she ceded ground to Jim Florio by saying and doing relatively little.

"She let this vacuum occur," says Congressman Rob Andrews, a young Democrat who holds the old Florio seat. "If she were out doing something, she could say the media is being unfair to talk about her gaffes, but she's not giving them anything else to write about. I see a total absence of any activity."

"First they had her in the candidate protection program," quipped Frank Capece on the eve of Whitman's vacation. "Now they've relocated her to Idaho."

"They've knocked off a third of the campaign and done nothing," says Florio's campaign manager Jim Andrews (no relation to the congressman) of his counterparts in the Whitman camp. "Caso's [Gun-a-Rama] was goofy. Horton was goofy. Their candidate is out on the road, and she's *not prepped*. Jim Florio's a seasoned politician in his fourth gubernatorial campaign. He's very savvy. She's running around, a candidate on her first try, and she's weak on the issues. The problem is not staff, it's *her*. She's changed staffs! She went through 1990 breezing around and did very well. Then in the '93 primary she bollixed up something every two weeks and won. What does that teach you? You can breeze around and make mistakes and win! That's what she thinks she can do."

Andrews says the Florio campaign is on track and doing fine. "People are paying attention to her more than she thinks they are. I don't think they're seeing anything. You had a lot of women candidates go out in '92 and get all puffed up [in the media]. Our intention was not to let that happen—to keep on her every day. And it hasn't happened."

Doug Berman, who managed Florio's '89 campaign and is a senior

advisor to this one, thinks the Whitman campaign is being cautious because Republicans all remember how Jim Courter said and did things in
the summer that wounded his candidacy. But Berman believes that's the
wrong lesson to learn from Courter. The real lesson is that the campaign
begins long before Labor Day. "If your opponent engages early, you have
to engage at the same level of intensity," he says.

The Whitman strategy, as outlined in an inch-thick black binder
that Dan Todd keeps possession of, is to use the summer to build relations
with constituency groups and to shore up support among Republicans,
not say too much, hoard resources for the final phase of the campaign and
for TV, and kick into a higher gear after Labor Day. The campaign is
relying on anti-Florio sentiment and worries about the economy to carry
it along. And it is counting on what it sees as Christie Whitman's charm, in
person and on television, to provide the winning margin of support.

The Whitman campaign is also determined not to get rattled or
thrown off stride by the aggressive tactics of the Florio campaign. Dan
Todd, in his colorful country way, told me, "Jim Florio is rolling tar balls
through the door here to see what sticks." In an interview with a print
reporter, he used the same line, adding, "I watch the door."

While there is worry and grousing among Republicans, there is
also confidence that the public hasn't "focused" yet, that the problems of
the campaign are all "inside baseball," and that the raps against Whitman
as vague or incompetent are overblown.

"Jim Florio when he ran for election [in '89] was not specific at
all," says Hazel Gluck, a fact that was especially true in the '89 primary
when his Democratic opponents, Alan Karcher and Barbara Sigmund,
ridiculed Florio for waffling on state finances and school funding. Gluck
adds, "Jim Florio hasn't said anything about the future, either. All he's
talking about is what he's done and the 'tough decisions.' For example,
how are you gonna handle bond debt refinancing in 1995? Raise taxes?
He's not talking about that."

Gluck thinks the Whitman campaign needs to be offensive, rather
than defensive. Carl Golden talks about being more "pro-active," staging
more events that have a theme attached to them and not simply accepting
invitations to drop by this or that gathering of fifty to a hundred people
and giving your stump remarks.

Last night and today the Whitman camp held a "retreat" at the Scanticon Conference Center outside Princeton. About twenty-five people attended the Sunday night dinner, including Tom Kean. On Monday the core group shrank to about fifteen. The idea was Dan Todd's. Whether a move was made there to wrest some power away from him, I don't know. But the talk was frank. Christie and John Whitman attended Sunday night and tonight, but not during the day. Outsiders see the retreat as an opportunity for Christie to shake up the staff and dislodge her brother. "I wouldn't expect that to happen," says a staffer. "The die has been cast. That's just wishful thinking on the part of some."

The Florio campaign is not sharing its private polling numbers, but one insider says the numbers show the race to be "neck and neck." A private Republican poll written up in a Washington newsletter but unidentified as to source has the race at Whitman 40 to Florio 36.

Glenn Paulsen, the Republican chairman of Burlington County, says, "I'm scared. She has to establish herself as a credible general election candidate and make no more missteps."

Jerry Hall, a veteran political observer at the New Jersey State Chamber of Commerce, says, "She needs to make a splash. I haven't seen great position papers. We need more substance out of Whitman. Her novelty—I don't know if that can really swing it."

But George Norcross, the Camden Democrat, says, "Florio's negatives are still high. If he wins, it'll be by her losing, and by him showing she's not a credible alternative. It's her race to win or lose."

★　Saturday, August 14　★

Go away, and you can be certain something good will happen while you're gone.

Three things happened in the race this week.

The most enjoyable to have covered would have been the flap that ensued after a Florio campaign film crew was spotted at nine o'clock Wednesday morning on the edge of Pontefract farm by Christie Whitman and two young aides (who were there at that hour because they are "bunking" at the farm this summer, Keith Nahigian and Jason Volk). The three of them got in a car and chased the Florio camera crew's van, while John Whitman called the Tewksbury Township police. The Whitmans say the three-person crew was trespassing. The Florio campaign says they were shooting from the road. Christie Whitman told Mark Magyar, of the *Asbury Park Press*, "We all expected to see some form of class warfare, but this goes a step beyond what anybody would consider acceptable." James Carville told the same reporter, "Nobody's spying on anybody. We just had a videotape camera out there taking pictures of the house where she hired the illegal aliens, broke several laws, got breaks on her property taxes, and lived when she didn't vote in a school board election. This has to be the silliest thing I've heard about. And this coming from the woman who hired the Willie Horton ad man."

Apprised that Whitman said three of the vehicle's tires were on her property and not the road, Carville told Magyar, "What's she runnin' for, state surveyor?"

The conclusion being drawn from the episode is that Florio plans to run a TV commercial attacking Whitman's farmland assessment tax break. "A lot of people are a little bit troubled by someone who pays $47 a year on fifty acres," Florio was quoted in the Bergen *Record* as saying the next day at the Sussex County Fair, where, ironically, he signed a bill expanding the farmland assessment program to make it easier for farmers to get tax breaks on certain buildings on their land.

The comical nature of the film crew incident inspired Carl Golden to put out a David Letterman-style "Top 10 Reasons Why the Florio Film Crew Was at the Whitman Farm," including "No. 9—They were in search of barnyard manure as the basic natural resource for the governor's television commercials," and "No. 6—The crew was searching for watermelons to use in the governor's next rifle demonstration." Jo Glading countered the next day with new lyrics to "Old MacDonald:"

> Mrs. Whitman had a farm, E-I-E-I-O,
> And on the farm she raised some hay, E-I-E-I-O,
> With a tax break here, a deduction there,
> Here a break, there a break, everywhere a tax break,
> Mrs. Whitman tilled for tax breaks, E-I-E-I-O.

In a front-page story today, Jerry Gray of the *New York Times* opined that the encounter with the film crew "backfired" on Whitman by foucsing public attention on her farm, "which is just what the Florio campaign wanted." What he didn't say is that some will find it sleazy that the Florio campaign was lurking outside Whitman's home.

The other significant development of the week was the National Organization for Women's "recommending" Whitman, one step shy of an outright endorsement. The Florio campaign had hoped that NOW would stay neutral. And later in the week, several chapters split from the 12,000-person organization to back Florio. NOW-NJ used some tortuous logic to support its decision. The group strongly opposes Florio's welfare reform law because the law denies extra benefits to welfare mothers who have additional children while on welfare, but Whitman supports the law. NOW says she told them she'd "look at it" with a more open mind than the governor, even though she supports it. On that basis, plus the argument that Florio has not appointed enough women to high office, the NOW board voted nineteen to eighteen to "recommend" Whitman. I suspect NOW-NJ president Myra Terry and ex-president Linda Bowker had a lot to do with swaying the vote. Terry, I know from interviewing her, is enamored of the idea of a woman governor. Bowker has been bitter at Florio ever since he overlooked her as a candidate for Congress to fill his old seat in 1990 in favor of the party regulars' choice, Rob Andrews.

What the NOW recommendation is actually worth is questionable. But it got a lot of attention this week, and has symbolic value.

In a third interesting development, another legendary Republican national figure named Roger has dumped on Christie Whitman. Roger Stone, the Washington-based former consultant who performed "dirty tricks" for Richard Nixon's re-election committee in 1972, then rose to prominence in the '80s, sent a memo to Whitman warning, "The opportunity to win the 1993 gubernatorial race is slipping away." Someone sent copies of it to Statehouse reporters (who suspected Stone himself, though his office denied it).

"In the coming weeks, Florio will continue to try to depict you as vacuous, wealthy, insensitive, uninformed, and vague: the only way to counter this is by being specific and by putting Florio on the defense on both the Clinton tax increases and corruption among his closest aides," the memo says.

Stone recommends that she call for a tax cut, as Tom Kean did when he defeated Florio in 1981. (Democrats have been speculating for several weeks that she might do just that, to revive a flagging campaign.) He also recommends that she hone in on Joe Salema and portray the Florio administration as corrupt. "If Florio knew Salema was corrupt then he is guilty of a crime," Stone snorts. "If Florio did not know what was going on around him then, he is incompetent." Another recommendation is to fire Ed Rollins. "He has no successful statewide campaign experience. That Rollins could not foresee the firestorm that would be caused by your campaign's association with a media consultant who was connected to the Willie Horton ad speaks to his lack of judgment. He does not understand New Jersey."

Stone was an unofficial advisor to Whitman in 1991, but she kept him at arm's length because of his reputation as the "Prince of Darkness," a name the newspapers always say he bestowed on himself but he says was bestowed on him by Tom Kean in '81. He has no role with this campaign, as Carl Golden was quick to point out.

"Roger has a long history of back-stabbing," Ed Rollins told Mark Magyar, but, interestingly, he said that, except for the suggestion of firing him, Stone's ideas are sound.

★ Monday, August 16 ★

A horde of journalists descended on Whitman's farm today. The campaign had decided on Friday to invite the media in for a tour, and whether out of interest in the election or curiosity about her wealth (or the free lunch of home-grown products promised), the number of TV vans and other cars parked in a field when I drove up was quite astounding.

Because NJN had moved to brand-new headquarters over the weekend and there was some confusion over where to find our vans and equipment, cameraman Ray Cordero and I arrived a bit late. An aide in the parking area directed us to the far side of a modern barn, where a bizarre scene was just getting ready to unfold. Against a backdrop of hay bales piled nearly to the roof, Whitman and various other casually dressed farmers and local folk sat on hay bales facing about sixty reporters, still photographers, and TV crews, many of whom were munching on beef-lamb-burgers, deviled eggs, tomatoes, potatoes, and peaches that had been served to them by agrarian types standing behind serving tables.

Whitman wore jeans, sneakers, and a short-sleeved red "Whitman for Governor" crew shirt. Her brother and husband, who have continued to get a rough press lately as the "heavies" who are controlling the campaign, hovered around the scene in country garb, Dan Todd wearing his Stetson hat, John Whitman wearing a baseball cap with the logo of the New Jersey Devils on it.

"You started all this," Todd said when he saw me, a joking reference to my visit there in May.

First came the testimonials. A local planning official told the assembled how pleased the community is that the Todd family has donated Pontefract to a conservation fund that will keep it permanently undeveloped. A farmer and a local legislator discussed the importance of farmland assessments.

Whitman then fielded a barrage of questions about this farm and Twenty Springs Farm, the fifty-three-acre property in Far Hills she and her husband used to live on and where they also get a tax break because they harvest trees. She parried them the way she has parried questions throughout the year about illegal aliens and campaign disarray. Some of the reporters grumbled later that they found her evasive. I didn't. She said she and her husband qualify for every tax break they get. Pressed on whether millionaires who don't farm for a living should still be able to take advantage of the farmland assessment program, Whitman shot back, "We pay over a million-three in taxes annually. That's not someone who's avoiding taxes. A million-three is a lot of money!"

She said her parents wouldn't have been able to keep this farm were it not for farmland assessments, and that she's proud to be part of the farming community in this state with its twenty-five thousand farms and its role in preserving land. "I'm part of what makes New Jersey green," she explained. "I'm part of what makes New Jersey the Garden State."

The press kept trying to get her to address the "perception" problem. On the estate in Far Hills, the *New York Times* reported yesterday, she barely surpassed the $500 income threshold for a farmland assessment in 1988 and '89 by selling cords of firewood for $100 apiece to her brother in Far Hills and her brother-in-law on Park Avenue in Manhattan. But Whitman wouldn't acknowledge that there is a problem. "Is there a law that says whose money is better than someone else's?" she asked incredulously.

A Florio goon/kid stationed out on the driveway passed out a ream of material, including a brilliantly funny "guide" to Pontefract ("Visit the taxpayer-subsidized estate of Christine and John Whitman in the rolling hills of Hunterdon and Somerset counties. . . . See: The fertile land that produced little last year but a bumper crop of income and property tax shelters. . . . Enjoy: Watching while the Whitmans 'materially participate' in their farming operation, as required under federal tax law in order to fully deduct the farm losses on their income taxes . . .").

After the news conference, as a walking tour began, John Whitman and I said hello, and he let off a little steam about the incessant and repetitive nature of the questions. I had asked Christie if she believed Americans were entitled to take every possible tax deduction they could. John Whitman quoted Justice Holmes to the effect that of course Americans should, and he said he couldn't believe I had asked the question. I told him just because I asked doesn't mean I hold the view expressed in the question. I tried to explain we play devil's advocate. We poke at candidates sometimes, just to see if they'll say something interesting, I said.

The media stampeded through the Whitman barns and coops and swarmed around Whitman herself, peppering her with questions. Cameraman jostled for shots of Whitman with the livestock, then trained their cameras on the animals for long, studied shots as if they'd never seen a pig or a cow before. No visitor was allowed within camera range of the house, the swimming pool, and the tennis court, and John Whitman patrolled the driveway to rein in any camera crew that strayed into that area.

Columnist Liz Auster of the Bergen *Record* captured the feeling best when she said the Whitmans looked unhappy for having to put up with this, and the journalists looked vaguely ashamed of themselves for inflicting it upon them.

After the barnyard tour and a mass of interviews, twenty cars and vans caravaned over to Far Hills for a quick drive-through of Twenty Springs, where the Whitmans lived until 1991. This was where they harvested trees and paid just $47 in property taxes last year on fifty of the fifty-three acres. An old stone wall about four feet high divides the property from the road. At the dirt-driveway entrance, where the wall rises up to form a big stone gate, Dan Todd in his Stetson sat on the wall, waving the cars in.

Today's event was a gamble for the Whitman campaign. Todd told me it was something they had always intended to do and that last week's incident with the camera crew made now the right time. Carl Golden told me they were doing it because there were so many "distortions" and so much "innuendo" going around.

Inviting the media in takes a little of the edge off a future Florio TV commercial about the farm. If the public has already seen it, the shock value of the pictures is lessened. And the Whitmans probably get some credit for being open.

But they are still on the defensive. They staged an event today to discuss something on the Florio campaign's agenda, not their own. Some will find the answers unsatisfactory and agree with the governor that Whitman is manipulating the system. And, though it was held on a farm, the event was a zoo and had little to do with governing the state of New Jersey.

I asked Dan Todd how it went. "I'll know tomorrow," he said, meaning after he looks at the newspapers.

★ **Wednesday, August 18** ★

While the Lady of Pontefract was showing off her farm, the Lord of Drumthwacket was at the National Governors' Association meeting in Tulsa, Oklahoma. He came back yesterday and renewed his attack on the Republicans in the senate, who on Monday voted in a private caucus not to strip John Dorsey of his senatorial courtesy privilege and, instead, offered the governor and Judge Marianne Espinosa Murphy a compromise: She can serve another seven years and then come up for review again. Murphy has said she won't accept that demeaning and unprecedented offer. She wants tenure to age seventy like most judges get once they pass their initial review. The governor got off an airplane in Newark, held an airport news conference, proclaimed the matter a "constitutional crisis," and vowed to explore legal options to continue the fight.

Florio had no public schedule today, but I attended a pro-Florio event up in Union City, the heavily Cuban enclave along the Hudson River above Weehawken and Jersey City. Three former Hudson County Republican party chairmen endorsed Florio, an event held today in an effort to counter tomorrow's more significant endorsement of Whitman by Jersey City Mayor Bret Schundler, the new Republican phenomenon.

From Union City I went to nearby Secaucus, where Whitman called a news conference and gave the first hint that she may indeed propose a tax cut.

The meeting room at the Meadowlands Hilton was packed with supporters. Whitman came out to applause and then, on TV monitors on each side of the podium, played excerpts from a tape of Jim Florio's August 1990 prime-time TV "mea culpa" speech in which he tried to explain his record tax hikes, admitted he may not have properly explained them before, and appealed to the public to give them time to work. In the excerpts there was a trace of the unctuous salesman about Florio, and the Republican crowd laughed as they heard his three-year-old promises about the tax hikes making New Jersey more stable and more attractive to business.

Then Whitman turned to some Ross Perot-style charts to illustrate how New Jersey's economy has actually suffered during the Florio years. As she peeled each chart off the easel, she handed it to John Whitman, who was out of view of the audience behind one of the TV monitors. The charts showed dramatically poorer performance here than in the rest of the nation in job growth, personal income growth, retail sales, and building permits. Two of the charts were expressions of "annual deviations from the trend," an economist's way of viewing things and probably too sophisticated for this type of presentation. It smacked of John Whitman's Wall Street world.

For Whitman to propose a tax cut now might seem to some like a transparent and irresponsible attempt to steal the election. A Florio insider told me he hopes she goes for one, because the media and the public will never buy it. "It would look desperate," he said. But Whitman laid the foundation for one today. In her prepared remarks, she warned of a "structural deficit" in next year's state budget and said the way to address it is, first, to cut spending, and second, to cut taxes to stimulate the economy.

"Governor Weld in Massachusetts and Governor Engler in Michigan have both closed budget gaps and lowered taxes in their state, and I intend to work closely with them both to bring their techniques to bear on the problems here where appropriate," she said, invoking the name of a fashionable "new" Republican tax-cutter, Weld.

About half a dozen of us in the press seats up front challenged her. Was she proposing a tax cut? Hadn't she said two months ago, when Florio and the legislature were talking about one, that a tax cut in the current climate would be "cynical"? Was she saying, as Florio had in '89, that she foresees no need for *new* taxes? Whitman danced around the questions and promised to make her position more clear sometime down the line. "When?" several of us shouted. Whitman stared at me sternly in the front row and shot back, "When-I'm-Ready!" which brought down the house and had her husband in stitches.

If she can propose a *credible* tax cut, it could be the arrow in her quiver that wins the election. John Whitman told me after the event that she won't propose one unless they can come up with one "that you'll accept."

He was wearing a small political button with a picture of a man's face on it. It was his grandfather Charles Whitman, and the button was from the New York gubernatorial campaign of 1915, which the grandfather won. "See, political campaigns aren't that different from what they've always been," remarked the grandson. "They had buttons, we have buttons." I took the remark as a subtle dig at all those who have complained of late about the Whitmans' not taking the advice of their hired professionals and of John Whitman's getting in the way.

Today's was a well-organized and well-thought-out event. The tape, the charts, the crowd, a twelve-page prepared text. It was even held in the same hotel Florio had repaired to for a rally after his August '90 prime-time speech—a point Whitman noted in her remarks: "After he delivered his television address three years ago, Jim Florio came to this hotel to celebrate. While the people of New Jersey had to work harder and longer to pay their tax bills to Trenton, Jim Florio and the Democrats had a party."

Finally, Whitman was talking substance, shifting the focus back to the Florio taxes, and the Whitman campaign was doing something it was supposed to do.

Her new media consultant, Mike Murphy from Washington, talked to reporters after the candidate was rather abruptly whisked away from too many more questions on her tax position.

Asked to assess today's event, he observed, "Offense is great."

★ Saturday, August 21 ★

A big, new, dark blue sedan pulled up to the Broad Street train station in Newark and out stepped Governor Florio. I was waiting on the sidewalk with cameraman Mark DiPietro. The governor glanced at a *New York Post* newspaper box behind us, and the tabloid headline puzzled him. "Zorba Is Stud?" he read quizzically. I explained it was about Anthony Quinn cheating on his wife and fathering a child at age seventy-eight with a woman in her thirties. The governor looked at me. "Judge not, lest ye be judged," he cracked, then quickly held his hand up toward the camera, horrified that we might have been rolling. (We were, but we'd never use such a thing.) The moment displayed both Jim Florio's wit and his seasoned politician's concern for appearances.

This has been the first week all summer in which the Whitman campaign seemed to have "won." If Whitman wins the election, this may go down as the week she turned the corner. The farm tour on Monday went well and played straightforwardly in the media. The tax event on Wednesday was well staged, and the hint of a tax cut is a potential bombshell. The reason I was at Broad Street station in Newark at eleven o'clock Thursday was that Whitman was getting endorsed an hour later in Jersey City by Mayor Bret Schundler, and I needed a reaction from Florio.

The mood inside the second-floor council chambers at Jersey City Hall that day was giddy, and the room was packed. In a county and city that have been crucial to Democratic politicians in statewide elections for nearly a century, the prospect of a Republican mayor endorsing a Republican for governor tickled the people present. "It's amazing the walls are still standing," said consultant Bill Palatucci, who was there as a friend of the mayor's. Indeed, three walls were lined with portraits of past Jersey City mayors, most of them Democrats, many of them colorful, and several of them legendary for the wealth and power they amassed in the service of the people.

The atmospherics couldn't have been better for Whitman's new media consultant, Mike Murphy, who was there with a film crew shooting material for possible use in a commercial. He followed Whitman and Schundler around Jersey City all day. Schundler is the Jack Kemp/ William Weld-wannabe of New Jersey politics—a moderate, antitax pragmatist with a touch of newspeak evangelism in his promises of innovation and change. Just thirty-four, with a Wall Street background, he reportedly conducts once-a-week Bible readings in his home and, as Jim Goodman of the Trenton *Times* put it, acts as if politics were a calling he has been summoned to rather than a profession. His twenty-minute endorsement of Whitman began like a sermon: "This is not about Christie Todd Whitman. It's about our state, and our city, and doing something for ourselves. She is just the vehicle in which we invest our hopes."

The Democrats had hoped to keep Schundler neutral (and reportedly had gone to considerable lengths to do so, including appointing a Schundler ally to a paying position). They failed, ostensibly because Schundler and Whitman both support a voucher program for Jersey City parochial-school families while Florio thinks vouchers will damage the public schools, but also because Schundler must endorse Whitman if he hopes to see his star keep rising in the Republican party.

"A Republican mayor endorsing a Republican gubernatorial candidate—I suspect there's nothing newsworthy about that," Florio said at the train station.

But there was enough newsworthy that NJN had three cameras at City Hall, one for a news piece by me on the reasons for the endorsement, one for a news piece by my colleague Sandra King on the impact of the endorsement, and a documentary crew that's working on a behind-the-scenes look at the Whitman campaign to air after the election. We *added* to the ambience!

No one knows whether Schundler can carry many voters along with him, but as he himself noted, no Democrat has ever become governor without carrying Jersey City by at least 19,000 votes. In 1989, Jim Florio carried it 37,082 to 8,827.

The Florio camp, meanwhile, is so fixated on destroying Whitman that it missed an opportunity to promote the governor. Instead of another fax ridiculing Whitman's shifting position on state taxes, the Florio campaign on Wednesday might have been better off trying to trumpet the governor's role in convincing the Clinton administration to drop the idea of pharmaceutical price controls. The pharmaceutical industry is one of New Jersey's most important. On Wall Street, drug stocks climbed on the news out of New Jersey that Florio, at the National Governors' Association meeting, had announced he'd been given assurance that mandatory price controls on prescription drugs would be left out of the president's health-care program. It was page-one news here. Some say letting Florio announce it was a gift from the White House to the governor. But the Florio campaign's press release for the day was a three-year compendium of Whitman quotes on taxes.

The governor had no real events this week, and on Friday he seemed to duck reporters. His one public event, set for 9:45 at the Statehouse, went off at 9:30 and was over by the time reporters straggled in. Maybe he didn't want to answer questions about news stories detailing the $130,000 he has received in campaign contributions from bond houses (Whitman got $12,000). Larry Stuelpnagel of NJN got in to see him after assuring Jon Shure the questions would deal only with senatorial courtesy.

★ Tuesday, August 24 ★

I laughed to myself when I saw Florio's and Whitman's schedules for today. Florio was being endorsed by labor unions at a construction site where three to five hundred jobs had been created. Whitman was holding a news conference outside a closed factory where six hundred jobs had been lost. The settings virtually define the central argument of the campaign.

Florio's event was impressive. The BASF Corporation is building a new headquarters in the international trade zone in Mt. Olive, up in semirural northwestern New Jersey. The project wouldn't have happened had Florio not approved a controversial land swap in 1991. Environmentalists had fought it. This morning several hundred men in hard hats came streaming off the construction site to watch their union leader endorse the governor. These men wouldn't have been working had it not been for Florio's decision, which kept BASF from pulling up stakes and moving to Atlanta. Most every one of the workers I asked said he liked Florio. These are the sort of people one imagines hating Florio a few years ago. To me they were like the watermelons that burst apart under a barrage of semi-automatic rifle fire: living proof that the governor's rhetoric is grounded in reality, in this case his argument that he is striving mightily to create jobs.

Whitman's event was at the Maxwell House plant in Hoboken that closed last year and whose sign is still a landmark on the Jersey side of the Hudson. She called Maxwell House a symbol of all the businesses that have shut down or moved away during the Florio era.

Not much press attended either event, but I did a four-minute piece tonight in which, through opposing sound bites, Florio and Whitman argued about job creation. Florio on camera said the Maxwell House plant closing happened in February 1990, just weeks after he'd become governor, and so was not really his fault. Whitman on camera said it happened in June, right after Florio's tax hikes passed. Both were right—it was threatened in February and announced in June—but I couldn't get into that level of detail in a TV piece. Most of the back-and-forth was Whitman saying what a poor job the governor has done creating jobs, and Florio challenging Whitman to stop being so vague and hiding behind "her little task force" and to tell the public what she would do to create jobs. Whitman's answer to me was that she would add $10 million more to the Department of Commerce budget (in effect, doubling it), create a "commission on competitiveness" that would report to her in 120 days, enact recommendations of her regulatory reform task force, and create a business ombudsman in the Department of State. Not a terribly convincing brew, but an answer.

She said the proposal being put together by her economic recovery task force would tell more. Florio wondered if voters would get to see it "sometime before the election." I reminded her there are just ten weeks 'til the election and asked when we'd see the plan, giving her another chance to come back with, "When I'm ready—as I told you before." She said it with such emphasis that I again made it the last word in my piece before the closing stand-up, which said: "New Jerseyans currently out of work or worried about the employment picture have a choice between

Florio's record and Whitman's promise. Whitman says Florio's record is poor. Florio says Whitman's promise is empty."

★ Thursday, August 26 ★

Last night about a thousand Republicans gathered at the Brunswick Hilton for a big $1,000-per-person Republican State Committee fundraiser. The featured guest was Senator Robert Dole, and the focus of the evening was how important it is to get Christie Whitman elected.

Dole, Whitman, Tom Kean, the legislative leaders, and Republican state chairman Ginny Littell met the press privately, then spoke in the ballroom. Dole was funny and wry in both settings. He's a better toastmaster for New Jersey Republicans at this kind of function than George Bush was, because he's looser than Bush, and New Jerseyans appreciate a man who can make them laugh.

The watchword of the evening was taxes, as it has been at every GOP event in this state since 1990. But now the national GOP is becoming a one-note party as well. Dole said, "You're paying taxes through the nose. You've been Florioized and now you've been Clintonized and I don't know where it's going to end." He urged the faithful to send the nation a signal in this race, one that will carry over into the 1994 congressional elections and beyond. Of the four big elections since Clinton took office, Dole noted, Republicans had won all four, in Georgia, Texas, Los Angeles, and even the lieutenant governorship of Arkansas. "We even carried Hope."

Tom Kean was the politician swarmed over by the media after the press conference, all wanting to know whether he will run for the U.S. Senate next year against Frank Lautenberg. He said he'll decide by Labor Day.

Christie Whitman used the occasion to call upon state treasurer Sam Crane, a Florio cabinet officer, to take a leave of absence because of his role in what's called the Lyndhurst controversy, or the Lyndhurst "scandal," as the newspapers have begun to call it. Last Friday then–Attorney General Robert Del Tufo released a full report on Lyndhurst in which Crane, a forty-two-year-old longtime Statehouse Democratic soldier, was portrayed as the operative who carried out a secret transfer of funds from one government account to another that enabled the state to funnel $1.5 million to the Lyndhurst Board of Education to keep a political promise. Del Tufo's report was ambiguous on Crane's degree of wrong-doing, but Whitman has been urged, and apparently is agreeing, to go after Florio on the "sleaze factor," as Republicans call it. Demanding that Crane step aside until a grand jury clears him is reminiscent of her call in early May for Joe Salema to take a leave. (Crane and Salema, coinciden-tally, are brothers-in-law.) When she blasted Crane last night in her speech, I noticed the legislative leaders applauding but not Tom Kean. Crane is a well-liked veteran Statehouse person, and Whitman's blast smacked of a cheap shot. A longtime lobbyist and Republican insider in the crowd, Alan Marcus, agreed. "It was beneath her," he said.

At functions like these you get to have brief exchanges with dozens of people it would take days to reach on the telephone. A lot of them think Whitman has "turned the corner" in the past week and a half. Congressman Dean Gallo thinks Clinton's tax hike spells big trouble for Florio. Marcus thinks the best thing Whitman could do for herself would be go on a long international tour so she can't do anything that might lose the race for her. "It's hers to win," is a line you keep hearing.

"Her faux pas of the summer don't seem to have taken hold," said Marcus, who helped William Cahill get elected governor in 1969. "Florio can't get over 40 percent. He can't get over that bubble. He's known by 99 percent of the public, and still he can't get over 40 in the polls. On paper, she can't lose. Of course, I remember when Ray Bateman was ahead of Brendan Byrne by 33 points in his own polls on Labor Day (1977). We should have sent him on a long international tour, too. Jim Florio misses Bob DeCotiis badly," Marcus continued.

> He made things happen. Florio's problem is, he's the best politi-cian in his organization now. Forget the consultants. This is about him and her, and Florio's a much better politician than Whitman. But losing DeCotiis and Salema and now Del Tufo [the attorney general, who just resigned for a lucrative job in private practice], it hurts. Why do you think they named an "acting" attorney general? They can't get anybody to take the job! Would you take that job knowing it could be over in a few

months? It's a perception thing—it sends a signal. Then again, I'd never count Jim Florio out of anything.

John Renna, the wily old GOP chairman of Essex County, is one of the many old-school Jersey pols who think geographically. Everything is seen in terms of counties. Renna told me Whitman would do well in Bergen, Morris, Somerset, Monmouth, and Ocean. That means Florio, he said, will have to do well in Hudson, Essex, Mercer, Middlesex, and Camden. In Hudson, the Democrats are still reeling from the election of Bret Schundler in Jersey City. In Essex, the party is divided into two warring factions. "That doesn't mean they'll vote for Christie Whitman," I said. "It means they won't vote," he said.

A reporter from New Jersey's talk-radio station WKXW-FM (New Jersey 101.5) asked if I'd heard, as he has, that the Florio camp is about to reveal some big dirt on Whitman. "They have something on her," he said. I said I hadn't heard that. What I didn't say is, that's the kind of rumor his station used to feed on, back in the days when it was teaming up with the *Trentonian* to fan the flames of the tax revolt.

Even Jim Courter was in the crowd! It was the first time I'd seen the defeated '89 GOP candidate at a state party gathering in four years. He left early, but I stopped him on his way out for a quick on-camera interview. His name has become synonymous with how not to run a campaign in New Jersey, so he was a good sport to do the interview. He said the mistake he'd made four years ago had been to think that the campaign began on Labor Day and the summer wasn't important—that, plus not appreciating the importance of hiring a "professional" staff (his campaign manager had been an underpaid Statehouse Republican operative with little experience). In hindsight, he said, he would have attacked Florio harder, earlier, the way Whitman is doing it, and "handled the abortion issue differently." Courter and I never particularly liked one another, but we had been through a campaign together, and I think we both felt a touch of nostalgia about finding ourselves on opposite sides of the camera again.

In the ballroom there was positive energy, within limits. Whitman pleased the crowd but didn't wow 'em. "She didn't do it," said Alan Marcus. "This has got to be the night you get them excited. If you don't get the party faithful screaming at a kickoff event like this, you don't send 'em off energized. And she didn't do it."

★　Saturday, August 28　★

The week just past was a draw. A lot happened, and there is getting to be a lot of infighting. Behind the scenes, the first TV commercials are being shot and edited. In public, the candidates are starting to appear more regularly and take daily swipes at one another. The Florio campaign is now sending out *two* faxes a day ridiculing Whitman or attacking her credibility. If you miss them at your office, the two college kids who trail Whitman, recording and videotaping as many of her statements as they can, will be sure to hand you one as you walk in to cover a Whitman event. Whitman now gives a good-natured hello to them and teases them, while her young aides play cat-and-mouse with them by luring reporters into rooms where a door can be closed to keep out the Florio spies, "video dweebs," as cameraman Tim Stollery dubbed them.

Jim Florio this week announced a major initiative to bolster and preserve the Highlands, a recently designated section of northwestern New Jersey near the New York border that takes in parts of six counties. Now that the Shore and the Pinelands have been secured, he said, it's time to take care of the Highlands—a broadly popular move that appeals to open-space advocates who've looked askance at the governor's criticism of farmland assessments; it is opposed only by some who own land up there and want to develop it or sell it. The next day the governor unveiled a new $6 million grant program for farmers, some of whom, it is said, were starting to resent his incessant carping about Whitman's farmland assessment. He also needed to mollify farmers after forcing a hike in the minimum wage for farm workers last year over Republican and farmer objections. It was $4.25. It's now $5.05.

Whitman and Florio both campaigned among women's groups on Thursday, Women's Equality Day, she talking about breaking the "glass ceiling" on women in the workplace, he touting bills he signed mandating insurance coverage for mammograms and "family leave" for workers two years before the federal Family Leave Act.

Yesterday, among their other stops, they gave back-to-back speeches at a conference of the Statewide Hispanic Chamber of Commerce at the Meadowlands Sheraton. I went to hear how they would pitch themselves to an ethnic group that is becoming increasingly potent. Hispanics were only 6 percent of the New Jersey population in 1980. By 1990 they were 10 percent. In a state of 7.4 million people, they number about 800,000, with about 188,000 registered voters, enough to swing a close election if they voted in a bloc.

Except for a large Republican-leaning Cuban-American community in Union City, Hispanics in state and local elections have traditionally supported Democrats. That may explain why Jim Florio got a standing ovation coming and going from the two to three hundred in attendance, while Christie Whitman didn't get one at all. Whitman, however, ended her twenty-minute stump speech with a couple of lines of fluent Spanish, which she later told reporters she learned in college.

Whitman made no special appeal for this group's vote and showed off her Spanish without fanfare. She talked about the economy and taxes, education and civil rights. She ticked off virtually every proposal she has made since January. She talked substance and delivered a no-nonsense, non-emotional appeal. Florio also had a prepared text but spoke with more passion. He retold the story of his administration and bits of his family history. He presented himself as someone who operates on the principle that, as he put it, "you can't run away from problems or else they fester." He extolled the virtues of work and family. He was eloquent and keyed up. He got a rise out of the audience when he called the water at the Jersey Shore this summer "as clean as the Caribbean," thanks to his administration's half-billion dollar "investment" in sewerage upgrades. He got a bigger rise when he said he expected to see New Jersey companies trading soon with a newly liberated Cuba. On this day, in this room, he out-performed Whitman.

Two bigger developments were unfolding at the same moment. The governor has decided to challenge the constitutionality of senatorial courtesy, and on Friday filed a lawsuit with the attorney general and Judge Marianne Espinosa Murphy as two of the plaintiffs, and Republican state senators as the defendants. The case will be heard this Thursday by a friend of mine, Judge Philip Carchman, a very bright man who will need all his faculties to resolve this clash of governmental interests, not the least of which is the judiciary's interest in keeping individual senators from squelching the careers of its own judges. The Florio campaign is still trying to drive a wedge between Whitman and those who support Judge Murphy by arguing that Whitman has changed her position twice and should have asserted more leadership to get the senate Republican caucus to override Senator John Dorsey and grant Judge Murphy a full hearing on her re-appointment. Whitman says she supports Judge Murphy but has done all she could. Yesterday she challenged Democrats in the senate to vote to end senatorial courtesy, predicting Republican votes would materialize. She is finessing a difficult situation.

Also yesterday the governor's office released a report by the state treasurer on the bonding practices of the Florio administration over the past three years. Last week it was the attorney general's Lyndhurst report released on a Friday afternoon so as to hit the Saturday papers, which are thought to be the least read; this week, the bond report. Republican legislators have been demanding this information for months and threatened earlier in the week to subpoena it. Although the report showed Merrill Lynch and Lazard Freres, two firms heavily written about during the Salema controversy in May, as the top bond underwriting firms during Florio's tenure, it didn't show much that was incriminating. Assembly speaker Chuck Haytaian said it was so sanitized "it would make the Ty-D-Bowl man proud," which sounds like a line thought up by two or three people in a room.

Another of those lines was Florio's response this week to Whitman's demand that state treasurer Sam Crane step aside over the Lyndhurst affair. "People who live in glass mansions shouldn't throw stones," Jon Shure said to me on the telephone an hour before Jim Florio said it on camera.

It was a cute line, but I wonder how many people who hear this stuff every day are starting to tire of Florio's constant allusions to Whitman's wealth. To me it's the cheapest note in the campaign so far (not counting whoever faxed parts of Florio's old divorce papers to reporters in June). The Florio camp's attempt to drum up resentment against Whitman solely because of her wealth is something I don't recall ever being done in such an overt way. To my way of thinking, people envy the rich more than they resent them, so the tactic may not even be working. In the meantime, it's socially divisive.

Shure had called me to tell me he had liked my piece the night before. I had taken a statement of Whitman's in Hoboken on Tuesday about Governor Florio "continually cutting" the Department of Commerce budget and had shown it to be inaccurate. My "trophy" was a Florio campaign press release on Thursday ("Wrong Numbers, Wrong Facts Are No Substitute for the Truth and a Plan") built around my report, with a full transcript attached. Whitman seemed a little cool toward me yesterday at the Hispanic event, unless I imagined it. Carl Golden, her spokesman, thought the piece had been a "bit unfair" though not enough to follow his normal practice in such an instance of picking up the phone and chewing out the reporter. What few people know is that early this week Brenda Bacon, Governor Florio's policy chief, whom I had interviewed at the Statehouse about health care, told me that up at Florio campaign headquarters people think I've been "soft" on Whitman this summer, that she has me "snowed." Having heard something similar from another Florio advisor a few weeks ago, I needed to dispel the notion. The next day Whitman made a false accusation against the governor and I seized on it.

★ **Monday, August 30** ★

The Florio campaign has its act together. Today, with both candidates having no public schedule, I tried to do a piece on two false statements I thought Governor Florio had made on Friday. It would keep things even. But the Florio campaign had the research to back up the governor's statements.

On Friday afternoon, while I was putting together my piece on the Hispanic event, Carl Golden had called me to say that if I was going into the issue of the minimum wage, Governor Florio in his speech had falsely accused Whitman of supporting a rollback in the minimum wage. (Someone from the Whitman camp must have stayed and listened to the speech.) So this morning around eleven, I called Jo Glading and asked if she could back up the governor's statement. About two hours later I got a transcript of Whitman remarks at some kind of town meeting in June in which she voiced skepticism about last year's hike in the minimum wage and said we'd better "study it carefully" to make sure it's not costing jobs. Glading also faxed a recent clip from a South Jersey newspaper, *Today's Sunbeam* of Salem County, in which Whitman implied the minimum wage should be rolled back at least for farmworkers.

I called Golden to tell him his candidate's support for the minimum wage was shaky. He tried convincing me that Florio was still wrong to say Whitman supported a rollback, but now we were into semantics and I wasn't buying.

The other statement I wanted to challenge was Florio's oft-repeated claim that by the end of this year he will have cut ten thousand employees from the state's payroll. I did some independent checking and was unable to contradict the governor, although the number may actually be closer to eight thousand or nine thousand. Glading, of course, weighed in with numbers supporting Florio's position, but by that time—two o'clock—I realized I didn't have a story. To help fill the news hour, I switched to a quick story on pharmacy owners upset about a big drug-company merger.

So on a day when neither candidate had an event, the Florio campaign still managed to deflect my planned piece on Florio's "misstatements," plus stage a Statehouse news conference featuring law enforcement and drunk-driving groups ridiculing a relatively minor proposal in Whitman's blueprint on crime, backed up, of course, by a scathing and fact-filled press release.

The Whitman campaign is not as hard-charging. That may reflect the personalities of the candidates, the greater resources available to the governor, or both.

★ Friday, September 3 ★

Sometimes an external event alters the course of a campaign. This week Superior Court Judge Paul Levy declared the Quality Education Act (QEA), the centerpiece of Governor Florio's first term, unconstitutional. The judge ruled that it did not do enough to close the gap between New Jersey's rich and poor schools.

Suddenly the political landscape is changed. The decision raises anew the specter of the 1990 tax hikes, $1.2 billion of which were from an income tax increase earmarked for additional school aid. The state supreme court in its landmark *Abbott v. Burke* decision was about to declare New Jersey's prior system of school funding unconstitutional. Anticipating the ruling, the Florio administration in its early, heady days came out with the QEA, which redistributed school aid to favor poor and middle-class school districts. The QEA created an uproar. Florio was called "Robin Hood" for trying to shift school aid from the wealthier suburbs to the cities. The legislature stepped in, in 1991, and redirected $380 million of the school aid to property tax relief in every town.

And now a state judge, in his final act before moving up to the appellate bench, has ruled the QEA was not enough. Despite all the backlash against higher taxes and the angst over the "levelling down" of New Jersey's best public school systems, the state must dig down deeper and find a way to give *more* school aid to Newark, Trenton, Camden, and the thirty-one other "special needs" districts in which half the school kids in the state are educated, or not, as the case may be.

The impact on the gubernatorial race is unclear and a subject of considerable speculation. Republicans are saying it refocuses attention on the governor's tax hike and his hasty overreaction in 1990 to *Abbott v. Burke* (which mandated spending only an additional $440 million on special-needs schools, not $1.2 billion on all schools). Democrats are saying it should help vindicate the governor by pointing up how bad the disparity would have been without his efforts.

But its most direct effect is to undermine Christie Whitman's preparations for announcing a tax cut proposal. The state already faces a likely $1 billion deficit in the budget the next governor will have to submit in February or March of '94. If Judge Levy is right, and is backed up by the New Jersey Supreme Court, the state will need to come up with $450 million more in school aid on top of the $5 billion it's presently spending. The head of a blue-ribbon task force created by Florio and the legislature to keep the issue *out* of the '93 election, former assemblyman Albert Burstein, is already saying a tax hike is inevitable, and the *Star-Ledger* gave it a big headline. Florio's education commissioner Mary Lee Fitzgerald is saying the same thing.

Taxes and schools are traditionally the most volatile issues in New Jersey state elections. The school funding controversy combines them both. It's been a battle for twenty-three years in this state, and many other states, most notably Texas and Michigan, are grappling with it, too. The accident of a judge's personal timing has reopened the debate here two months before the election. David Blomquist of the Bergen *Record* probably got it right on "Reporters' Roundtable" this week when he said it hurts both Whitman and Florio. "It puts an issue onto the table that neither side wanted to deal with so soberly," said Blomquist.

I was on my way to the Eagleton Institute of Politics at Rutgers to interview five professors for a feature on the governor's race when the QEA decision was announced and my beeper went off. I phoned in, then turned around. While another reporter handled the straight story, I did a piece that night focussing on the ruling's impact upon the race.

The next day Jim Florio went to the Shore, and I decided I'd do a piece on how Florio has been taking credit for the clean ocean water this summer. I went to the Shore, interviewed the governor briefly, and we sent a Newark desk assistant and cameraman to Morris County to ask Whitman some questions I'd messaged up.

Back at the station, Carl Golden called to complain about the desk assistant having asked Whitman whether the clean water and the good season at the Shore might be a political omen. "What kind of stupid question is that?!" he bellowed when I got him on the phone. We argued for ten minutes. What really galled him was that I did a piece at all linking the governor to something the weather was primarily responsible for. "The last time I looked, Michael, it was spelled GOV not GOD," he said rapidly, then accused me of pandering. "You rolled him a softball!"

I defended the piece, told him the views of his candidate and beachgoers would be well represented, and suggested maybe he look at the piece before attacking it.

"Michael, I got so many nicks in my television set from throwing things at it lately, I don't know if I'll even get a picture," he shot back, and since NJN is the only TV station covering the race steadily, I knew who the comment was aimed at. I looked out my cubicle and noticed half the people in the newsroom listening avidly to my end of the conversation.

Golden was jawboning me, trying to get me to drop the story, bend it his way or make it up to his candidate the next time. The piece aired, and the next day Florio's spokesman Jon Shure complained that the beachgoers I'd interviewed didn't want to give the governor much credit. "What question did you ask them?" Shure wanted to know. I said I'd asked whether they thought Florio deserved some of the credit for the clean water, and had followed up by telling them about the sewage treatment plant upgrades and then asking again. "No wonder," said Shure. "You didn't ask the question right. The way you asked it, nobody's going to give credit to a politician."

So both spokesmen were upset, Golden with the premise, Shure with the execution. Maybe that means it was a good piece. Maybe not. After seeing the piece, Golden today apologized, but I had to initiate the call and coax it out of him.

★ Labor Day, 1993 ★

It's hard to believe that ten months of gubernatorial politicking since the presidential election have passed. The election is just eight weeks from tomorrow. It's all supposed to kick into high gear now.

What I'm looking forward to are the debates, the TV commercials, the polls, the visits by Clinton and Gore and whoever the Republicans send in, the arguments, the feverish stumping that will take place in the final ten days, and the unexpected elements that crop up in the last stage of an election.

We are no closer to knowing who will win than we were on Primary Day, June 8th. Although the most recent poll, done by the *Asbury Park Press* three weeks ago, had Whitman ahead 38 percent to 37 percent for Florio, with 22 percent undecided, stylistically and on points, Florio won the summer. His organization appeared more in charge of itself than Whitman's. The governor staked out winning positions on guns, on mandatory sentencing of criminals. He gave the appearance of being concerned about job creation and of working hard to make strides in that area. He didn't put his foot in his mouth, shake up his staff, suffer an indictment within his circle, or have to alter a major policy or backtrack on a major statement.

And yet he could lose. That vacation he was supposed to take right before Labor Day at the Jersey Shore turned into just a Saturday and Sunday off. He worked last Friday and worked again today, stumping at a street fair in Rutherford, where Christie Whitman also stumped. A sign of concern?

Twice last week he exhibited an impatience with reporters. At a news conference in his outer office a few hours after the QEA ruling came out, he chided reporters for asking questions about something they hadn't fully read: "It's gonna be an interesting discussion here today, since nobody has read in any depth the decision you're all gonna write about authoritatively," he said, and repeated the point several times. Afterwards, when a handful of reporters gathered around him at his lectern as they customarily do and Dan Weissman of the *Star-Ledger* tried to ask him some questions about the bond deal investigations, Florio turned nonresponsive, saying no one had done anything wrong and dismissing the veteran Weissman, who's been dispassionately covering Florio virtually every day for four years, with a curt "That's a nonquestion."

Back at the station, looking at the tape of the news conference, Larry Stuelpnagel, who had double-teamed it with me, called me over and played the part where Florio got testy. "Who does it remind you of?" he asked. I didn't know. "The old Florio—Florio in '81," he said, referring to the election in which a less mature, harder-edged Jim Florio came off to many people as a cold, shrill technocrat and blew a big lead.

But enough of this attempt at psycho-political analysis. Florio may well win this election, maybe even handily! Whitman has not shown great leadership ability or daring or cunning. She has shown geniality and good humor, but not much more. She has shown *politesse*, but not great skill at politics. Her organization is thinner than Florio's. Her rhetoric is thinner than Florio's. She did not use the summer to advance any issue position beyond the basic tax-economy-jobs critique upon which her entire campaign seems to depend. She spent much of the summer on the defensive. And yet she, too, could win handily! The voters may simply prefer her to Florio, or want change, or still dislike the governor so much that any reasonable alternative is worth trying.

A reporter for the Bridgewater *Courier-News*, Pat Politano, wrote yesterday that James Carville will be more of a presence after Labor Day. Jo Glading told me Carville has been "up and down" from Washington a couple of days a week, but for such a famous consultant, he's been mighty invisible. For that matter, Ed Rollins, too, is not frequently seen or quoted in the media.

I expect to learn this week whether Florio and Whitman will do a debate with me alone as moderator. NJN and the CBS affiliates in New York and Philadelphia are cohosting one of the two sanctioned debates, and I'll be on the panel, but my colleague Dan Noonan, our executive producer for public affairs, also invited Whitman and Florio to debate in a sixty-minute studio talk-show format with me asking the questions. Dan Todd seemed inclined to go along the one time we discussed it. Doug Berman, who's handling debate negotiations for Florio and who met with Todd last week for the second time, told me beforehand he thought it "unlikely" the exclusive NJN debate would come off. "Each campaign has to communicate in the way it thinks most effective," he had said to me cryptically, leaving me to wonder whether NJN's audience is too small or it had something to do with me.

On television right now are two commercials put out by the Republican and Democratic state committees. The Republican spot is about taxes, and features average New Jerseyans complaining about how badly they are hurting under the Democrats. The Democratic spot is about assault weapons, and features an Uzi being fired at a watermelon and, for a second or two, at a little blond girl's head; it's very graphic and says the NRA is coming to wage war on the Democrats, and we should stick up for the Democrats because they stuck up for us. Both state party chairs, Ginny Littell and Ray Lesniak, held news conferences last week at which they unveiled their commercials and blasted the other party's. It was all terribly predictable.

Although I haven't seen it, Jo Glading tells me the Florio campaign also brought out its first TV spot this weekend, a spot about welfare reform that is running on cable stations. So much for the pundits like

David Blomquist who predicted with such certainty that Florio's first TV commercial would be a brutally negative attack on Whitman. This one is just Jim Florio talking positively to camera. On the other hand, the fact that it's running only on cable means the buy is small, and perhaps the motivation was simply to confound the pundits and be able to say Jim Florio's first ad was positive.

Four years ago auto insurance was the big issue in the gubernatorial race. Last Friday the Florio administration disclosed that the Market Transition Facility, its answer to the despised Joint Underwriting Association of four years ago, is running a deficit that has built to $900 million and going higher. This was the third week in a row the administration tried to bury bad news by releasing it on a Friday. There is an opening in this auto insurance news for Whitman, if she is sharp enough to exploit it.

So it's on to November. And may the best person win.

PART THREE

Fall

Day one of the *real* campaign. Christie Whitman stumped with Jack Kemp at Miller Homes, a public housing project in Trenton. Kemp was in the state to help the assembly Republican majority raise money at an evening fund-raiser. Jim Florio visited a factory in Bergen County helped by his Economic Development Authority, then went south to Cherry Hill to a high-tech pharmaceutical firm to talk to the workers. In my morning call to the assignment desk at 8:10, I suggested we do two pieces today, the first day of campaigning after Labor Day. It seemed to me we would get more content that way. So I covered Whitman, and Larry Stuelpnagel covered Florio.

Whitman and Kemp arrived separately at the high-rise project. Miller Homes is a success story. Once known as "killer homes," it has been transformed by its tenants' association into a place people are trying to move into instead of out of. Tenant initiative. People power. It's a good Republican theme, and both Kemp and Whitman elaborated it after a fifteen-minute tour of the place. As HUD secretary, Kemp apparently did a lot for Miller Homes, because one of the residents, Alberta Williams, the head of the Trenton Housing Authority and a Democrat, gave him a heart-felt, teary-eyed thank you as she handed him a plaque.

Kemp made obligatory noises about Whitman, saying he likes her because she's for lower taxes and more "empowerment" of people. Whitman spoke about "bringing people into the process and giving them the tools to make a difference in their lives." When I suggested she hasn't said much about cities so far in this campaign, she grinned and said, "I have. You just haven't been with me," and reeled off a laundry list of generic solutions (more jobs, less regulation, more enterprise zones, less disparity between the rich and poor schools).

The Whitman camp must be feeling the heat over its lack of an economic plan, because today Whitman said she'll be announcing it "sometime next week." I'll be there.

That means Jim Florio has just a few more days left in which to taunt her for not having offered any specific proposals for improving the economy and creating jobs. Today he had a good line, saying she's offered nothing in the way of a plan after three years of running. "Mrs. Whitman, the lights are on, the curtain is up, and as Lennon said—John Lennon—we'd all love to see your plan." That's a line out of "Revolution," a Beatles song, and you just know Jim Florio wasn't listening to the White Album over the weekend. Come to think of it, he was at his lawyer friend Carl Poplar's beach house in Sea Isle City Saturday and Sunday; maybe he heard it there, though it probably is the work of a staffer.

Florio was sharp in Stuelpnagel's piece tonight. Asked about ethics, he shot back about illegal aliens and not paying taxes, and said he's "ready for ethical discussions" with Mrs. Whitman.

I crossed paths with Whitman again at the Republican fundraiser at the Marriott in Plainsboro, where I did a live interview with Kemp for a slot halfway through the newscast, and where she made a brief stop before heading back to NJN in Trenton to appear on our nightly call-in program. On that show she answered Florio's ethics line when the host, Mary Cummings, threw it up at her, by saying that "unlike Lyndhurst and the bond deals, nothing I did cost the taxpayers a penny"—a good response.

But she has a big problem on school funding. She told Cummings the way to come up with $450 million more for urban schools is not to raise taxes but to "reallocate" a portion of the $5 billion we currently spend on schools. That can only be done by taking it away from wealthier school districts, and that's what killed Florio and ignited a suburban revolt and the wrath of Republican legislators in the first place: the idea that the QEA involved the "levelling down" of New Jersey's best schools. Now Christie Whitman is advocating much the same thing, and she's supposedly an opponent of QEA!

★ Wednesday, September 8 ★

If Jim Florio is having a hard time figuring out how to attack a woman, as some Republicans still assert, I sure didn't see it today. Florio went to another thriving company, USA Detergent, in North Brunswick, makers of private-label laundry detergent and fabric softener. He soaked up the soapiness of the company's success, which couldn't have happened without a low-interest Florio administration EDA $2.75 million loan. He also used the occasion to accuse Whitman of distorting his record, renewed his attack on her lack of specifics, and mocked Dan Todd for having told the *Philadelphia Inquirer*, "We want to stay general as long as possible. It's driving Florio nuts that we're not being specific."

"Well, ladies and gentlemen," Florio told the two hundred or so assembled, "this election should not be about who can drive Florio nuts but about who can provide a plan that the people of New Jersey can have some faith in." I was tickled to hear him refer to himself in the third person, since he once told me he doesn't like hearing broadcasters call him Florio again and again without saying Jim or Governor.

Whitman was at a senior citizens picnic in Sandy Hook, at the northern tip of the Shore. We were back down to one package today and sent a cameraman to shoot her event.

I had called Carl Golden in the morning to see if I could interview Whitman later, at her headquarters. He said she wouldn't be there.

"Where do I have to go to see her?" I asked.

"If you don't tell anybody? You have to go the hairdresser," he said. It had been awhile since her last visit, he added, implying she'd be out of commission all afternoon. "Men can get a haircut and be out in fifteen minutes. With women it takes a little longer." Apparently, he doesn't go to any barber I've been to in the last twenty years.

I asked Golden if Dan Todd might be available. He said he'd see.

After Florio levelled his charges in North Brunswick, I called again from there and got a message to come on up to the headquarters in Clark, that Todd or, if not him, Golden would give me a response. But when I got there, Golden said neither of them would go on camera. "Dan Todd's not gonna respond to the governor," he said as if the idea were suddenly unthinkable now that the governor had taken a swipe at Todd directly.

I got some off-camera responses from Golden to use in my piece, and asked for a shot of the two of us talking to show that I'd been there and tried. Golden invited me back to his office to get a copy of Whitman's schedule for the next day, and as I passed Dan Todd's open doorway, I said hello. He was reading clips, looking haggard and depressed, and wearing around his neck his trademark bandanna, which I thought maybe he would have abandoned after Florio's dig at it, except that his pride alone is probably enough to prevent that.

He didn't particularly want to talk, but I stayed long enough to check on the prospects of the debate I'd like to moderate. He said the Florio camp wants to do only three debates, four at the most, including joint appearances on Sunday morning New York talk shows. He seemed disgusted at their unwillingness to debate more. Plaintively, he said, "I think we've got a good horse that can go around the track. They've got one that breaks down at the quarter-pole." He meant, no wonder they don't want to run it.

In his office Golden and I had a brief discussion of the fairness of my coverage, a subject I generally try not to raise but did this time because I'd sensed a little coolness lately. He said he defends it but "others here with less experience" have gotten upset at what they think are "impertinent" questions I've put to Whitman. He said he reminds them I'm the one who asked Florio about the wisdom of bringing Joe Salema back. "They think public television is an arm of the governor's office," he said, adding he's tried to explain NJN is at least as much a creature of the legislature. (State government provides half of NJN's funding, and, unlike in most states, in New Jersey public television is a state agency. We in the news department do our best to ignore that.)

Florio's most pointed attack today was on statistics Whitman uses to show that retail sales, building permits, and new business incorporations were all down in the Florio era. The governor countered with numbers showing that all three categories were up in 1992 and '93. The Florio campaign's press release contained footnotes that provided a citation to back up every factual statement in the governor's speech. Twenty-one footnotes! In a press release! I had never seen that before, and it's a testament to the strength of the campaign's research arm.

One small problem. The governor's campaign schedule said he would visit USA Detergent to meet "the one thousand new employees" and their families whose jobs had been made possible by the EDA loan. The president of the company, a young Jewish man whose Lubovitcher relatives and partners stood out in the crowd of salesmen and suppliers, told me on camera he had "more than a hundred employees" at this plant "and maybe double that." On a day when the governor was talking about factual accuracy, his campaign exaggerated the story line by at least a factor of five. I pointed this out in my piece tonight.

Arm of the governor's office, indeed.

★ Saturday, September 11 ★

The Florio campaign has opened another battlefront. On Thursday Jim Florio proposed tightening the welfare system by requiring single mothers on welfare to provide the name of the fathers of their children or else lose their monthly grant. It was one of several proposals Florio presented to the White House task force on welfare reform at a hearing in North Jersey. It looked like a blatant appeal to "Reagan Democrats" and other conservative voters who disapprove of the welfare system or resent the people on it.

The Whitman campaign went ballistic. Carl Golden issued a statement that afternoon under Whitman's name that accused Florio of "playing to the most vicious stereotype of a welfare recipient in the most demeaning and degrading way possible.

"What is the Governor's next idea in his headlong rush to embrace extreme right wing radicalism? A program of tatoos for welfare mothers? A badge sewn on to their clothing identifying them as welfare recipients? Creation of colonies, like leper colonies, where welfare recipients would be forced to live? How about an involuntary re-location program into camps?

"Is the governor willing and eager to see women and their children thrown into the streets by a loss of welfare benefits? How many cardboard boxes will become a child's next home?"

The statement was written by Golden. Whether it was cleared by Whitman, who was stumping through Burlington County that afternoon, I do not know, but it was certainly hyperbolic, as if the Whitman campaign sensed that Florio's idea might not sit well with many women, child advocates, and liberals, and so they played it up.

That night we taped "Reporters' Roundtable," and two of the panelists used the word "pandering" in regard to the governor's proposal.

The next day "a stern-faced and testy Mr. Florio," as Jerry Gray in the *New York Times* put it, called a noon Statehouse news conference and blasted Whitman for issuing a "knee-jerk, intemperate statement before she even had a chance to study the proposals." He called her statement "viciously worded" and said it is "an insult to victims of the Holocaust to make allusions to Nazi Germany, which is clearly what is being done here." Florio defended his proposal passionately. He said it was designed to force fathers to take responsibility for their children, nothing more, nothing less. He said it grew out of two-and-a-half years' worth of study and discussion of welfare, and the fact he was presenting it now, seven weeks before the election, had nothing to do with politics. (I don't think anyone in the room believed that.) Jim Goodman of the Trenton *Times*, the dean of the press corps, kept asking, what about the child who gets hurt as a result of the mother's being denied benefits? Florio said no child will be hurt, the families would still get food stamps and Medicaid. That skirts the question of how the family gets by without cash. Echoing his social-policy advisor, Brenda Bacon, Florio took great umbrage at the question, what if the woman doesn't know who the father is? Bacon says the question is based on a horrible stereotype that is patently false, as most women who get pregnant know who the responsible party is. I asked, what about women who may have multiple sexual partners? Florio called that a "condescending" suggestion and "not one that I am willing to base policy on in this state."

"[This is] what being governor is all about, being able to take leadership positions on things of importance to all our people," Florio said, appealing to the reporters to understand he is dead serious about this. Florio has become something of an expert on welfare reform. His embrace two years ago of Assemblyman Wayne Bryant's ideas on welfare, including that welfare mothers be denied extra benefits for extra children, led to the state's Family Development Program and Florio's being selected to head the National Governors' Association task force on welfare reform. At his news conference, Florio said he is for "change" and for trying to fix the "broken" welfare system, while "[Whitman's] for keeping it where it is."

Whitman was holed up at Pontefract Friday afternoon with a small group of advisors, working on her economic plan and unavailable for a response. Once again, the Florio campaign has set the agenda, and the Whitman campaign has been forced to respond. Florio appears to be trying to outflank Whitman on the right, on this issue and on crime. The approach is comparable to Bill Clinton's trying to be a centrist Democrat during the '92 campaign, and, as such, it bears the signs of Carville and Begala. Hazel Gluck calls it a "base appeal to blue-collar bigots . . . the basest possible." But Jo Glading said, "It's not pandering, Michael. You know the governor is a very serious-minded man." Florio seemed annoyed at me for pestering him at his news conference about the political motivation.

Welfare reform must be polling well for the governor, because his past accomplishment is the subject of his first cable ad and now comes this new thrust. It joins guns as the issues he wishes to push. The Florio camp's first over-the-air TV commercial (as opposed to just on cable) began running Tuesday night. It's a gun commercial that suggests the NRA is behind the Whitman campaign and prepared to spend $1 million to defeat Jim Florio. "Whitman and the NRA, Perfect Together," says the tag line. Even Republicans admit it's a clever ad, but the Whitman camp thinks the election is about the economy, not guns, and sees no need to respond to the commercial.

I was in Burlington County Thursday covering Whitman when NJN news director Bill Jobes decided he wanted my story to be about TV commercials, not Whitman's day on the stump. Some monkey business had been discovered in the spots the Republican and Democratic state committees had put out; the Republicans' man-in the-street spot had featured two relatives of local Republican party officials; the Democrats had doctored a newspaper headline. I'd known that and passed on it, but Jobes thought it was a good story, better than another day with Whitman on the campaign trail, so after putting up some token resistance, I agreed to shift gears, even though it was 2:30 and I was forty-five minutes south of Trenton. We lumped three things into my story: the errors in the ads, the new Florio anti-NRA commercial, and a letter sent the day before to seventy TV and radio stations by the Florio campaign's lawyer, Angelo Genova, threatening a lawsuit against any station that accepted a commercial from the NRA or any other group that "distorts Governor Florio's record or infringes on the privacy rights of the Governor, his family, appointees, associates, or friends." Christie Whitman found that laughable, coming from "somebody who sent a couple of people onto my property and sent two photographers to my sister-in-law's in New York to ask questions about 'the Whitman' who lives there." She accused the governor of not understanding the first amendment.

The Florio campaign must be trying to inoculate itself against negative ads, but threatening to sue the media is a hardball tactic that won't win friends in station board rooms. "I think they're cracking up and don't know what to do with themselves," observed Hazel Gluck, the Whitman co-chair.

The Genova letter coincided with the joint announcement of a debate schedule. There will be three debates: two, big multisponsored ones as required by the public financing law, plus one joint appearance on Gabe Pressman's Sunday morning show on WNBC-TV in New York. Out of seventy invitations, just three were accepted. A joint statement bore all the markings of the Florio campaign, especially the tightly drawn language restricting joint appearances ("If the candidates are to appear before the audience at the same time, namely, when one candidate is speaking the other candidate is also present before the audience, then no questions to either candidate, whether from the audience, the moderator, or any other type questioner, are permitted. Each candidate will give only his or her appropriate statement."). I didn't get "my" debate, but the uptightness of the guidelines reassured me that it probably had little to do with me or NJN and a lot more to do with Jim Florio's aversion to giving Whitman too much side-by-side exposure. The New York Times Magazine asked the two to pose together for a photo, to accompany an upcoming story about the race; the Florio camp said no.

Meanwhile, as I write this, Judge Marianne Espinosa Murphy's term on the bench expires in twenty-five minutes—at twelve midnight Saturday. My friend Phil Carchman, the judge, ruled that neither the executive branch nor the judiciary can tell the senate how to conduct its business. The state supreme court heard an appeal Wednesday but, surprisingly, has not ruled. The senate has called a special session for Monday to reconfirm Murphy for another seven-year term, as opposed to the lifetime tenure she sought. But the judge has said she won't demean herself and her fellow judges by accepting, and Governor Florio insists she can't legally be reconfirmed unless he renominates her, which she has asked him not to do. The senate thinks otherwise. Yesterday Florio and senate Democratic leader John Lynch made one last appeal to senate president Donald DiFrancesco and to Christie Whitman to whip the Republican caucus into line and do the right thing, to no avail. This morning's *Star-Ledger* front page carried an emotional account of the farewell party thrown for Murphy yesterday at the Morris County courthouse by her fellow judges.

And as if the news itself were not enough to occupy one's mind, our coverage of the campaign is a constant issue for me. First thing Thursday morning I got a call from Carl Golden, furious at NJN over unequal treatment of the candidates on "New Jersey Tonight," the station's call-in show. Whitman had been the guest Tuesday night and gotten several calls from obvious Florio-campaign plants. Florio came on the next night and the first caller congratulated the governor on how courageous he'd been to hike taxes, and there were no hostile calls after that. Whitman plants apparently weren't able to get through. Golden said the Whitman camp is convinced that NJN "is an arm of the governor's office." He said he didn't necessarily believe that, but that lots of people around Whitman and in the legislature have seen us at the station become "handmaidens of the governor's office" and that they were going to make it an issue. I said, obviously they don't understand how the media works. "They may not know the media, but they know what they see," he said, and then, *sotto voce*, warned me, "If she gets elected, you guys are in for a rough ride." Realizing a threat had been issued, he quickly softened it.

In Burlington County a few hours later, I asked Jason Volk, one of the two young men who drives Whitman around, whether I could ride with her to her next stop and discuss the NJN situation. Whitman okayed it, and I got to ride in her little aquamarine Mercury Sable, me in the back, she in the front craning her long neck around at me as I explained that what happened on "New Jersey Tonight" must have been sheer coincidence because there was no way the station was working for Florio. She said she wouldn't have thought so, but that after enough unfair incidents "you start saying to yourself, hey, there's gotta be something going on here." She complained about the time an NJN reporter asked her questions off a sheet of paper that were direct quotes from a Florio press release that hadn't even come out yet. I tried to explain how that happens innocently. The conversation ended abruptly after four or five minutes when we arrived at Whitman's next event, but I think I had mollified her.

Back at the station, I called Jo Glading for some information. She told me that I had taken a "cheap shot" at her the night before, when, in my piece, I had pointed out the error in her press release about the number of employees at the plant Florio would be visiting. The error was in the "schedule," not the press release, she said, and why hadn't I called her for an explanation. Right—at four o'clock in the afternoon, from a van with no phone in it, when just getting a three- or four-minute piece with both candidates in it on the air every day is often a near-miracle. I told her she can't expect to be able to respond to every little thing that comes up.

I hung up the phone, rushing to get back to writing my script, when cameraman Rafy Rosario poked his head into my workspace. "Hey, man, I thought your piece last night was good but a little, how you say, one-sided?" Against who? I asked. "Against Whitman." Thanks, Raf.

An election like this one becomes very consuming for those involved in it. It has a way of shutting out other news and affairs. You say, the Israelis and the PLO made peace yesterday? That's nice. What's Christie doing tomorrow?

The Clinton administration is beginning to weigh in. On Friday, health and human services secretary Donna Shalala appeared with Florio, at a New Jersey Women's Health Network conference. Today, Attorney General Janet Reno lent the governor her considerable popularity, making three stops with him on what was ostensibly a nonpolitical fact-finding tour. In Hackensack, they looked at assault weapons together and called for a national ban similar to New Jersey's. In Piscataway they went to a school and talked to kids about violence. In a poor neighborhood in Trenton they visited a community-run "mini–police station."

I picked up the tour in Trenton, where Reno did her job well. She spoke highly of New Jersey's crime-fighting initiatives and of the leadership that inspired them. Are you here to help the governor get re-elected? I shouted to her at an outdoor press conference. No, she said, that was not her purpose. She was here to get ideas and see how New Jersey could be helped by the federal government. Right.

Whitman called the visit by Reno "inappropriate," given that her U.S. attorney for New York is reportedly investigating bond sales that center around key allies of the governor. Whitman, in Atlantic City to give a speech, asked what kind of signal that sends. But Reno shook off the criticism and proclaimed that nothing she said or did here would have any effect on any investigation. Florio, standing next to Reno, wouldn't even comment on Whitman's charge. "I'm not getting into politics today," he said, trying to foster the illusion that this was an official visit and nonpolitical.

I got through to James Carville in Washington today after several unsuccessful attempts this summer. He had to jump off and take a call from Greece, where he's also doing some consulting this season, but he got right back to me. I had written asking him if he would appear on television with Ed Rollins, who was willing, but Carville said he didn't see how it would benefit Jim Florio. He said he was "dumbfounded" by the Whitman camp's reaction to the welfare reform proposal, having expected her to agree with it. And he suggested the New Jersey press corps take a close look at Lawrence Kudlow and Steve Forbes, Whitman's economic advisors who are shaping the proposal she'll unveil soon. They're the same people who brought us trickle-down economics and the huge federal budget deficit, he said, and they are much more newsworthy right now than he. "My influence is on a TV spot that runs for a week. Theirs could be on the economic performance of New Jersey for the next four years," Carville said.

I asked if the Florio campaign's been keeping him under wraps. To the contrary, he said. They want him to do more things, like talking to reporters. Although he's in Washington much of the time, he talks to New Jersey four times a day and has "a great working relationship with Jim Andrews," the campaign manager.

The strategy for beating Whitman, he said, has been "to prevent her from getting traction by being aggressive at every juncture"; to have the governor be gubernatorial and get into the fray later; to "show people she doesn't have the understanding or judgment to be governor; above all, to be aggressive and refute everything they try to do.

"Attack when possible, refute when necessary," he said, summing it up.

As we spoke, an example of the strategy was on display at the Statehouse, where a Jewish Holocaust survivor, a rabbi, and a relative of Holocaust victims were holding a news conference to blast Whitman for her insensitivity in comparing Florio's welfare reform idea to the practices of the Nazis. They did not do this on their own. A Florio aide would later say to me, "Of course we rounded up Jewish leaders to respond."

★　Wednesday, September 15　★

"Seven weeks to go—how are you holding up?" I asked Dan Todd.

"All I know is, there's one day less than yesterday. It's just like calvin' time. Take 'em as they come," said the cowboy–campaign manager.

We were in his office. His sister was holed up in her office across the hall knocking off previously scheduled press interviews with the *Village Voice* and the African-American *Philadelphia Tribune*. I needed a reaction to today's Bergen *Record* poll, so I interviewed Todd, who today was wearing a purple kerchief and a royal blue t-shirt under his oxford dress shirt. I teased him about adhering to his style despite the governor's criticism. (Back at the station tonight, in the control room during the news, you couldn't hear Todd's first bite because too many people were commenting on "that thing around his neck.")

The *Record* poll had the race a tie! Forty-three percent for Florio, 43 percent for Whitman. The percentage of undecideds is down to 13, with 1 percent for "other." Those 13 percent theoretically will decide the election. How to win them over? Tighter welfare rules? A tax cut?

Florio seemed less encouraged by the poll results than Todd, who argued that given all the advantages a sitting governor enjoys, plus the fact that Florio's TV ads had started running and Whitman's hadn't, a dead heat was good news for the challenger. Florio's line was, we knew all along this would be a tough race and, given that I'm the underdog, we're doing better than you might have expected. It was the same line Jo Glading had given me over the phone early this morning. It was impossible to budge Florio off that answer today. I tried twice.

I've seen both candidates the past two days. They are starting to criticize each other's mind-set. It's subtle and hasn't been picked up by the press yet. Whitman told a luncheon of state worker union shop stewards that with Jim Florio everything is "us against them," that there is something inherently divisive about Florio's approach to issues and that he's too political; everything he does, he injects politics into, and it's time to open things up and let a little fresh air in, Whitman said.

Florio told a bunch of environmentalists gathered to endorse him on a boardwalk in Spring Lake that Whitman is focusing so narrowly on economic issues she fails to see that crime and welfare reform and the environment are important also. "I see problems as connected to one another. She doesn't," he said and went on to explain that weak policies in any of those areas can all have economic consequences, as we're seeing in Florida, where random murders of tourists are killing the tourist industry.

Both observations have a ring of truth to them.

Another difference I noticed today is that there is a more guarded and controlled style around Florio and a more open style around Whitman. Ask Whitman or Dan Todd a question on camera, and you get a fairly straight and spontaneous answer, whether you agree with it or not. Ask Jim Florio and, if it's on the issue of the day, you get the line of the day. At

the environmental endorsement, Jon Shure noticed a man on the periphery of the crowd holding what looked like a folded-up sail or dropcloth of
some kind under the arm of his windbreaker. Worried that the "sail"
might be a banner with a negative message on it, Shure tapped Rich, a
young advance man, and together they moseyed over and cased the guy,
ultimately asking him what he had under his arm. Once a first-rate reporter, Shure at that moment had evolved into a leader of a protection
squad. Also indicative of the different attitudes of the two camps is the
fact that the Whitmans are allowing an NJN crew and producer to follow
them around for a semi-behind-closed-doors post-election documentary;
Florio, who was asked first, turned down the project. (Of course, that
could be attributable to the Whitmans simply having more stars in their
eyes at the thought of a sixty-minute documentary memorializing a six-
month period in their lives.)

"The 'control' you're talking about is everyone just heading in
the same direction," said Audrey Kelly, another top press aide in the
governor's office, when I tried out my observation on her. "Everyone has
the same ideas. That's why you won't see us making as many stupid
mistakes as the Whitman campaign. Our control is self-imposed.
Everybody's on the same message. Her spontaneity is really 'out of
control.'"

The joint endorsement of Florio by the New Jersey Environmental Federation and the Sierra Club are meaningful and deserved. Although he has tilted toward business in the past year, compelled to by the
alarm over unemployment and his impending re-election fight, the governor has a good environmental record. He signed the Clean Water Enforcement Act and the Pollution Prevention Act, two tough pieces of environmental legislation. He pushed recycling over waste incineration and is an
advocate of mass transit. And today, with the Atlantic as his backdrop and
a beautiful sunny sky, he gave himself credit, again, for the clean water
and clean beaches this summer and talked up his Highlands initiative as
the next great frontier for preserving New Jersey's precious resources.

Whitman got a boost yesterday from a large state worker union
local, the Communications Workers of America (CWA) Local 1037. You
would think that with all her talk about cutting government spending,
state workers would be the last people in her corner. But Governor Florio

has been at odds with the CWA for most of his governorship. In an effort to control spending, he tried to break the union contract one year. He takes pride in having cut the state workforce, and he and the union have dueled over whether enough of those cuts have come from the higher echelons of government where, according to the union, the "cronies, the fat cats, and political appointees" push paper, do political errands, and feather their nests. Whitman was the boss of 400 Local 1037 members when she was president of the Board of Public Utilities, and the leader of the local told me on camera yesterday, "She was the best employer we ever had, bar none." A straw poll of the local's members went 700-plus for Whitman to less than 200 for Florio.

The Florio campaign started running a new TV spot last night. It says Whitman's assault weapons position, her proposal that drunk drivers be given special license plates if they need to commute to work instead of having their licenses suspended for six months, and her opposition to more mandatory sentencing, put her at odds with most New Jerseyans on matters of crime control. "She just doesn't understand," says a disapproving narrator. It's a strong commercial. If you didn't know anything about Whitman—and the *Record* poll says 24 percent still do not—you could think the woman was a loon.

Florio had a strange lapse yesterday. At a training institute in Newark, he visited a class of welfare recipients learning how to use computers, then delivered remarks aimed at Whitman's criticism of his welfare reform proposal. Afterwards, talking to reporters, he said his proposal would take away only 20 percent of a welfare mother's grant if she failed to name the father of her child. That was a change from what he had said last week, and several of us told him so. No, no, look at the proposal, he said. It's a 20 percent cut. Florio ducked into a room for an interview with the *Washington Post,* and Jon Shure tried to explain the confusion; under current law the grant could be cut by only 20 percent; eventually, the governor would try to get a federal waiver so that the whole grant could be cut off. It seemed disingenuous of the governor, if that's the case, not to have said so himself.

Florio came out, got into his car with Jerry Gray of the *New York Times,* who was riding with him all day and all over the state, and left.

Later, back in Trenton, Shure called me to say that in the car the governor realized he had been mistaken. His proposal *is* to cut off the entire grant. "He misspoke," I said. "He misspoke," Shure agreed. It was unlike Jim Florio. Both David Wald of the *Star-Ledger* and I put it in our stories. When I saw Florio today, I expected him to say something about his mistake of the day before, but he didn't. He had forgotten, or it was unimportant to him, or he had too many other things on his mind, or he doesn't like to acknowledge mistakes.

His campaign staff, however, impressed me yesterday. I had interviewed Whitman about the welfare issue at the CWA luncheon in Cranford. She had said some inflammatory things about welfare mothers not wanting to name the father because in some cases it was their *own* father or brother, and the woman would fear retribution. The Florio kids who follow her with a camcorder and tape deck were taking it all in. I went to Newark to cover the governor, then drove back to Trenton to edit, and when I got there a Florio press release was on my desk. It contained Whitman's remarks to NJN, Jo Glading's commentary on them, and was headlined, "Shame on You, Mrs. Whitman."

The Florio rapid-response machine is relentless.

Florio is slashing at Whitman. He can be deliciously cutting or, as they say in Maine, wicked good. In a little room of welfare mothers and Newarkers yesterday, Florio began the attack portion of his remarks this way: "Every time she leaves her estate and goes out to campaign. . . ."

It almost didn't matter what he said next. That said it all.

★ **Friday, September 17** ★

Whoops! The Florio campaign has committed a boo-boo. Yesterday, while picking up the endorsement of the state AFL-CIO in Atlantic City, the governor lashed out at Bill Haines, Jr., a Burlington County farmer who serves on Christie Whitman's economic task force. Florio told the labor leaders, here's a man facing fines for violating pesticide regulations on his farm and providing inadequate toilets to his migrant workers. Only problem is, the Florio campaign had the wrong Bill Haines, Jr. As many agricultural people in New Jersey seem to know, there's "peaches Bill," and "cranberry Bill." Both are big-time Burlington County farmers. But it's "peaches Bill," a state senator, who faces the fine. It's "cranberry Bill" who heads Whitman's agriculture advisory committee.

Whitman wasted no time in trying to capitalize on this rare Florio mistake. She changed her schedule and called a Statehouse news conference for 3:30—only her third sit-down Statehouse news conference all year! With Ed Rollins and Hazel Gluck looking on, she expressed outrage at Florio's attempt to smear her by smearing her supporter and demanded an apology.

The gaffe got pretty good play in the newspapers, perhaps in part because it is so unlike the Florio campaign, which prides itself on being thorough, meticulous, and on target. As Carl Golden put it, "They work hard to project the image of a well-oiled machine. When you have that image, and you make a mistake, you fall farther and harder." He also thinks the episode "reinforces the image many people have of Jim Florio" as a hard-driving, aggressive, go-for-the-jugular campaigner.

I barely caught Florio for an interview this afternoon as he was leaving the Statehouse for Drumthwacket. He said he was sending a note of apology to Mr. Haines, but when I asked if he might also apologize to "Mrs. Whitman" his eyes got a little steely and he said, "This is someone who started the campaign by attacking my wife incorrectly, and I haven't heard from her since then." He was referring to the Whitman radio ad last April that questioned the expenditure on Lucinda Florio's staff, an ad that never ran because the amount was inflated. Either it really angered him, or it gives him an excuse to express a little indignation, because there was also the slightest quiver in his face as he defended his wife.

What I didn't know at the time, but learned later, was that as Florio was in his office deciding whether to wait around for me to arrive or stand me up and go home, Harold Hodes walked in with a bowl that contained two pieces of fruit. This is a peach and this is a cranberry, advised the governor's confidante.

If Florio goofed yesterday, Whitman did something worse: she flip-flopped. On the governor's welfare reform proposal, no less. That's what happens when you expose yourself to the Statehouse press corps; you run the risk of making news you may not have intended to make.

After berating Florio for his Bill Haines error, Whitman was asked about the welfare reform debate of the past week. To my shock when I subsequently heard about it, she said she agreed with the thrust of the governor's proposal requiring welfare mothers to identify the father of a child, except that she would cut the woman's cash grant by 20 percent instead of taking it away entirely. This from the candidate whose statement last week called the proposal "cruel, heartless, vicious," part of a "headlong rush to extreme right-wing radicalism," and compared it to practices associated with Germany under Hitler!

I can only assume that Whitman has been trying to retreat from that statement since it came out. Though I've been told Carl Golden wrote the statement, Golden will not confirm that for me. Nor will he tell me whether Christie Whitman approved it before it went out. A person close to Whitman says she did not. If it hadn't caused trouble, I think Golden would tell. That he won't leads me to believe he, or somebody, screwed up. "Carl's been doing a lot of damage control lately, don't you think?" said Channel 9 reporter Brenda Flanagan to me this morning as we both watched Florio give a speech. Yeah, I thought, and maybe some damage.

Golden and Whitman, of course, both deny that there is any flip-flop here or even an evolution! Golden is very clever. The original statement blasted Florio for seeking a total cutoff if a welfare mother is "unable" to name the father. That's still her position, he says. She would penalize women who *refuse* to supply a name, but not totally and not if the woman is unable to because she doesn't know, or is legitimately afraid to name, the father. The tone of her position has changed completely. Gone are the inflammatory references to camps and leper colonies. But Golden and Whitman—who was interviewed on the subject for my piece today by NJN reporter Mary Cummings on the boardwalk in Wildwood— say nothing has changed.

The Bergen *Record* caught the essence of the day. Its headline across the top of page one this morning said: "CONFUSION ON THE CAMPAIGN TRAIL," and beneath it, "Whitman now backs sanctions, too," on one side, and "Florio camp issues apology after attack on wrong man" on the other.

A veteran observer of the state scene said to me this week that the campaign has been pretty low-level so far and that both candidates have disappointed him. "Jim Florio has a story to tell, and he's not telling it," said Tom O'Neill, of the Partnership for New Jersey.

I think there's some truth to that. I saw a commercial for New York mayor David Dinkins, who's also standing for re-election this fall, that named some of Dinkins's accomplishments. They were all news to me, and they were impressive.

I think Florio needs a similar commercial. His two over-the-air TV spots attack Whitman without even saying his name. On the stump, he tells the schmaltzy story of his grandfather Giuseppe, the immigrant, his father, Vincenzo, the shipyard worker, himself, the high school drop-out who becomes governor, and now his daughter at whose medical school graduation he spoke in South Carolina this spring, Dr. Catherine Florio. It's a touching story about the American Dream, but it's not likely to win the votes of people worried that the American Dream may be over. On the stump he also defends his record and gives some of its highlights. But to me a large part of the Florio story is the many good bills he has signed and sensible policies he has backed that people are not generally aware of.

The commercial I think he needs is the one that says:

Did you know Jim Florio raised the minimum wage in New Jersey to five dollars and five cents, eighty cents higher than the rest of the nation; that he required insurance companies to cover routine mammographies; that he banned discrimination against homosexuals, established an office of minority health, and established a family-leave policy in New Jersey three years before the federal government got around to one? Did you know he pushed recycling to the point where we now recycle 60 percent of our waste; that he fixed it so health insurers cannot turn someone down because of a pre-existing condition; and gave crime victims the right to attend parole hearings? Jim Florio, fighting for you.

Instead, his ads ridicule Whitman, as if a calculation has been made that you can't get undecided voters to vote *for* Florio. You have to convince them the alternative is worse.

★   Sunday, September 19   ★

I think they are breathing a little easier at Florio headquarters. A new *Star-Ledger*/Eagleton poll has Florio up by 9 points, 47 percent to 38. A poll by the *Asbury Park Press* has Florio up by 6 points, 42 percent to 36. This is what the Florio campaign's own internal polls have been showing as well, a lead in the high single digits. I learned that from a campaign staffer a few days ago, and it explains why the Florio camp was a bit disturbed when the *Record* poll had the race a dead heat.

The secondary numbers in the polls suggest Florio's support is soft. They confirm that taxes and jobs are people's number-one concern, but that crime and assault weapons, education, the environment, and welfare are matters they care about.

The most interesting statistic concerned gender. In the Eagleton poll, men were about evenly divided between Florio and Whitman, 44 percent to 42. But women favored Florio by 51 percent to 32. Pollsters say women tend to support Democrats more than men do, but this is the year a woman is trying to become New Jersey's first female governor.

Were women voters impressed by Jim Florio's sustained and well-publicized attempt this summer to save the career of Judge Marianne Espinosa Murphy? A few perhaps, but more are probably moved by his attempt to rid the state of assault weapons and wish he'd go further. Women tend to be big supporters of gun control, say the pollsters.

★   Monday, September 20   ★

While I stayed in-house today and put together a feature piece on the way the two campaigns have kids recording and videotaping virtually every word the rival candidate says, Jim Florio was getting endorsed by the New Jersey Fraternal Order of Police (FOP), and Christie Whitman was holed up at Pontefract briefing key legislators and her campaign co-chairs on the substance of the economic plan she will unveil tomorrow.

The Florio campaign is so active it's almost hydra-headed. While the governor was receiving the FOP endorsement in Hoboken and, later,

Cherry Hill (once in each media market), Congressman Bob Torricelli was holding a news conference at the Statehouse for the Florio campaign to lay out the case against Christie Whitman's handling of the sale of watershed land by the Hackensack Water Company when she was BPU president. This was an issue Cary Edwards tried to raise in the final days of the GOP primary, without much success. Now the Florio campaign is trotting it out again. If Christie Whitman were given to the sort of country answers I got from Bill Clinton last fall, she'd say, "They're not gonna make that watershed dog hunt on me." (With Clinton, it was "tax" dog.)

As if they are not busy enough, the Florio campaign has the governor going to Newark tomorrow morning for a breakfast and press conference to announce Business Leaders for Florio, a group of about two dozen CEOs, including the heads of Merck Pharmaceuticals, Liz Claiborne, and the state's largest bank, First Fidelity, which is hosting the event. It's an obvious piece of counter-programming on a day when Whitman presents her economic plan.

The importance of that event is very much on my mind tonight. The outcome of the election could hinge on what she says tomorrow at 2:30 at the Ramada Inn across from her headquarters in Clark.

★ Tuesday, September 21 ★

There was an air of urgency in the hallway outside meeting room G at the Ramada. Two kinds of people milled about, waiting for the big event: reporters and Republican notables. A makeshift security blockade was set up to check reporters' IDs and keep out the Florio spies. Inside the room, filled with cameras and tripods, more people waited, and there was a sense in the air that the election was about to be altered dramatically.

"Are you ready now?" David Wald asked Whitman as she collected herself behind the podium and prepared to speak. He was teasing her for having gotten such mileage out of "when I'm ready."

"I was just about to say it," she said, looking down at Wald in the first row, two seats away from me. To the roomful of people, she explained the reference, and then, with a sense of occasion, said, "I am now ready."

Standing behind her on the stage were the two legislative

leaders, assembly speaker Haytaian and senate president DiFrancesco. Soon a late-arriving Tom Kean would take a place up there with them. Off to the side were the two Republican budget chairmen, Senator Robert Littell and Assemblyman Rodney Frelinghuysen, and Littell's wife, Ginny, the Republican state chair. Seated in the small audience were Steve Forbes and Larry Kudlow, the twin towers of Whitman's economic team. Every key member of the Whitman cabal was in the room, including media consultant Mike Murphy and his fancy film camera. He actually clapped a clap-board in front of the camera as Whitman entered the room.

A month ago, when she first started hinting about a tax cut, I thought it would be a potent weapon that could tip the election in her favor. The tax cut proposal I heard today is grander than anything I had imagined—a 30 percent cut in the state income tax—and yet it seems flimsy.

Whitman proposed cutting the income tax rate by 10 percent a year for three years in a row, for married couples with taxable income under $80,000 and single taxpayers under $40,000. People in higher tax brackets would get slightly smaller cuts. The top state income tax rate, which Florio doubled, would come down from its current 7 percent level to 5.6 percent; people now paying 3.5 percent would pay 2.45 percent. At the bottom of the scale, she would raise the threshold at which state income tax kicks in from the current $3,000 to $7,500, freeing 350,000 low-income New Jerseyans, by her estimate, from the tax rolls. She would also repeal Florio's extension of the sales tax to telephone and fax machine bills, end a surcharge on the corporate income tax, and eliminate a special fuel tax paid by truckers. "My message," she said: "New Jersey is open for business again!" So far so good.

To pay for all this, however, she promised to find $500 million in savings through "management reforms," such as voluntary worker furloughs, privatization of services, "unnecessary overhead," cutting back on "professional services," and ending "double coverage" of state workers whose spouses have health insurance through private employers. Not very convincing. On top of that, she promised to hold the growth in spending to 3 percent a year, the rate of inflation, and to use her line-item veto and impoundment powers to a degree no New Jersey governor ever has before.

She also promised immediately to "reduce the number of workers holding patronage jobs at salaries above $50,000 a year, sell the governor's helicopter, cut the governor's office staff by 20 percent, end the system of forcing taxpayers to pay for three residences for the governor, chauffeur-driven cars for thirty-five state officials, and the statutorily mandated practice of buying art works for public buildings." All of which would save a few million bucks.

To many reporters in the room, it didn't add up.

"Look in your packets. The numbers are all there," Whitman said several times. But they weren't, and several cranky reporters let her know it. "We'll get that to you," she said.

She was skating.

How are you gonna plug a $500 million hole next year, and $1.2 billion eventually, when there's already a structural deficit of at least a billion dollars in the next budget? reporters asked.

"I'm not accepting a billion-dollar deficit right now," said Whitman, though she herself had used that number all summer, and the reporters reminded her so.

The faces of the bigwigs behind her started to droop.

What about school aid and the likelihood of a court order that $450 million more be spent on urban schools? What about all the spending increases mandated by law, like Medicaid and pensions? What was she gonna cut? If you cut school aid or municipal aid, property taxes will go up. Whitman said she wouldn't cut those, or the homestead rebate program. "All we have to find is four-and-a-half cents on every dollar the state now spends. I'm convinced we can do it," she said. But the press was far from convinced.

In their hands, reporters held copies of a Florio press release containing all of Whitman's past put-downs of quick-fix tax cuts. "It insults the intelligence of New Jerseyans and shows contempt for their finances to dangle election-year handouts before the voters only to take them away once comfortably installed in office," she had said back in February. As recently as June she said, "In an election year, the governor should resist the cynical call to promise tax cuts for the purposes of re-election."

Now here she was, doing just that, and saying that with her it would be different "because this is a carefully worked-out three-year plan and the numbers add up." Unfortunately, the numbers on her own handout didn't even add up; the column of management reforms that said it totalled $500 million when properly added totalled $430 million.

Kean and Haytaian chimed in to support the plan, DiFrancesco as well, but he spit out the words reluctantly and with difficulty. A contentious half-hour news conference was cut off by Keith Nahigian, one of the two young aides who drive and shepherd Whitman everywhere and keep her on schedule.

Back at the station, reaction was negative. My colleagues thought the plan "desperate," "irresponsible," "bullshit." After seeing some tape, several commented on how "shaky" Whitman had seemed. "She didn't believe in what she was saying," observed a top producer. I said I hadn't noticed a wobbly demeanor so much as wobbly content.

The story led our newscast. "Christie Whitman went for the long bomb today," said back-up anchor Trish Degasperis, reading the lead I'd written while screening tape in the back seat of a van that was tearing down the New Jersey Turnpike toward Trenton in the late afternoon.

Whitman has her first TV commercial out today, a spot in which she looks straight into the camera and promises to "cut your taxes every year for the next three years." I saw it today at Florio headquarters, where they had taped it off the air, and where I stopped on my way to Clark so that I could tape a sit-down interview with James Carville for use later in the week. The mood there was almost giddy. Carville, Doug Berman, Harold Hodes, Ray Lesniak, Jim Andrews, Jo Glading, plus three recent imports from elsewhere in the Florio-Clinton apparatus, Rich Gannon, Jon Shure, and Brenda Bacon—the whole Florio gang was there, plus CNN and four print reporters all wanting a piece of Carville or just hanging out between shows (Florio had done a morning event in Newark). Everybody was anticipating Whitman's big speech. The fax machine was churning out anti-Whitman handouts. The hubbub was infectious, the chatter between the reporters and the Democratic operatives very chummy.

By tonight the Florio campaign really had not reacted yet to the Whitman plan—which may be why the Whitman camp pushed back the time of its unveiling from the original 1:30 to 2:30, to give the Florio camp a smaller window of response time before the evening newscasts and the newspaper deadlines. But I can imagine how they are going to skewer it.

They'll say it's a fraud and a hoax. They'll ask how she'll possibly fix the school funding problem. They'll say that holding state aid down will inevitably hike local property taxes. They'll ask how she'll pay for rising entitlements like Medicaid and pensions, and what programs she'll be forced to cut and what institutions she'll be forced to close. And they'll ask if she's really *serious!*

I am not always right about these things. My feel for the public pulse is probably no better than yours. Maybe people are hungering for this new direction Christie Whitman wants to go in. But I think she lost the election today.

★ Wednesday, September 22 ★

Governor Florio was incredibly cutting in his remarks today about the Whitman plan. He held up two pages of the four she handed out to reporters yesterday. "Two pages," he said, waving them for effect. "Three years in the making."

He scorned the plan for its vagueness on the spending cuts. He called it welfare for the rich, arguing that the top 5.5 percent of the economic scale will get 40 percent of the tax breaks. "This isn't a plan. It's voodoo re-do," he said, another of his good lines.

And there were more.

> This plan is not about helping New Jersey through the next four years. It's about helping Mrs. Whitman through the next six weeks. No one in history has cut taxes 30 percent, not Ronald Reagan, not Tom Kean, not the 3 to 1 Republican legislative majorities in Trenton.
>
> Let me remind Mrs. Whitman she's running for governor of New Jersey—not Fantasyland.

The remarks were delivered at another job site, the Rutgers University football stadium, where a state-sponsored expansion project that Whitman once criticized was putting men to work. Yet as sharp as the attack lines were—lines that included a derogatory reference to her Wall Street advisors—Florio did not look like a man who had just been handed the election. On the contrary, he was intense, as if he were digging his heels in deeper for an even tougher fight.

On the phone this morning at Whitman headquarters, Carl Golden was fairly upbeat. He said the campaign had gotten the headlines it wanted: Whitman calls for 30 percent cut in taxes; "and, not to be cynical, Michael, but most people don't read past the headlines and first paragraph." I mentioned there had been a fair amount of skepticism in the room yesterday. He said, of course there was, and didn't Christie show toughness in handling it. "We've made the contrast now," he said. "People kept saying she isn't giving the voters a reason to vote for her? Now she has."

"You rolled the dice," I said. "We'll see if it comes up seven, eleven, or snake eyes."

He objected to the metaphor, but soon called up another one from the world of games. "Michael," he said, "isn't it true, when you're trying to win a close game, throw deep?"

Since the voters are the ultimate arbiters of all this, we decided at the 11:30 news meeting that I should talk to some, so I interviewed a dozen people in downtown New Brunswick at lunchtime. Five said right away they like Whitman's proposal. Seven expressed sharp reservation or deep skepticism.

★ Friday, September 24 ★

The parallels between this race and the 1977 New Jersey race for governor have been much commented upon this week. In '77 a nice-guy Republican from Somerset County, Ray Bateman, had a big lead over incumbent Democrat Brendan Byrne, who was unpopular for having instituted the state income tax the year before. Then in September, Bateman, with the help of financier William Simon, unveiled a plan to repeal the income tax and replace it with a one-cent sales tax hike, some budget cuts, and a repeal of the newly enacted homestead rebate. The public didn't buy it. Byrne labeled the Bateman-Simon plan the "BS plan," and "one-term Byrne," as he had been called, rolled to victory.

Yesterday, at the behest of the Florio campaign, Byrne held a

Statehouse news conference to commemorate the sixteenth anniversary of the day Bateman presented his plan. Byrne, known for his wit, called Christie Whitman's plan "BS Too," and "the half-witman plan," and the "Whitman simpler."

Editorial writers are weighing in heavily against the plan. The *Star-Ledger* called it "irresponsible," The *Philadelphia Inquirer,* "an intentional fraud perpetrated by a desperate candidate," to quote a few. The *Atlantic City Press* began its editorial, "Christie, Christie, Christie. What happened?" Even the *Trentonian,* which hates Florio, asked who Whitman thinks she's trying to fool. Only the *Wall Street Journal,* the *New York Post,* and the *Home News* of New Brunswick praised the plan. The *Journal* opined knowingly that "Ms. Whitman will . . . face the hostility of some New Jersey elites, especially the state press partisans. . . . But the thrust of her plan is exactly right."

"We knew we weren't gonna win the battle of the editorials," Carl Golden told me. "Editorial writers are conditioned to react this way. She said tax cut, and all over the state their knees started jerking in unison."

Republicans are publicly supportive. Ginny Littell, the Republican state chair, says, "At least she defined herself. And she got the focus back on the economy." Roger Bodman, the lobbyist and NJN analyst, says, "She had to do something startling. Florio was dominating the discussion."

But privately, while some Republicans accept the logic of her proposal, others are dismayed by it. Many think she went too far, and listened to the wrong advice. Tom Kean, for example, advised her to call for new deductions on the state income tax—for such items as property taxes, charitable giving, and capital gains—but not to cut rates until the second or third year and only if the economy picked up. Others talk about a 10 or 15 percent cut in rates, but not 30! There is talk that she didn't take enough advice from the Republican legislative budget experts, that help was offered by prominent Rutgers economists who worked for the Kean administration and the offer fell on deaf ears. The architects of the plan are said to be John Whitman, Dan Todd, and Lawrence Kudlow, not one of whom has ever worked on a New Jersey budget. Doug Berman, the Florio advisor, says he was at Giants Stadium last Sunday and Chip

Stapleton, chief of staff to senate president Donald DiFrancesco, came by. Stapleton had been at a briefing, so Berman asked how big the tax cut would be. "John hasn't made up his mind yet," said Stapleton. As Berman tells the story, Stapleton then said, "Make that, John hasn't made up *her* mind yet."

Democrats are said to be jubilant. Many think Whitman has handed them the election, and they are trying hard not to show it. Yesterday the Florio campaign started running a commercial that opens with Whitman's commercial in a TV set and then it freezes and an announcer goes, "Unbelievable!" He says this is the same Christie Whitman who pays $47 in taxes on fifty acres of land, the one who was fined by the IRS for not paying taxes on her illegal aliens. A female voice then quotes Whitman saying, last February when the GOP-controlled assembly proposed a tax cut, "it insults the intelligence of New Jerseyans and shows contempt for their finances to dangle election-year handouts before the voters," and the male voice returns and says, "You got that right, Christie." The commercial is vintage Carville. It puts the opposition candidate's face on the screen and lets her hang herself with her own words. It's this year's version of the famous "C'mon, Pete, be real," commercial that Carville used to kick off Frank Lautenberg's media campaign in 1988 against Pete Dawkins. The fact that it was on television two days after Whitman unveiled her plan is yet another testament to the speed of the Florio campaign. "A few people were up very late," Jo Glading told me. In New Jersey or Washington? "Both."

Jim Florio took the day off today, but he called the campaign office several times to check up on things and pester people. A staffer described him as "antsy." Carville, in our interview the other day, had described Florio as "someone who leaves few things to chance" and suggested the campaign reflected the candidate.

Relations, meanwhile, are beginning to tear between NJN and the Whitman camp. Carl Golden called news director Bill Jobes yesterday and chewed him out for sending a young woman desk assistant out to ask an embarrassing question about Whitman's getting the endorsement of trash-mouth radio star Howard Stern. Stern said on the air he'd endorse the first New Jersey gubernatorial candidate who called him. Someone who heard it called Whitman in her car, she called Stern, and he endorsed her on the spot, adding that he liked her body and expected her to wear a thong bathing suit to her inaugural. Desk assistant Annemarie Caprario was told to ask Whitman how she felt about getting the endorsement of someone who has been fined by the FCC for obscenity and whom many find offensive. Whitman handled it with good humor, as she does all such questions, but Golden at least—and perhaps Whitman as well—was livid.

Yesterday her aide Keith Nahigian tried to prevent another young woman associate producer we sent out from getting some questions answered, and today Whitman walked away from rookie reporter Rich Young, who was asking tough questions about school aid that I had fed him for a piece I was doing. Staffing shortages dictate that we can't always have senior reporters out with the candidates, but the Whitman camp doesn't like it and thinks, mistakenly, that sometimes the questions are spoon-fed by the Florio campaign.

"She's not a big fan of NJN, lemme tell ya, Michael," said Golden on the phone this morning.

★ Monday, September 27 ★

Six days out, the Whitman economic plan is playing a little better than I had thought it would, but not much. It's not the unmitigated disaster it looked like upon first encounter.

Republicans are complaining about the Whitman campaign not selling the plan hard enough, but they're not complaining about the plan. Veterans like Kean, Gluck, and Rodney Frelinghuysen say it's "doable." "I've been in government. I know there's a lot of waste there," Gluck told me. Republican legislators, all of whom must now run for re-election on their standard-bearer's plan, have not risen up and rebelled, not even in the Trenton area, where the state workers whose livelihoods would be threatened by budget cuts form a powerful voting bloc. Others, like Essex County Republican chair John Renna, talk defiantly about the skepticism that attended the last round of Republican budget cuts, in 1992, when the legislature cut the sales tax by a penny and cut a billion dollars out of the budget. "Everybody said the state would go to hell, and it didn't," Renna says.

Some Democrats inside and outside the Florio campaign recognize that even if the voters judge Whitman's plan a crock, they still might vote for her on the grounds that she's likely to do part of what she says. "I think our euphoria is a little misplaced," Democrat Frank Capece says.

The media have been going all out on the plan, interviewing voters and economists, as well as the plan's architects. New details have spilled out, such as that the plan went through many permutations and at one point was a 40 percent cut. Contrary to the gossip, I'm told that outside advice was solicited; Beth Gates, the senate Republicans' budget expert, helped put the plan together, and former state treasurer Michael Horn was asked to vet it. Rutgers economists may have been left out, but two Princeton economists were consulted.

It was Christie Whitman who settled on the 30 percent figure. Despite plenty of advice that it was too high, she chose a dramatic number. She and her advisors say it's because she wants a mandate, if elected, to take the drastic action she truly believes is needed to turn the state's economy around. It may also be that she was trying to jolt the electorate into noticing that she's for "cut and save," as she calls it, while Florio's for tax and spend.

The Whitman campaign was so focused on last Tuesday's announcement that it forgot to plan for Wednesday and Thursday. Second-guessers are saying the campaign should have had corporate CEOs, or a Republican governor, or a labor union, lined up to endorse the plan. Finally, today, Whitman held an event in Newark with about twenty small-business owners from around the state, who talked up the plan. Whitman came armed with a new statistic: the state lost ten thousand jobs in July and August, according to Florio's own labor department.

Unfortunately for her, the reporter for Channel 2 in New York, Ren Scott, came armed with some numbers, too. He had the results of a *New York Times*/WCBS poll that showed Florio leading Whitman 51 percent to 30 percent. Insiders have been talking about this poll for days, spreading the word it would be good for Florio, but nobody thought it would be this good. Sixty-one percent think Florio has the honesty and integrity they like to see in a governor, to 36 percent who think Whitman has. Forty-five percent think Florio was right to raise taxes, the same percent that thinks he was wrong. Fifty-nine percent think Florio understands the problems of "people like you," to only 30 percent who think Whitman does. Only 10 percent think Whitman will lower their taxes if elected; 36 percent think she'll hike taxes.

Having the numbers sprung on her at a news conference, Whitman responded as best she could, saying there was plenty of time for people to change their minds and, "don't forget, you're looking at someone who was told two days before an election in 1990 I was gonna lose by 16 points at best and most likely 32. I lost by 2."

But as she headed off for Washington this afternoon, to raise funds and attend a forty-seventh birthday party in her honor at the home of her sister, Kate Beach (a former deputy U.S. treasurer), she has to be worried. The poll was begun the day she put out her economic plan.

★ Tuesday, September 28 ★

To read the *New York Times*/WCBS poll is even more devastating for Whitman than simply to hear the numbers. The *Times* played it on page one, top left, and the first paragraph says Florio has "taken advantage of a lackluster Republican challenge to revive his reputation." That word "lackluster" must not have looked too good to Christie Whitman down in Washington this morning. Writer Iver Peterson goes on to say Florio "has come to dominate the terms of the campaign. . . . The poll shows that Mrs. Whitman has suffered from each principal charge Mr. Florio has made against her: that she is rich and out of touch with ordinary voters, that she is too close to the gun lobby and that she lacks the experience and judgment to govern." Right there on page one. Before the jump.

Florio's moods don't go up and down very much, according to an aide. He was not visibly excited today. U.S. interior secretary Bruce Babbitt came in for a tour of the Highlands region, the third Clinton cabinet officer here in the past three weeks. Babbitt was to have awarded the state $2 million in federal funds for land acquisition, but he forgot the checks and promised to put them in the mail right away.

It was a gorgeous day—the gods are smiling on Florio—and the governor took Babbitt to two beautiful spots in North Jersey, the Skylands

Manor mansion high on a hill in Ringwood State Park near the New York state line, and the Palisades Park Commission headquarters overlooking the Hudson River in Alpine. The day illustrated that with Florio one gets a range of policy interests, while Whitman clings to her one-note portfolio. Florio on a given day will talk about welfare, crime, economic development, open-space preservation; Whitman will talk about tax cuts spurring job growth, period. "Where's plan B?" David Blomquist asked awhile back on my show. Now is the time for it, whatever it is.

It's crisis time in the Whitman camp, again.

I don't know how much time Florio took to savor the *Times* this morning, but an item in the *Wall Street Journal* caught his attention. In it the head of the gun lobby in New Jersey, Rich Miller of the Coalition of New Jersey Sportsmen, suggested that Florio was being demagogic in his fight against the NRA. "I've read about this kind of campaign before. It ended in a bunker," Miller was quoted as saying. Another reference to the Holocaust by an opponent! Some would skip over it as just a small, crude remark, but not the governor who leaves little to chance. He called Jim Andrews early in the morning and told him to do something with this new ammunition. Then he called Jon Shure from his State Police helicopter while flying up to Ringwood and urged him to do the same. Apparently it's a Florio trait to call several aides and place the same order with each of them. Staffers who think they are perfectly capable of executing a command don't understand why the governor needs to place the same order with other lieutenants, but they accept it as his way of making certain something gets done.

Sure enough, by mid-afternoon a fax arrived in my newsroom on Victory '93 letterhead, the election arm of the Democratic State Committee, in which state chairman Ray Lesniak blasts Rich Miller of the gun lobby for his wildly intemperate statement to the *Wall Street Journal* which insulted Jews by again raising the specter of the Holocaust. Score another one, however small, for Jim Florio.

Ironically, and perhaps to clear up any misconception about her campaign's earlier allusion to nazism, Whitman toured the Holocaust Memorial in Washington today before heading home for a fund-raiser tonight thrown by a group called Republican Women of the '90s. Hazel Gluck was Whitman's surrogate tonight live on our newscast, saying don't believe the polls and watch out for Christie's new thrust.

Ed Rollins saw Kayla Bergeron, the longtime Whitman aide, outside Narda's restaurant in East Orange yesterday morning, waiting for Christie Whitman to show up for an event. They greeted one another. "The gloves are off," Rollins was overheard telling her.

Inside, behind closed doors, before the event, with Whitman at his side, Rollins told a small group of Essex County Whitman supporters that he was going to take charge of the campaign now. Since the *Times* poll came out, Republicans have been swamping the Whitman headquarters with phone calls, begging for a tougher fight. Rollins promised them they'd get it. I put him on camera an hour later, and he said the campaign was about to get more aggressive. The morning papers had articles in which Whitman aides were promising the same. "She wants to talk about issues," Rollins told me. "If we can't win talking about issues, we'll talk about Florio's record." He said England and Israel have thirty-day elections, "and that's what we'll have here."

I stopped in at Whitman headquarters between her two events and mentioned to Carl Golden that people are saying Rollins is assuming a more active role. "Oh, that was always in the works," said Golden, assuring me it meant nothing. Whitman herself was true to form at her two events today. She took a few shots at Florio's taxes, but if anyone expected her to re-invent herself and start calling him names or unleash an attack on his ethics, they were mistaken.

Around six-thirty that night, while the newscast was in progress, an NJN colleague got a tip that Dan Todd had been fired. If true, the news director wanted to put me on the set for a quick "*this just in.*" I called Golden and waited ten minutes while he finished up with someone else. When I told him what we'd heard, he feigned shock and said, "Dan Todd is sitting right here. Dan, have you been fired? No, Michael, he has not been fired." He said there had been a "slight shift" in responsibilities. Rollins would run the media side, Todd would run the political side, and since media was important in the final five weeks, it meant more involvement by Rollins. But that was all. Not enough for us to interrupt the newscast.

I went to the newsstand early this morning and was shocked to see front-page headlines saying: "Whitman shakes up staff"; "Whitman puts Reagan talent at helm of slumping campaign"; "Whitman's brother out of lead role"; "Whitman demotes her brother." I felt foolish. I had been at the headquarters—had spoken to Golden, Rollins, Todd, and Whitman during the day—and every reporter but me seemed to have the story, and they had probably never left their desks. I was furious at Golden. He can be difficult, but I never thought he would lie to me.

After reading the stories, I could see that Golden had said the same things to the other reporters. They had gotten their tips and their confirmations elsewhere, from unnamed sources.

I reached Golden by phone from the New Brunswick Hyatt where I was covering Florio this morning. I told him how angry I was at him when I saw the morning headlines.

"Michael, the fact that everybody overwrote the story is not my problem," he shot back. He said the notion of "shake-up" and "demotion" is "in the minds of the media."

"This place is a fucking Johnstown flood," he added, meaning it leaked. "You think you're angry? I'm absolutely livid." He said the leaks had come from the Republican State Committee, which occupies the adjoining suite of offices. He named the leaker, a second-level official, and implied serious problems existed between the Whitman campaign and "the people over there."

That still didn't explain why he hadn't been more straight with me.

"I talked to you *twice* yesterday," I said, still agitated. "I had egg on my face this morning."

"I would never do that to you or any other reporter," he said. "I would never publicly screw a reporter." He adhered to the line that "nothing unusual" had happened and castigated the media for its "obsession with process."

"I don't think anybody out there in TV viewer land gives two goddam hoots whether Dan Todd is in charge, do you?" he asked.

In Jersey City this afternoon, Christie Whitman stood with Mayor Bret Schundler, in the same ornate council chambers in which he'd endorsed her a month ago, and laid out a get-tough crime plan. Life without parole for repeat violent offenders. Adult trials for juvenile offenders if they're seventeen. But once again, her message was lost in a maelstrom of questions about her campaign. As Jo Glading put it in a quote I saw in several morning papers, Whitman has now been through three campaign managers, three press secretaries, and three media consultants this year. What kind of leader is this? What kind of governor would she be if there's this much instability around her?

Whitman clung gamely to the explanation that Rollins's stepped-up role had been part of the plan all along and that her brother had never wanted the title campaign manager in the first place and would now be free to do what he liked—travel around with her, meet people, organize surrogate speakers, and be a "supersurrogate" himself. It didn't wash, but she did a good job of trying to sell it.

Several Republicans I spoke to today are heartened by the move. The *Times* poll was a shock to them. Many were down on Dan Todd anyway; now they had good reason to call for his head. The decision was made at a meeting Tuesday morning in Washington at the home of Kate Beach, Whitman's sister. In attendance were Rollins, Lyn Nofziger, Mike Murphy, Christie, John Whitman, and Dan Todd. In their minds, I'm told, they were just speeding up a planned transfer of power. They had no idea the media would pounce on it as big news. To the media, however, it meant the candidate had finally acceded to the wishes of all those on the periphery of her campaign who had been saying, in effect, get the ama-teur out of there and put a professional in. Todd is bright and likeable, but, as several newspapers have delighted in reporting over the past few months, the last campaign he managed was Lew Fleege's successful run for chief of the Winifred, Montana, Volunteer Fire Department. He thought he and his sister could save everything for the end. He let the beginning and the middle get away from them.

The unkindest cut of all today was Jim Florio announcing that he had found a new chairman for the Legalized Gaming Study Commission, a body that is to report by the end of this year. Cary Edwards will head up this important effort, the governor told a gathering of addiction experts. As he said the name, he looked like the cat that swallowed the canary. Questioned later about whether this implied political support on the part of the former Republican candidate, Florio merely repeated Edwards's outstanding credentials for this very important undertaking.

We haven't even had a debate yet, and already conversations about the governor's race are starting to sound like post-mortems. Whitman never gave people a convincing reason to vote for her. She didn't show a deep enough grasp of the issues. She let Florio "define" her. She made too many mistakes. Steve Salmore, a Rutgers professor who consults for Republican campaigns, says part of the problem with the Whitman campaign is that it's been "too closed, too small, too insular." Salmore worked for Cary Edwards in the primary and wanted to work for Whitman in the general but was shut out. Bewildered at finding himself regarded as untrustworthy, he blames the Whitman inner circle for not opening itself to Republicans who may not have been with Christie from the beginning. In politics you get even with your enemies after the election, he says. "They settled scores before they won."

"They didn't reach out enough," echoed Tom Kean, a co-chair of the campaign, in a recent conversation. "When you're the candidate, you've got to give everybody a stake. If you keep it close, secrets are preserved among people who have your interests at heart 100 percent, and that's nice. But it's better to bring in as many people and the best people you can. Jim Florio learned that the hard way. He kept it too close in the government. He decided everything within his inner circle. It hurt his administration.

"The primary is of necessity a small group, but then you reach out and broaden; in government, even more. You reach out to Democrats and independents."

We taped "Reporters' Roundtable" yesterday, and the discussion dwelt upon Whitman. Florio was barely mentioned. In ten days, she's been hit with a triple-whammy: her economic plan bombed, the *Times* poll half-buried her, and replacing her brother signaled her own recognition that she's in trouble. Asked for an assessment of Whitman's condition, Rita Manno of the *Courier-Post* said, "The patient is on life support."

On the same show Jerry Gray of the *New York Times* said he's heard that Cary Edwards is miffed at not having been asked by the Whitman campaign to do anything, and that Edwards, who had said during the primary that "Florio and Carville will eat her alive," now runs through the halls of his law firm yelling, "I told you so." (After the show Gray said he'd heard all that from Edwards himself.) My news director, Bill Jobes, heard what Gray said on the air and decided we should get Cary Edwards on our news program last night and find out where he stands. When I got Edwards on the phone, he said, "I told you I'd be back in this race," and he was agreeable to coming to our Newark bureau for a live interview. I prepared a minute-and-a-half package to set up the interview, then interviewed Edwards live. He said he was totally supportive of Christie Whitman for governor, and he thinks she can win "if she gets her message better focused." The appointment by Florio had nothing to do with politics, he said. It was a slow news day; the Edwards story led the newscast, and Cary indeed had resurfaced.

Digression: I am an aging weekend athlete. Soccer has been my game for the past thirteen years. Governor Florio occasionally teases me about my game, because until recently we played on a field near Drumthwacket, and he and Lucinda sometimes stroll by on Saturday afternoon. The governor remarks upon how slowly he sees me moving out there; I reply that he must have walked by late in the game, and that I'm just happy to be out there with guys half my age.

Not much could pry me away from my weekly soccer, so when I heard the Whitman campaign was unveiling its new attack ad for reporters on Saturday at the Princeton Hyatt at two or three o'clock, I hoped for the latter. Luck was with me; they called it for three-thirty.

Freshly showered, and limping slightly, I walked into the Hyatt. To get to the press conference, you had to walk down a staircase through a mezzanine lounge, where James Carville, Doug Berman, Jim Andrews, and Jo Glading, all dressed in casual Saturday clothing, were conspicuously seated around a table near the stairs. Ostensibly they were there to give reporters a video cassette of *their* newest TV ad. But really they had come to haunt the Whitman event! Jo Glading had said to me on the phone this morning that they might have "someone" there. "It's Carville," she had said, meaning this was his idea and his modus operandi. She gave no hint that such an august contingent as this would be in attendance. She also didn't tell me that Carville was in town for a debate preparation meeting at Drumthwacket that morning.

Jim Goodman of the Trenton *Times* showed up at the hotel with a red bandanna tied around his neck. Dan Todd was there with his kerchief on too. While he and his sister and about two hundred Republican supporters, operatives, and legislators were holed up privately in one room, Ed Rollins and Carl Golden were in the next room, welcoming reporters. Only seven or eight of us showed up. Rollins played the newest Whitman commercial. It opens with Florio in a 1989 debate saying "I see no need for new taxes," then on comes the ominous music and the headlines about record tax hikes, followed by statistics and grim visuals about job loss and business failures, and ending with the narrator saying, "Jim Florio, he may be the worst governor New Jersey has ever had."

"This is the beginning of a tough, aggressive campaign," Rollins announced. He was clearly speaking as the new man in charge, the man who was going to give the Whitman candidacy one last good try. "When we get through, voters will have two clear visions to choose from. His has already turned out to be a nightmare. Hers is the only one that offers some hope." He badmouthed the *Times* poll, called upon assembly speaker Chuck Haytaian to defend the economic plan, and joked about being too old for the harrowing task of running a campaign day-to-day. The last campaign he ran was Ronald Reagan's in 1984, he said. "There are only three people alive today who have run presidential races," he added, and he mocked himself for having his career path run in reverse: normally, one would do gubernatorial races and then a presidential.

"If you think either James or I enjoys this," he said without finishing the thought, referring to Carville, who is his closest neighbor in the Blue Ridge Mountains of Shenandoah National Park, where they both have second homes about two hundred yards apart and about sixty miles from Washington.

In the next room, Whitman was promising supporters a new vigor in her campaign, soliciting their ideas, sharing poll data with them, and urging them not to give up. Since we couldn't get in, several of us reporters moseyed up to the lounge to talk to the Democrats.

"The Republicans have nominated a candidate who clearly has no idea where she wants to take the state," Carville was saying, in answer to someone's question. He and Berman proceeded to run down Whitman's candidacy. There was a clear pecking order among them. Carville, the only one with a million-dollar book advance, was dominant, followed by Berman, then Andrews (the day-to-day campaign manager on this side), then Glading, who, though she didn't speak much here, is said by at least one Florio insider to have become a "star" in this campaign.

The Florio team is not over-confident. And they refuse to take credit for derailing "Mrs. Whitman," as they all call her and we do, too, when we're among Florio people. (Among Whitman people, it's "Christie.") To them, her floundering campaign is a function of a pure and simple truism: She is not in the same league as Governor Florio. I asked what they thought about her changing campaign managers this week. "The spokes change. The flat tire is still there," said Carville. He joked that the Republicans would be in better shape if they'd made Ed Rollins the *candidate* this week instead of just the campaign manager. "Then, I'd be nervous."

We were seven or eight people seated around a low coffee table, not eating or drinking, just consuming the governor's race. The Whitman rally below broke up, and Whitman people started streaming upstairs. It was interesting to see Hazel Gluck come over and hug Jo Glading, Ed Rollins come over and shake Carville's hand, Carl Golden shake hands with Glading, and Chuck Haytaian give Carville a respectful greeting ("Hi, Jim") and get a deferential one back ("How y'a doin', sir"). Haytaian even gave Berman a "Hi, Doug," despite having railed against him publicly and privately on many occasions. There is a camaraderie among political people that can transcend party warfare, and it's nice to see.

To Carville, Whitman is a candidate out of step with New Jersey voters. He runs through his litany: She thinks the gun ban is lousy legislation; she opens her general election campaign in a gun shop; she hires illegal aliens and says good help is hard to find in America; she misses her school board vote; she's for weakening the drunk driving laws; she's for cutting taxes 30 percent, but when she hands reporters her two-page plan the numbers in one of the columns are added wrong; and now she's talking about maybe cutting taxes 50 percent in urban areas. I tell them that I think these are all inadvertent acts or statements that they in the Florio camp have seized upon and magnified in a skillful and successful effort to undermine Mrs. Whitman's credibility. She's not really as bad as you've painted her out to be, I say. Oh, yes, she is, they argue, and Carville decides it's time to go home to Washington. He gets up, puts a bright blue United Steelworkers jacket over his yellow turtleneck, and heads out with Andrews.

Poor Ed Rollins has to go back to the Ramada Inn in Clark, where he's taken a room for the duration of the campaign. Although at fifty he's only two years older than Carville, he looks like he hails from a prior decade. But down in the polls and trying to pull it out for an old friend, as he describes Christie Whitman, he is allowing himself only twelve hours a week at home in Washington, from Sunday night at seven to Monday morning at seven, and then only to "make sure my wife still lives there."

Asked if Christie Whitman is still a viable candidate, he says sure, but adds, "If we're having a discussion ten days from now on whether she's viable, she won't be."

★ Sunday, October 3 ★

The headlines in the Sunday papers catch the mood of the moment. "It's make-or-break week for Whitman campaign," says the Trenton *Times*. "CAN WHITMAN OVERCOME BOTCHED CAMPAIGN?" asks the tabloid *Trentonian*.

Carl Golden tells me that Christie knows she is behind but also knows that candidates have come from further back and won. Her camp thinks she's five to eight points down. Tom Kean was eight to ten points behind Jim Florio on October 15th twelve years ago. George Deukmejian was nineteen points behind on October 1st and went on to become governor of California. Whitman herself trailed Bill Bradley 55-27 and 54-22 in two mid-October polls in 1990.

"There is cause for concern, but not panic," says Golden.

He also admits, for the first time, that Dan Todd was "out of his element" as campaign manager. "No question about it," Golden says. "He tried hard, but he was out of his element." He adds that Todd has been unfairly trashed in the media this week by people "in the campaign and at the state committee" who had it in for him all along and "played the hyena role, constantly on the phone with reporters."

Like the editorial writers, their cousins the columnists have had a field day with Whitman's economic plan. Bob Herbert of the *New York Times* called it "breathtakingly irresponsible." Steve Lopez of the *Philadelphia Inquirer* wrote, "You listened to it, and it took maybe two, three seconds, before you realized what it reminded you of. Remember those junior high term papers you threw together at the last minute?"

The Florio campaign's fourth commercial—and they are spending heavily right now, gambling that now is the time to move in for the kill—was nothing but a litany of quotes from editorials about the Whitman economic plan. To hear and see the adjectives piled onto one another had a devastating impact, I thought. Ed Rollins must have thought so, too, because on Saturday he admitted he was pleased to see it was coming off the air. Replacing it is a new Florio commercial that mocks Whitman's stand on welfare reform (". . . Mrs. Whitman, who should pay? The fathers or the taxpayers? Whitman on welfare reform? Out to lunch.").

Florio yesterday got endorsed by the state Policeman's Benevolent Association, the largest police union in the state, with thirty-thousand members. The ceremony was on the steps of City Hall in Woodbridge, and the governor used the occasion to ridicule Whitman's crime plan. If her tax plan taxes credibility, he said, her crime plan is itself a crime. It contains ideas that he's already implemented, he said, like putting more cops on the street. And Whitman's call for putting three-time violent offenders away for life is totally inconsistent with her earlier position of being against mandatory minimum sentencing, he charged. "I could go on," he said, "but I think the men and women in blue know the real thing when they see it. And when they look at Mrs. Whitman, they see someone out of touch—someone who is changing her position almost weekly in a desperate effort to revive a campaign that appears to be going nowhere."

If you're going to try to kickstart a campaign in the final four weeks, you need the media's help, so Christie Whitman's event today was a Statehouse news conference. The Whitman campaign has not courted the press all year and in fact has come to resent the press for several perceived shortcomings and imbalances; now it decided to put on a show for the press on the first day of the first week of the new Rollins-led campaign. Whitman stood with four Republican legislators and played a videotape of excerpts from Florio's appearance on NJN's "New Jersey Tonight" last month. Florio explained why he raised taxes three years ago. Whitman and the legislators debunked the explanations, arguing, for example, that when Florio says he inherited a $3 billion deficit, he's lying by $2.4 billion. These are old arguments, but they are being revived because the Whitman strategy now is to focus on Florio's record and hack away at it.

Whitman's top brass were all there this time, and Carl Golden cut the press conference off a bit early. As Whitman walked down the hall toward the front door of the Statehouse, reporters scurried alongside her with tape recorders and microphones pointed at her face, asking more questions. They continued out on the sidewalk, and Gene Dillard, a veteran radio man who files stories with public radio and other stations, wouldn't quit. Christie got in her car and Dillard stuck his microphone in the window. Christie was still talking and Dillard's hand was still in the window as Jason Volk, the driver, put the car in gear and drove off. It called to mind the time Jim Courter walked away from the Statehouse press corps on a sidewalk in 1989 after a particularly contentious session on his feelings about homosexual teachers. I heard then there's an unwritten rule in Trenton that you never walk away from the Statehouse press corps, but I guess the Whitman camp didn't know that.

Meanwhile, the Sunday Bergen *Record* had a story that said the securities firm that hired Melvin "Randy" Primas, former commissioner of community affairs, received $100,000 in fees for its role in a Housing and Mortgage Finance Agency (HMFA) bond deal, despite the fact that it sold no bonds and that Primas had been chairman of the HMFA just five months before the sale. Primas is a Florio ally and was a key member of the cabinet before he left for the private sector. I asked Florio about the story at his PBA event. He deflected the question and touted his executive order requiring competitive bidding on all future bond sales. I tried three times and still got the stone wall treatment.

Within an hour Jon Shure and Audrey Kelly were reaching out to me to tell me the governor misunderstood my question, hadn't read the story, feels his answer would sound dumb, and, without saying so, asked me not to run it. I called my newsroom to see if we were planning to do anything about the Primas story. We weren't. So we decided not to force it just because the governor didn't handle the question very well. But we vowed to come back to the story.

Whitman looked awfully downcast this morning as she listened to the president of the New Jersey Women's Political Caucus tell reporters what a wonderful candidate she is and why the group is endorsing her. A new Bergen *Record* poll out this morning had Florio leading her 50 percent to 37, an improvement over the *Times* poll but a far cry from the 43 to 43 tie in the *Record* poll of three weeks ago. Worse, the new poll had 72 percent expressing doubt about Whitman's ability to cut taxes by as much as she promises. And while men split 47 to 40 for Florio, women again were decidedly pro-Florio, 53 percent to 33.

The event was at the Statehouse. Whitman perked up once the press corps started firing questions at her. She even became biting in her remarks about Florio, saying that one reason he was a better campaigner than she is that "I happen to be hampered by something called principle."

"She's pissed," said an aide, who didn't want to be identified. At Florio? At the media? "Both."

Republicans hope some of that venom percolates in her tomorrow night during the first debate.

Her sister, Kate Beach, who has been with her this week, says Whitman is a little tired but is holding up amazingly well. "My mother was affectionately known as the Hurricane in the family," Beach said. "I think Christie has inherited her strengths and stamina."

But a public information officer for one of the state government departments, who says he's a Republican, told me today he can't vote for Whitman. "She's made too many bad decisions."

Florio today hosted yet another Clinton administration official on a supposedly nonpolitical visit, drug czar Lee Brown. They talked to a business audience at Forsgate Country Club about keeping drugs out of the workplace; this was Florio sticking to his knitting. Don't talk politics.

Don't talk polls, tactics, strategy. Talk about a serious social problem: that is the reason you were elected.

But after it was over, Florio sat down with the media and lambasted Whitman once again, blaming her drop in the Bergen *Record* poll on her economic plan and pulling the two sheets of paper out of his breast pocket and waving them for the cameras again. "I carry it around with me. Two pages. Nothing on the back," he said, holding them up and turning them over. "The numbers on this page don't add up to the numbers on this page. The *Inquirer* called it a fraud. That's a little harsh but not inaccurate."

The Florio camp was secretive about the governor's debate preparations, telling me only that a woman was playing Whitman in a mock debate. Whitman went off to a TV studio in Morris County to practice with Ed Rollins, Mike Murphy, and Carl Golden, among others. On her way out of the Statehouse, I asked her who plays Jim Florio. "Whoever's in the nastiest mood that day," she said, striding off.

★ Friday, October 8 ★

Last night's first televised debate between Florio and Whitman was stellar. The questions hit all the right nerves. The candidates were sharp and keyed up.

It took place in the Trenton studio of WPVI-TV/Channel 6, the Philadelphia ABC affiliate. The combatants walked into the studio like fighters entering a ring, first Florio, then Whitman. They shook hands briskly for the photographers, who coaxed them into doing it several more times. Then the media cleared out. Only five people watched in the studio—Dan Todd, Ed Rollins, and a close friend of Whitman's from Washington, Nancy Risque Rohrbach, in one row, and right behind them Lucinda Florio and chief of staff Rick Wright.

From the outset, Florio showed he is a master at one-upmanship. Whitman took the first question and said, before answering it, she just wanted to express her condolences to the families of two New Jersey soldiers slain this week in Somalia. It was a slight pander, but politically correct, and showed she had the big picture in mind. Then it was Florio's turn. "First of all," he said, "let me join Mrs. Whitman. When I spoke to the families of the two young men who unfortunately were killed in Somalia yesterday, I did extend to them the condolences of all of our people." He, too, sounded the correct note but with a hidden message: *I am the governor!*

After some early banter about whether or not Whitman was blowing the campaign, Florio was asked why he refuses to take a no-new-taxes pledge. "If there's anybody in the state who knows the price you pay when you lift taxes, I suppose it's me," he said. "I know about bumper stickers. I know about toilet paper thrown on your front lawn." (The Florio tax hikes extended the sales tax to paper products, a hike that produced so much backlash it has since been repealed.) But a pledge would be irresponsible, the governor said, and, besides, the state is fiscally sound now. Whitman, in rebuttal, said Florio will raise taxes.

Nora Muchanic of Channel 6, who covers Trenton, asked Whitman to be more specific about the spending cuts that are at the heart of her economic plan. This is a key question. Whitman's credibility is wrapped up in it, and predebate speculation suggested she might be wise to reveal new spending cut proposals. Instead, she said, "If you're able to double people's taxes in one year, as the governor did in six months, why is it so incredulous [*sic*] to people that you can lower taxes 30 percent over three years? What we're talking about doing, it's five cents on the dollar!" She repeated her pledge to hold spending growth to 3 percent, and she threw in a couple of new examples of waste in government. "When I see numbers that tell me that $10,000—tens of thousands of dollars—are spent by the Department of Corrections to buy Adidas sneakers for prisoners, those are the kinds of things we can cut."

"Well, $1.5 billion dollars' worth of Adidas sneakers is a lot of sneakers," Florio drily remarked when it was his turn, underscoring the gaping hole in Whitman's plan, the $1.2 to $1.5 billion in lost revenues she'll need to offset. Then he held up a sheet of paper in each hand, as he had two days before with reporters, and said, this is the plan, the numbers on one sheet don't add up to the numbers on the other, and "it really is promising people pie in the sky without telling anybody where the dough is going to come from."

Jim Gardner, a Channel 6 anchor and one of the debate's moderators, asked Florio the Republicans' favorite question lately, what's your plan?

"My plan is sitting on the runway up at Newark airport—Kiwi Airlines. Go talk to Bob Iverson, the CEO, who will tell you that but for state loan guarantees . . . that whole airline would not have gotten off the ground. My plan is the Rutgers University stadium that we are building, that Mrs. Whitman opposed. My plan is the convention center in Atlantic City that is being built right now, that Mrs. Whitman opposed. My plan is the performing arts center. . . ." It was a terrific answer, but as Florio drifted back into criticizing the Whitman plan, he started sounding a bit shrill. "Tonight we heard the first degree of specificity forever. Adidas sneakers are going to be taken away from inmates, apparently. Well, you've got to make up $1.5 billion. Weather vane politicians really just won't cut it anymore. . . ." This was what the Florio people were afraid of—that Florio would be so disdainful of Whitman that he would come across as strident or nasty. "All we have to do is keep him from losing his temper, and we're fine," a top aide had confided to me earlier that day.

Whitman's goal, as Carl Golden had put it earlier in the day, was to "show that she can stand on the same stage with the governor" and to look competent; perhaps, also, to rattle him and try to bring out that streak the Florio camp hoped to keep under wraps. So Whitman reeled off lots of facts about the sorry state of the economy and about crime, to demonstrate familiarity with the issues. After she said her approach to health care was to stress preventive medicine, Florio came back with, "It's kind of interesting, because all the things Mrs. Whitman has been advocating, we're doing already," but by now he was starting to talk a little faster, and his voice was getting slightly higher pitched. He was not about to yield this woman an inch!

Throughout the sixty-minute debate, the TV viewer saw him look at her exactly once. She would periodically look over at him, to make a point or for effect. Florio is supposed to be the experienced performer, but Whitman was the one who frequently made eye contact with the camera and talked directly to the viewers. It made her appear forthright, and comfortable. By contrast, as Florio spoke, his eyebrows would arch, and the lines around his mouth would sharpen, and his face would take on an angry, serious cast. She smiled every time a tough question or accusation was thrown at her. He stopped smiling after his opening statement.

She talked. He had a tendency to lecture, especially when he was disput-
ing someone's assertion or the premise of a question; occasionally it sounded
as if he were putting the questioner down. When the subject of school
funding came up, she mentioned the $1.5 billion in new money Florio had
put into public schools, and the fact that a judge now says the problem is
worse and the state is $450 million short, then turned to Florio and said,
"Jim, where did all the money go? The people have a right to know where
the money went," implying it went down ratholes in corrupt city school
systems, and calling the governor by his first name, something no state
politician does in public.

Before the debate, Whitman had looked nervous. Her husband
then added to the air of tension by freaking out when he saw Florio walk
in with papers in his hand. "There are supposed to be no notes!" John
Whitman protested to his wife and anyone else within earshot. The candidate tried to calm him down. "Go talk to Michael," she said, presumably
meaning Mike Murphy, the media consultant, who could take up the
matter with the producer and sponsors. A moment later, John came back
and gave Christie a stack of papers. If Florio was going to have notes, so
was she, godammit, though she never used them.

Once she got rolling, Whitman came across as patient, concerned,
and sensible, so much so that one observer remarked, "She could have
been the dean of Bryn Mawr or Wellesley." She also managed to convey
emotion. When she expressed indignation at the way Florio had supposedly twisted her welfare position—"It doesn't mean that [I think] women
on welfare are promiscuous. It means there's a question here [sometimes]
of abuse, family abuse, spousal abuse. That's the kind of thing—you can't
just throw those children out onto the street if their mothers have that
kind of fear governing their lives"—her passion called to mind the late
Millicent Fenwick, another wealthy political woman from the Somerset
hills, whose sympathy for the downtrodden sounded phony until, like her
colleagues in Congress, you saw it up close and realized how genuine it
was. For a moment, Christine Todd Whitman became a young incarnation
of the grande dame of the New Jersey Republican party.

Darlene Superville of the Associated Press asked Florio why, in
light of the fine contributions made by the Kennedys, the Rockefellers,
the Fenwicks, and the Keans, he keeps attacking Whitman for her wealth.
"This is not about wealth," Florio replied. "This is not about credit

cards, it's about credibility," Florio said, but then he quickly darted to safer ground, attacking Whitman for her gun position and suggesting it shows she is out of touch. Whitman said he hadn't answered the question. Superville asked it again. This time he talked about the $47 in property taxes she and her husband pay on fifty acres of land, about the four pay hikes she voted herself as a freeholder, comparing it to his restraint in not accepting the full pay allotted him by law, $130,000, instead sticking with the old gubernatorial salary of $85,000. "I suspect she'll never be eligible for food stamps, but the fact of the matter is she took the salary increases and voted for them herself," he said. (Whitman failed to point out the salaries ranged between $13,000 and $17,000 a year.)

Minutes later he brought up the Somerset Trust Company and her votes to keep county funds in that family-controlled bank, "as blatant a conflict of interest as I've ever heard." He asked why to this day she has not disclosed her 1990 tax return. And he accused her of operating by a double standard (though he never explicitly mentioned illegal aliens). This was tough stuff, and it was coming out of a searing Jim Florio.

Whitman eventually hit back, satisfying those who feared she might not show enough toughness next to Florio. "For this governor to talk ethics," she said, "when there's a federal grand jury investigating this administration, there's a state grand jury investigating this administration, the Securities and Exchange Commission is investigating this administration. He had a chief of staff who left with a subpoena in his pocket!"

Bill Beutel of WABC-TV/Channel 7 in New York, the debate's other moderator, asked Florio, what about Joe Salema and the problems with state bond sales?

"There were no problems," Florio said, stonewalling Beutel and several hundred thousand viewers as he had stonewalled reporters in the past. "The reason why Mr. Salema resigned is because people like Mrs. Whitman jumped on him and immediately called for his resignation. He perceived this was clearly going to be something that would divert attention from my ability to talk about welfare and job creation and assault weapons, and said he didn't want any part of it. There have been no charges raised whatsoever. By the way, I welcome investigations in any part of the whole government so that we can find out if everything is going well."

"I love it. I'm glad the governor welcomes investigations, 'cause he's sure got enough of them going on right now," Whitman shot back. She had let his $47-on-fifty-acres charge go unanswered, but now she allowed herself a little more indignation and pushed out the fact that she and her husband paid over a million dollars in federal taxes last year, over $200,000 in state taxes, and over $30,000 in property taxes. "Maybe because, Jim, you haven't paid property tax in the last three-and-a-half years, you've forgotten what it's like." *Zing*.

By this point the debate was white hot. Watching on a monitor with the rest of the media out in the lobby of the office building in which Channel 6 has its studio, I wrote in my notebook, "THEY'RE BOTH GREAT . . . HEROIC." They were getting in every lick I'd heard from them and all their spinners all summer. Whitman was giving a performance one imagined her father would have admired, laughing off Florio's insults and clawing back. Florio was using his intelligence like a scythe, hacking through the misinformation to defend his record and justify his policies, and constantly trying to cut her off at the knees.

In her closing statement, Whitman pulled the debate's first and only ploy. Bemoaning all the "distortions and half-truths that have been projected on the airwaves about me," she said, "we need to change both the way we govern and the way we campaign," and she challenged Florio to accept a truce on negative advertising. From here on out, she said, let's have it be just "you talking about your record and what you're gonna do for the future and me talking about my economic program." She yielded the balance of her time to Florio, who launched into his closing statement without looking at her or even acknowledging her challenge, just sticking to his script, which asked voters whether they really want to go back to "the theories of the '80s that brought us so much pain." Only when moderator Jim Gardner, blessed with a few extra seconds, reminded the governor that Whitman had just thrown a challenge his way, did the governor respond with, "Well, I will tell you, we have not been having negative advertising. Talking about the record may seem negative to Mrs. Whitman. But when I talk about her saying it was a lousy law, she *said* it. When I said that she wanted to water down the drunk driving law, she *said* it. So what we're talking about here is the facts, and Mrs. Whitman is not comfortable with the facts."

After the debate, the doors to the studio opened and first the handlers, then the media, were allowed in. Florio and his wife stood at his lectern, thronged by reporters, as Whitman and her husband were similarly confronted behind hers. When a reporter asked John Whitman what he thought, he surprised himself and us by breaking a self-imposed rule of not giving on-the-record comments during the campaign. "As far as I'm concerned," he said, "I think this gave Christie and the people of New Jersey a chance to see how the governor has distorted almost every position that he talks about. He refuses to stand up for his own record. . . ." Throughout the studio, reporters were thrusting microphones and little cassette recorders at strategists and operatives, grabbing quick quotes and sound bites for stories that had to be filed soon. Ed Rollins said into my microphone that while Jim Florio gave probably his best performance, "there was more warmth to her than the governor, she was very confident, and my sense is that she did what she had to do. Anybody who was watching this debate is gonna take a second look at her." Paul Begala, James Carville's partner, who was in the state to help prep Florio for the debate (he had helped prep Clinton last year) and to be chief spin doctor for the day, recited a poem each time a reporter asked for his reaction:

> Oh, somewhere the NRA is laughing,
> And somewhere Republicans shout,
> But there is no joy in Far Hills,
> Mrs. Whitman has struck out.

People I've spoken to think Florio let his dark side show last night. In his zeal to whup her, he showed how haughty, how intense, how wrapped tight, and how combative he can be. One of his aides today, speaking on deep background, used the term "attack dog" to describe the performance—"all they had to do was throw red meat out there and he'd go for it." An ally said, "On content? We won. On style? We got our f——ing clocks cleaned." A reporter said he saw "the old Florio straining to get through the new Florio." The old Florio is the cold technocratic shouter who lost to Tom Kean in '81. The new Florio is the soft-spoken humble servant who, throughout the '89 campaign, held the hand of his pretty new wife, a wife who has been rather absent from her husband's side during this campaign, except on weekends and big occasions. A Florio insider predicted we'll see the governor next week around a lot of kids, and women, and Lucinda, to make him appear softer. "It's time to dust Lucinda off," he said, laughing.

★ Saturday, October 9 ★

Whatever bounce Whitman got from the debate was offset yesterday by President Clinton, who came to New Jersey and praised Jim Florio. Clinton has a fair amount of moral authority at the moment. His health-care plan, unveiled two weeks ago, has the country taking him seriously and liberals seeing him as visionary. So when Clinton stands in the atrium of the Robert Wood Johnson University Hospital in New Brunswick and tells the national media and a gathering of three hundred or so, "We need more people in this country who will call them like they see them, who will try to identify the problems and try to get up every day and try to do something about them, and I'm proud to be associated with Jim Florio," it means something.

What made it more impressive was that the president was linking his health-care plan to Florio's assault weapons ban. One way to control health costs is to cut down on the gun violence that is filling our emergency rooms with human tragedy, Clinton argued. The visit was billed as nonpolitical, just as the visits of Clinton's cabinet officers were. Had it been a political visit, the Democratic State Committee would have had to pick up $100,000–$150,000 worth of costs associated with the trip. But I'm told the DSC was prepared to pay, and it was the president who insisted on making this an official visit. He is trying hard to sell his health-care plan. Last weekend he barnstormed California for three days pitching it. "When you come to New Jersey, you reach twenty million people," Paul Begala had told me by way of explaining Clinton's preference. I had never realized the number was so large, but it's true that a media event in central New Jersey will get beamed into New York, Connecticut, and Pennsylvania. "Besides, New Jersey and Connecticut are big health-care states—lots of health corporation headquarters, and they're important to this," Begala said. He and Carville are advising Clinton on the selling of the health-care plan at the same time as they consult for Florio.

The Whitman campaign complained to reporters about the sham of this being a nonpolitical visit. But listening to Florio and Clinton on the stage at the hospital, you understood even more why they preferred it this way. Each wants to be taken seriously as a policy leader. And each sounded like one yesterday. Taking credit for the "toughest assault weapons ban in the country," Florio called on Clinton to enact a national ban, and he welcomed the president to "the fight against the NRA and the gun lobby." Clinton gave a sober talk, without a prepared text, in which he deplored the level of gun violence in the country, the "culture of violence" that lies behind it, and said the time had come to "change our ways as a nation." Sounding more like a gun-control advocate than I'd ever heard any American president sound, Clinton called for a five-day national waiting period for handgun purchases and a national ban on assault weapons. "Let's . . . prove that we can do in America what you are doing here in New Jersey," he said.

The visit and the message fit like a hand in the glove of Florio's re-election effort. Health-care reform and assault weapons ban: perfect together.

"I was elated when Jim got the John F. Kennedy Profiles in Courage Award last spring," Clinton told the crowd. "I know he hasn't always made people happy—but I also know what kind of trouble New Jersey was in, and I know you need to balance the budget, and you now have the best credit rating in the Northeast."

While this was going on, the Republicans were holding a rally on the Statehouse steps to proclaim Christie Whitman the winner of Thursday night's debate—except that the two top billed speakers, Tom Kean and Cary Edwards, didn't show up.

★ Tuesday, October 12 ★

"CHRISTIE'S STILL ALIVE," said the headline in the Sunday *Trentonian*, crediting her "poise" in the debate with "rejuvenating" her campaign. A number of pundits, columnists, and editorials have remarked upon the governor's humorless demeanor Thursday night, while Florio defenders, like Brenda Bacon, have said to me, "The governor takes this job very seriously, so it's difficult for him to smile his way through a debate. Is he humorless? Absolutely not. You know it and I know it."

In the meantime, Whitman is being cut an awful lot of slack. She was wrong when she said the Department of Corrections buys Adidas sneakers for inmates; the department pays $8 per pair for nondesigner sneakers and has never purchased Adidas, its spokesman says. She was also wrong in the debate when she said the Olympic sharpshooting team would be arrested if they landed at Newark airport because their rifles are on the assault weapons list; good research by the Florio camp quickly turned up the fact that Olympic marksmen shoot only single-shot weapons. After all her big mistakes, these little ones are going unremarked upon, except by the governor, who brings them up each day.

Today, she pulled a flip-flop of a higher order. Anticipating a Florio press conference on the subject of her 1990 taxes, she stuck to her guns in the morning, telling reporters she had released enough tax returns and this was a trick to divert people's attention from the real issues.

Florio had called a press conference for 2:30 at his Edison campaign headquarters. But in the morning James Carville called WKXW— New Jersey 101.5 and for ten minutes harangued Whitman on the air for not disclosing her 1990 tax returns. By 1:00, the radio station was reporting that Whitman had changed her mind and would release her 1990 returns by the end of the week. Why the sudden shift in a two-month-old position, no one outside the Whitman camp knew.

Florio went ahead with his event anyway. He suggested Whitman was being hypocritical for withholding one year's return after promising to set "a new standard for ethical disclosure," and after asking him for copies of the last four years of his tax returns. It goes to credibility, he said. And now that she has apparently decided to release them? Well, that goes to decisiveness, he said.

The cast of characters at his first-ever news conference at the campaign office included James Carville, Harold Hodes, and Lewis Katz, Florio's longtime chief fund-raiser and friend. Carville looked crazed. Katz, who's very funny, said James just gets antsy with three weeks to go in a campaign. The governor used blow-ups of Whitman's tax returns and a big black cardboard with "1990???" on it as visual aids. He also had visuals to support a Top Ten List, à la David Letterman, of reasons why Christie Whitman won't release the return. All of them were Whitman quotes, and the last six were attributed to "NJN postdebate interview"— I had asked her about 1990 after the debate and had included part of her answer in a piece later that night. The Florio camp, which tapes every, thing, had gotten six "reasons" out of one twenty-second sound bite.

The governor's presentation was good theater.

"We wanted to talk about issues. Florio wants to talk about watermelons, sneakers, and tax returns," said Carl Golden in reply.

"The person who frames the race always wins. The person who dominates the agenda always wins," Roger Stone, the Washington-based former Republican consultant, told me recently, by way of explaining how Florio had bested Whitman over the summer. Now, Florio is doing it again. His charge today, and her about-face, led our newscast tonight. "Politics is a shouting contest," said Roger Stone, bringing it all down to a very simple principle.

★   Wednesday, October 13   ★

Every day I make a little movie. The stars are always the same, like the old Hollywood studio system in the early days of film. You have your little stable of actors—Jim Florio, Christie Whitman, James Carville, Ed Rollins, Dan Todd—and every day they perform for you and rarely do they disap- point you. At night, thousands of people see the movie. It's what makes it easy to get out of bed and leave the house every day.

Today, Rollins had the lead role. He held a Statehouse news con- ference at which he blasted Florio for violating state election finance law. The charges are technical, and the Florio campaign quickly disputed the facts. But Rollins believes the Florio campaign may have gotten an unfair jump on general-election expenditures, and that belief enabled him to accuse Jim Florio of being willing to "lie, cheat, and do whatever it takes to win election."

"I've seen people steal a campaign on the day of the election, but never—and I've been in this business thirty-two years—have I seen some- one try to steal an election two months before it starts," he said.

Backed up by charts, the campaign's lawyer, and two Republican legislators, Rollins also explained to a room packed with newspeople that the visits by President Clinton and his cabinet officers never would have been passed off as nonpolitical by the Republicans when they had the White House. He read aloud the official White House policy on political travel from the Reagan-Bush years, and it clearly said that for the kind of travel the Clintonites have been doing, the campaign of the state candidate would have to reimburse the U.S. treasury at least in part for the travel costs. Rollins bemoaned the lower standard the Clinton White House has apparently adopted.

"Are we supposed to close the borders of New Jersey to the president of the United States just because Mrs. Whitman happens to be running for governor?" asked Jo Glading in response.

Whitman was in Atlantic City giving a speech while her pit bull was attacking. Florio attended a Bristol-Myers Squibb expansion groundbreaking and visited a computer software firm that recently decided not to leave New Jersey.

The Florio camp also unveiled a radio commercial for reporters today. It seems Whitman has been mailing "urgent-grams" to state voters in which she says vote for her, and it will mean $1,000 in their pockets. An asterisk points to small print saying, in three years, if you make $70,000 or above. The Florio campaign made a satirical commercial in the style of the old Crazy Eddie ads. A fast-talking pitch man shouts, it's amazing! she's promising a thousand dollars! After fifty seconds of such blather, he says, Christie Whitman—her promises are insane! (a play on "Crazy Eddie—his prices are insane"). After the campaign treasurer says, "paid for by Florio '93, Bob Long, treasurer," the announcer comes back on and says softly, "Act now and she'll throw in the ginsu knives."

Jo Glading, who unveiled the spot at the Statehouse, said the Florio campaign first saw the Whitman urgent-grams yesterday, and last night wrote and produced the spot (although she wouldn't say if the spot would ever air, and in fact it never did). It's hard to say which is more impressive, the "Saturday Night Live" humor or the speed.

But it was Rollins who dominated the agenda today and the Whitman campaign that gets the bigger headline.

★　Thursday, October 14　★

While I was covering Whitman in Bergen County today, someone in her small entourage told me that the sixteen-year-old son of Emma and Antonio Franco, the Portuguese couple who have worked for the Whitmans since 1986, had died on his school's soccer field yesterday. Apparently, the boy had a heart attack.

It came up because I asked this person how Whitman was feeling. "She's very upset today," the person said, and proceeded to tell me why, but asked me not to tell anyone. I said this was the kind of news that was going to come out. A few minutes later, as Whitman was giving her speech, I could see she looked a little pale and could hear a lack of verve in her voice.

Between stops, over a slice of pizza, I weighed the situation. The Francos are not public figures. But when any child dies suddenly on a ball field, it's news. I thought of *USA Today* forcing the late Arthur Ashe to disclose he had AIDS; I didn't want to be like that. But I also thought about my obligation to our viewers and how other media might treat the information. If David Wald, for example, was going to have an eight-inch story about it in tomorrow morning's *Star-Ledger*, should I suppress it? Shouldn't our viewers know that they can get all the news from NJN?

I called Trenton. The news director was off, so I asked for the executive producer of the news, Michael Fairhurst. His inclination was to report it—confirm the story, protect the initial source, and report it. I could ask Whitman herself about it at her next stop, but did not want to get the source in trouble and did not want to give her an opportunity to say, "yes, it happened, but please don't publicize it." Fairhurst and I decided I should call Carl Golden.

Golden got back to me in our Newark bureau in the late afternoon and confirmed the story. He said Christie would really appreciate it if the media would not report it, but that he understood it was news, and we would have to make our own decisions. Am I the first call about this? I asked. The second, he said.

The first had been from the Bergen *Record*. Before writing a stand-up and shooting it, I called David Blomquist, with whom I've sat for five years on "Reporters' Roundtable." I prevailed upon that bond to ask if the *Record* was going to report the information. Yes, he said, at the end of their story about her meeting this morning with their editorial board. He told me he had walked upstairs with Whitman to that meeting, and she had described being at the emergency room for much of last night. Blomquist and Golden both said she was deeply upset. She knew the boy well.

An hour later, I was on television reporting the day's campaign events and ending with a stand-up that told how a personal tragedy had "touched" the Whitman campaign.

Thus are journalistic ethics practiced.

★ Friday, October 15 ★

There are eighteen days until the election, and the Whitman campaign essentially wasted another day by inviting the press in to examine Whitman's 1990 tax returns. On the other hand, although the Whitmans made more money in '90 than in any other year we've seen so far—$4,195,553!—there doesn't appear to be anything damaging in the returns, and the Florio camp looks a little silly for having made such a fuss about it.

The bulk of the earnings, $2,599,300, was John's year-end bonus from Prudential-Bache. The rest was mainly capital gains ($850,800), interest and dividends ($259,692), rents, partnerships, and trusts ($214,966), and schedule C business income ($49,177). The Whitmans' total tax bill for the year was $1.3 million. At one o'clock today, Carl Golden handed out the returns in his office, alternately busting reporters' chops for their dumb and nosy questions, trying to be helpful, and joking about the size of their bonuses relative to John Whitman's.

Ed Rollins, Dan Todd, and various staffers wandered through the scene. The candidate herself was giving a speech in Bergen County again and then had to attend the funeral of Victor Franco. (The Trenton *Times* and Bergen *Record* reported the death; the *Star-Ledger* and *Asbury Park Press* have not so far.)

The Florio camp had little to say about the 1990 returns except to chide Whitman for waiting so long.

There's a new optimism in the Whitman camp. Frank Holman, a former state GOP chairman and a crusty old pol who's been consulting for the Whitman campaign, said to me today that things have "perked up" in the past two weeks. Rollins says his tracking polls put Whitman five or six points down; he could be telling the truth or he could be trying to influence opinion. I sense that Whitman is closing the gap, and I can envision her winning again. I don't think she will, but it's possible. Her debate performance stabilized her. Florio is starting to look like the heavy in certain settings.

The Florio camp is tight-lipped about its tracking polls, but a source tells me they showed the gap between Florio and Whitman at 11 points two weeks ago, then down to 8 the Monday after the debate, and now back up to 11.

A line going around reflects how a significant number of voters apparently feel about the choice being offered them: "They'll go in and they'll hold their nose and vote for Florio—or close their eyes and vote for Whitman."

★ Sunday, October 17 ★

Scanning the Sunday papers would be depressing this morning if you are a Whitman fan. The *Star-Ledger*/Eagleton poll has the race at 52 percent for Florio to 40 for Whitman; if accurate, that leaves not enough undecideds to tip the scale the other way. The *Philadelphia Inquirer* has a front-page article by two writers who spent six weeks studying the New Jersey economy and concluded that there really *isn't* a New Jersey economy, certainly not one that a governor can be held accountable for. And the *New York Times* has a wonderful magazine profile of Florio by Richard Reeves, plus a piece headlined "New Jersey Race Is Seen as a National Bellwether" in which Washington GOP consultant John Sears is quoted as saying, "She just didn't run a very good race, and she's going to lose." He was trying to say, don't read too much into this election, but in the process he buried the Republican candidate.

When you're up close to something every day and someone from the outside comes in and takes a quick, broad view of it, the results can be illuminating. Especially if the someone is as smart and knowledgeable a writer as the syndicated columnist Richard Reeves. In a few thousand words, he penetrates as close to the essence of Florio as anyone has. He calls Florio "driven" and "self-program[ed]" and describes him as an oddity in politics. "He is exactly the opposite of most professionals; he doesn't much like people in the flesh. He is comfortable alone and he is comfortable with silence," Reeves writes. But he praises Florio's commitment to principle, his toughness, and the piece paints a picture of Whitman as a bumbler running against a saint. Reeves says part of what makes New Jerseyans like Florio is that he has "brought New Jersey some respect in the national news media"; as a Jersey City native, Reeves understands what he calls the state's traditional "inferiority complex." Ironically, the piece—entitled "Jim Florio's Red-Hot Ice-Cold Politics: The fall and rise of New Jersey's kamikaze anti-social anti-politician"—itself burnishes the governor's national media image two weeks before the election.

Whitman is a likeable person, but every day she stands up and has to talk about how *bad* things are. Her stump speech is a litany of grim economic statistics, peppered with anecdotes of people she's met who are out of work or out of business, and followed by a pitch for her tax-cut plan ("if Jim Florio can double taxes overnight, I can certainly cut 10 percent a year . . ."). If the only voters in the election were the 300,000 people who held the jobs that have been lost under Florio, Whitman's appeal would be on target. But three million New Jerseyans *have* jobs. Day in and day out, she delivers the speech primarily to people who are well-dressed, being served food at tables while she speaks, and who are probably thinking how fortunate they are not to be like the people she's talking about. Cognitive dissonance is the psychological term for what's happening at her events. And she must come across to some as whining about conditions. Jim Florio calls it her "glass half empty" view, and while she is expounding a pessimistic outlook on the current moment in our history, he is out saying things aren't so bad and, in fact, they're getting better. The sunnier personality is selling the more sour message.

Meanwhile, her campaign is not setting a news agenda, not getting a media message out on very many days. Whitman is just giving her stump speech to groups of seventy-five or a hundred people two or three times a day, and the print reporters dutifully regurgitate it but without any excitement or sense of *news* (as in, hey, folks, something new happened here today, and you should read this).

Her TV commercials are hitting Florio increasingly hard, and that is obviously what Rollins is counting on. Her latest, number four, finally plays the ethics card. It mentions that two grand jury investigations are focusing on the Florio administration, backed up visually with headlines, and ends: "Jim Florio—rising unemployment, corruption, high taxes. We can't afford more. Christie Whitman—a change for the better."

But Florio's commercials are even tougher on Whitman. His latest, number five, opens with a car swerving down a residential street, as an announcer says, "Who'll lead New Jersey forward? Christie Whitman wants to let drunk drivers back on the road . . . and put assault weapons back on the street . . . proposes an unbelievable election-year tax cut . . . Whitman talks about jobs but hires illegal aliens, saying she can't find American workers. . . ." Although it goes on to tout Florio's "leadership," it is the fifth straight ad that essentially attacks Whitman.

The drunk-driving thrust is a perfect example of how Florio, Carville, and whoever else set the strategy have so far won this election. During the primary, Whitman put out a blueprint on crime, a seventeen-page document that was not very well thought out and had the feel of something thrown together by an outside advisor. Among the thirty or forty ideas it contained, one was to consider adopting an Ohio program that allows people convicted of drunken driving to obtain special orange-colored license plates allowing them to drive to and from work only, so that the conviction does not also cost them their jobs. It is a perfectly reasonable proposal, although it presents problems, such as what if someone else in the family wants to drive the car? Questioned in May on "NJN News," Whitman said it was just a proposal she was putting out for consideration. But the Florio campaign seized upon it. In New Jersey, you lose your license for six months for a drunk-driving conviction. So, as the Florio campaign puts it, Whitman wants to "weaken" the drunk-driving laws. It's true that the state's crackdown on drunk driving has greatly reduced the number of alcohol-related highway deaths. But, as Whitman keeps trying to point out, she is the mother of two teenaged children and is hardly trying to allow more drunks on the road. But her meek protest gets drowned out by the Florio campaign's incessant hammering—on the stump, in press releases and literature, and now in hundreds of thousands of dollars' worth of TV time. "If all you knew of me is what you got from the ads, I drive drunk at night with my Uzi hanging out the window shooting women who are having their cars stolen," Whitman complained to the *Asbury Park Press* editorial board on Wednesday, the last phrase referring to her questioning of the mandatory-sentence aspect of the new law making carjacking a separate crime.

The same phenomenon overtook her on the gun issue. She called the assault weapons ban a "lousy" piece of legislation once, in early July, to a TV reporter. The Florio campaign has quoted her a thousand times.

Attack when possible—refute when necessary.

★ Monday, October 18 ★

Another day, another demonstration of the Florio campaign's superiority. While Christie Whitman merely delivered her stump speech again, this time to a gathering of state worker union representatives, Jim Florio raised a new issue: property taxes, which he called New Jersey's "most oppressive tax." At an electrical workers' union hall, he argued that he has stabilized property tax rates, and that Whitman's economic plan would trigger "humongous" increases. The 1990 income tax hike raised funds for municipal aid and school aid; thus, after years of double-digit increases, Florio was able to announce today that the statewide average property tax increase was only 4 percent in 1992, after going up by only 1.5 percent the year before.

The Florio campaign backed up the event with a press release, clippings, and a text of the governor's remarks. And coincidentally or not, the *Star-Ledger* carried a front-page piece today headlined "Property taxes rise a modest 4%." Florio's treasury department was the source of the information in the *Ledger*, which often gets government documents handed to it first and which I overheard a colleague today call the *Star-leaker*.

The Whitman campaign issued no piece of paper today. Whitman's news coverage tomorrow will be her reaction to yesterday's poll, her reaction to Florio's property tax jab, her reaction to the *Daily Record* in heavily Republican Morris County endorsing Florio. All defense. "Where is Ed Rollins?" someone asked me today. Wasn't it Ronald Reagan who pioneered the theme-for-a-day approach to campaigning?

Instead, the Florio campaign orchestrated a media message today, while Christie Whitman was left out on her own to flounder.

"Everybody was saying, 'just relax, don't get excited,'" Hazel Gluck says of the Whitman inner circle's attitude all summer. "They've been too laid back. You can't be laid back with a kid from Brooklyn. *I'm* from Brooklyn. He's a tough fighter."

Florio looked relaxed and happy today. Whitman, to her credit, showed no sign of being shaken. The *Star-Ledger* poll, she said, contradicts the "incredibly positive" reaction she gets on the street. The second death in a week has hit her family—her uncle, Reeve Schley, Jr., who was eighty-five and had had a stroke the day Whitman's mother was buried. When you're running for office, life goes on around you. "We lost a father, mother, and brother in fourteen months. That makes you pretty philosophical," says Dan Todd of his sister's reaction to the deaths.

Nancy Risque Rohrbach, Whitman's friend from Washington, told me that Christie even cooked dinner at Pontefract last night. (Her housekeepers are mourning their son.) Rohrbach stays there during the week now and travels with the candidate each day, then goes home to D.C. on weekends. She said Christie is holding up fine. "We still think it's doable. You may not, but we do, and that's what's driving us."

Rohrbach is a tall, stylish, dark-haired woman in her forties who worked in the Reagan White House and met Whitman twenty years ago when they were both doing GOP work in Washington. Of her friend, she said, "She's a dream candidate—so committed, so intelligent. And sometimes she isn't such a dream candidate. You ask her a question, she wants to answer it—and some of the professionals tell you, that's wrong, don't answer the questions. But that's her."

The Birchwood Manor in Whippany, Morris County, is a stately, colonial catering hall that has been home to so many New Jersey political debates that it feels to me the way a baseball stadium must feel to an old ballplayer. Seated on its stage last night with two other questioners, Ren Scott of Channel 2 and Ken Matz of Channel 10, I looked across at Florio and Whitman. It was two minutes before air time. Whitman, looking pale, took a breath and flexed her jaw muscles. Florio looked over at me and Scott and held up his yellow legal pad, to show us the happy face he had drawn on it as a reminder to smile.

A new *New York Times*/WCBS poll had come out two hours earlier, showing Florio with a 15-point lead, 49 percent to 34. It was less than the 21-point margin in the last *Times* poll, but it was a bigger gap than in the Sunday *Star-Ledger* poll, and it must have hit the Whitman camp like a fist in the stomach. The secondary numbers were terrible for Whitman; for example, 65 percent find her economic plan not credible. To release the numbers right before the debate was almost cruel.

You don't see a debate as clearly when you're part of it as when you're sitting back in an audience or watching on TV. But from my vantage point, this was Florio's night. He was on top of every question, and, although she's the one behind, he was the one who kept attacking her the whole hour, nonstop. Her economic plan will raise property taxes! he warned. He'll match his ethics with anyone's in the room!

Whitman was spunky and showed flashes of anger at the governor. She conceded that her ad is wrong, he is not the worst governor New Jersey has ever had. "I give that honor to Benjamin Franklin's son, who was taken out of the state in handcuffs for supporting King George's tax increases," she said, garnering a good laugh, even from Florio. But it seemed to me no new ground was broken in the debate, and certainly the dynamic of the election was not altered.

An audience of nine hundred watched at the Birchwood Manor. My colleague Kent Manahan moderated, which enabled me to sit back more and enjoy it. As soon as Kent said good night to the viewers at home, the governor looked over at us on the panel, put his hands out in front of him, and gave a little clap, as if to say, thank you for helping me win tonight. Whitman came over and shook our hands. "Good luck the rest of the way," I said.

For the next half hour, in the midst of the hubbub of reporters interviewing the candidates and their staffs, I gathered on-camera reaction for a piece to air later that night. Spin alley, an NJN producer calls this ritual in which the media debrief the consultants. Carville was there, and the media swarm around him like bees drawn to honey. Of the eighteen people I interviewed, the one who made the strongest impression on me was John Whitman, who was almost rabid in his denunciation of Florio for criticizing "my wife" for not presenting a credible plan when Florio hasn't presented any plan whatsoever. Out in our big "location" truck, feeding sound bites via microwave back to Trenton, I sent that one down with seven others, and the editor taking it in down there, a woman, said to me over a phone line, "That man needs an attitude adjustment."

Today, Hillary Rodham Clinton came in for Jim Florio. I don't think it's any coincidence that Bill Clinton visited New Jersey the day after the first debate, and now the First Lady arrived the day after the second. What better way to dampen news coverage of the debates in the event that Whitman scores well. Give the media some big meat to distract them, and do it right away.

This morning I went down to Cherry Hill to cover her and was shocked to see three thousand people rounded up on a Wednesday morning at the racetrack, Garden State Park, for a grand, old-fashioned rally. The Camden high-school band played triumphal marches, the banners and placards were multitudinous, and Hillary Clinton was on fire. She poured on the praise and roused the crowd. Jim Florio is a man of courage and responsibility. He took on the national gun lobby and started a revolution in this country. Re-elect him and you send a powerful message to Congress and the nation that it's time to stop the madness! She was almost spellbinding. Whatever Florio did to help the Clintons last year, she paid back. Carville and Begala clapped mightily as she spoke. Florio's staff was moved. "It's days like this that remind us why we do what we do," Jon Shure would say later.

To its credit, the Whitman campaign today began a three-day, fourteen-county bus tour. At last, a gimmick! A hook for the media! Looking at the itinerary, seven stops in North Jersey today, thirteen in South Jersey tomorrow, I'm almost surprised that the Whitman campaign is deep enough to put something like this together (and not too dispirited to bother).

But where are governors Weld and Engler of Massachusetts and Michigan? They should be in here for Whitman, standing up for her plan. Where are Reagan, Bush, Ford, Dole, Elizabeth Dole, Nixon? Anybody! To counter the Clintons! The party of Web Todd is not rushing in to save his daughter.

Maybe that's one of the things Rick Wright, Florio's chief of staff, was alluding to when he said to me cryptically at the debate, "If they'd have done what we anticipated, they'd be in good shape."

* Thursday, October 21 *

Wheels of Change, says the sign on the windshield of the bus carrying the Whitman inner circle across New Jersey. Inside, in about as comfortable a setting as a customized bus could offer, the candidate is giving a TV interview, while Lyn Nofziger is reading pulp fiction and eating a big box of Cracker Jacks, John Whitman is in the seat behind him talking on a portable cellular phone, and Lonna Hooks, Christie's former aide at the BPU, is seated next to John, her corn-rowed hair facing us as she gazes out the window. Behind her Dan Todd and his daughter, Whitney, are each reading books. Kate Beach, the eldest of the Todd children, is reading an Edith Wharton novel, and Nancy Risque Rohrbach, who wears big eyeglasses, is doing needlepoint.

George Bush used this same bus in 1988. Dan Quayle, in '92. It's housed in Alabama, but it travels when Republicans call. The driver says, some people like huntin', and some people like fishin'. He likes campaignin'. He keeps souvenir photos of Bush and Quayle scotch-taped to the windshield visor. You can see from the photos that Whitman is sitting where Bush sat, the first full double seat on the right, the seat of honor apparently. Most recently the bus was used in a Georgia U.S. Senate race by

Paul Coverdell, who won. Each time it pulls into a scheduled stop, the driver cranks up Willie Nelson's "On the Road Again" and blasts it out of loudspeakers on the roof.

This morning the bus took the Whitmans to Glassboro, Woodstown, and Malaga, three dusty boroughs so deep in the South Jersey farm country that you might as well be in Alabama. At each stop, several dozen supporters carrying Whitman signs greet the bus. The candidate today wore jeans, sneakers, and a red Phillies jacket; the Phils are down three games to one in the World Series, but Whitman is sending the right message here where the Philadelphia TV signal is still strong. The Philly stations are here covering her. If elected, asks the Channel 6 reporter, might she try to lure any of the Philadelphia sports teams over to South Jersey?

That's the kind of question a candidate who's been beaten up by the press doesn't mind answering. In fact, John Whitman's first words to me today were, "This is fun—more fun than having to answer questions from you guys," meaning the political reporters, followed by, "Is this going to be the one in five of your pieces that's fair?"

He and I would kick that around later on the bus. He thinks the media are quick to jump on Christie and very slow to jump on Florio. He used the example of Adidas sneakers. We jumped all over her for making that mistake, but when the Whitman camp put out a list of thirteen "lies" Florio supposedly uttered in this week's debate, we didn't follow up on a single one. He has a point, but we jumped on Adidas because it was flat-out wrong and because Florio himself led the attack by holding up a pair and mocking Whitman, whereas the "lies" are more matters of opinion and Whitman does not personally level the more serious charges at Florio. Her name is at the top of the press release, but there's no way of knowing if she has seen it before it went out, because she doesn't say anything to back it up. (An attack line out of a candidate's mouth works much better on television than an attack line off a piece of paper.) John Whitman gets very agitated as he makes his argument. He accuses NJN—not me, but the station—of tilting toward Florio. Nancy Risque Rohrbach jumps in and separates us before John gets any more hostile.

At each stop, Whitman goes inside a supermarket, a diner, or restaurant, shakes hands, asks for votes, and spreads the charm that Dan

Todd thought would be enough on its own to topple Jim Florio. She seems to have a nice, human touch. And the people know her. Many of them, when asked, say they'll vote for her. "Change" and "taxes" are the words they use the most. Others say they can't vote for her because her tax plan is baloney.

Back on the bus, the two aides, Keith Nahigian and Jason Volk, who live at the farm with the family, are finishing up the Cracker Jacks and opening the prize. They crack up when they see what it is—a little hologram of a cowboy wearing a kerchief! I crack up, too.

The bus tour is getting good play in the media. It's a good image for Whitman, touring the heartland and reconnecting with the people after a month of commercials and editorials that portrayed her as out of touch and out to lunch. And it seems to be serving as a tonic for her and the others on the bus. They think they can win. Lyn Nofziger says he's *seen* it happen. So, while Florio was in North Jersey getting endorsed by former Reagan press secretary and gunshot victim James Brady, the Whitman clan was breezing through the rural south, generating fresh momentum, and possibly spinning a delusionary fantasy.

★ Saturday, October 23 ★

"Whitman, Aboard Bus, Is on Upbeat Roll," says the headline in today's *New York Times*. That seems to be the conventional wisdom. Florio aides keep saying they expect the race to tighten, and the Whitman camp keeps talking about tracking polls that show them down only two or three points. On "Reporters' Roundtable" this week, three of the panelists now gave Whitman a slim chance of winning, and the fourth, David Wald of the *Star-Ledger*, said she has a decent chance.

One of the barometers I use to gauge a New Jersey election is videotape editor Joe Martin. He has been looking at film and tape of state politicians for twenty years. After months of editing nightly stories about two candidates locked in combat, he has developed a feel for which one is coming across better on the air, and he believes that whichever one looks better on NJN will win the election (because the inside crowd watches

NJN, and they influence the larger community). A month ago, he told me Florio would win, no doubt in his mind. I asked again this week. Florio, he said. I asked why. "She contradicts herself. She can't get her facts straight."

It's true that Christie Whitman has shifted her positions an awful lot this year. She has backtracked a lot, too. A month ago, she promised to unveil an urban agenda; there has been no urban agenda. In August she put Jim Wallwork in charge of a campaign task force on regulatory reform; he gave her a nine-page document in September and, in October, according to him, twenty-four "good examples of government waste," and yet there's been no mention of his task force and no press conference on waste in government.

She said a tax cut would be "cynical" in an election year, then proposed the biggest tax cut in state history. She said she would reallocate education aid if forced to, but says different things at different times about whether that means taking aid away from the wealthier school districts (which is the only way it *can* be reallocated). She calls for more spending on commerce promotion, crime prevention, juvenile rehabilitation, plus a tax break for farmers and less reliance on fees and fines to support the Department of Environmental Protection and Energy—all within the context of a major cut in state spending, about which she gives few details.

She denounced Florio's welfare reform proposal, then slid closer to it. She went on record as being against further use of mandatory minimum sentences, then proposed a crime plan whose hallmark was mandatory life sentences for three-time violent offenders. She projected her tax-cut plan would create 450,000 jobs over three years, then, after an independent economist projected 36,000, said it would probably take much longer than three years. She stressed themes six months ago and three months ago that she has completely dropped now: more openness in government, less reliance on bonded indebtedness. Some of her better proposals, we never hear about anymore: doubling the commerce department's promotion budget, creating a business ombudsman in the secretary of state's office, and amending the state constitution to do away with one-year budget gimmicks.

She has been all over the place.

Jim Florio, meanwhile, has not budged, has not wavered, has not altered a single position or backtracked on a single statement. He may have pandered, evaded questions, and supported his arguments with facts carefully selected. But "waffled"? Never. You know where he stands, as he told the Business and Industry Association at the first joint appearance of the campaign in June.

It is difficult to come up with tough questions to ask Florio in a debate or out in the field, because he offers no inconsistencies a reporter can expose. In the last debate, I found it much easier to come up with questions for Whitman than for Florio.

Last night the Whitman three-day bus tour ended with a rally at Liberty State Park. I did a live shot at six o'clock with Ed Rollins, and when the bus pulled in around 6:20, I hustled Whitman over to the camera position for another live interview. If the campaign were building momentum, a Friday dinnertime rally in the beautiful old railroad station with the majestic skyline of Lower Manhattan looming behind it would be the place to feel it. With Bret Schundler in charge, and all of Hudson County invited, and all of Whitman's ethnic coalitions invited, there should have been twenty-five hundred people there. Instead the crowd numbered about five hundred, and there was no buzz in the air. I left before the rally ended, and as I was walking toward the parking lot, several other early-leavers, recognizing me from TV, solicited my opinion. "She's gonna lose, isn't she?" said one. "She's run a lousy campaign," said another.

Talk about exit polls.

★ **Sunday, October 25** ★

What wonderful scenes politics produce. Today we were inside Rockefeller Center, in the news studio of WNBC-TV on the sixth floor (a place I'd never been before), for the third and final televised debate. The whole gang was there—media, consultants, aides, Whitman family members, Whitman children. On their way into the studio Jon Shure and Jim Florio congratulated me on having been named "Geek of the Week" in this morning's *Trentonian* for a debate question I'd asked Whitman about the wisdom of doing away with perks for top officeholders. Shure and Florio press secretary Audrey Kelly have been similarly honored.

The press and the Whitman camp watched the debate together in a partitioned-off area of the studio. We sat on folding chairs and watched on a monitor as the debate took place about twenty feet away. Reporters occasionally made faces at the questions being asked by host Gabe Pressman and his sidekick, Larry Kane, of sister station KYW-TV in Philadelphia. The Whitman group watched, poker-faced, as their candidate traded jabs with Jim Florio over ethics, guns, welfare reform, drunk driving, tax cuts, and property taxes. The Florio camp was one floor above us in a conference room, making noise, yelling at the TV set, and phoning in rapid-response instructions to the Edison headquarters, where Jo Glading and researcher David Bocian would quickly throw together a press release debunking a statement Whitman had just made in the debate. Glading would then fax the release to the conference room, where a Florio staffer would quickly xerox it and bring it down to the sixth floor to distribute to reporters. Four times during the hour, a Florio advance woman walked past or leaned over the Whitman group to hand reporters a press release saying, in essence, Mrs. Whitman is full of shit. The Whitman camp produced one such rebuttal piece at the end of the debate.

Hanging over this match-up were new Sunday morning poll numbers from the *Asbury Park Press* showing the gap down to 5, Florio, 45 percent, Whitman, 40 percent. "I'm the one who always said it's going to be a close, tight race," Florio told reporters. Ed Rollins saw the numbers as vindication of his recent remarks about tracking polls.

The debate itself was noteworthy mainly for its loose, talk-show format, and the disconnectedness from the campaign of the two people asking the questions, especially Larry Kane. After Pressman opened with a question about character, a question designed to elicit instant head-banging, Kane followed with a plaintive scold in which he asked, "Don't the voters deserve a better campaign?" A slightly taken-aback Florio responded with, "Well, these are the questions that are coming forward." In other words, get off your high horse, Larry, it's your fault. Nearly ten minutes was taken up with a discussion of how the two candidates would handle negotiations with the '76ers, the Flyers, and the Yankees on moving to New Jersey. ("This is the biggest embarrassment I've ever seen," said Mark Magyar under his breath to other reporters.) And yet, it was a wonderful debate in that Florio and Whitman sat three feet apart at a desk and were able to tee off on one another. Who got the better of it is hard to say. They each had their moments.

Toward the end, some good talk-show questions got asked. What if you lose? Pressman asked each. Whitman said she'll stay active. Florio said he knows both winning and losing, and "I'm like Sophie Tucker. I've been rich and poor and rich is better. Winning is better." Kane asked if there was anything about the other each liked? "I don't dislike Mrs. Whitman," Florio protested; it is just her policies he dislikes. "I don't dislike him," said Whitman, and she conceded he'd done some good things as governor. "Nobody does everything all wrong."

Pressman asked who had the most influence on them during their earlier years. Without hesitation, Florio answered, "Robert Kennedy," recalling that Kennedy came to the Trenton Statehouse in 1968, and saying, "he was serene in his idealism" (an odd but nice choice of words). Whitman said her parents, because they stood for something and because they taught her "good government is the best politics."

After the debate, spin alley happened in the lobby near the elevators. Florio got away quickly, then Whitman, leaving Carville and Rollins to toss phrases at a media corps hungry for sound bites.

A few minutes later, on my way out of 30 Rockefeller Center, I saw Jim Florio in the ground-floor coffee shop ordering lunch at a table with his gang: Carville, Harold Hodes, Doug Berman, Paul Begala, Jon Shure, Jim Andrews, and a screenwriter friend of someone's who was gathering material for a movie about campaigns. They were laughing and talking animatedly, like boys who had just been in a street fight and were swapping war stories. It occurred to me later, they were having their fun in a building built by Webster Todd, the father of the woman they hope to demolish.

★ Tuesday, October 26 ★

"It's about people! It's about creating jobs! It's about hope! It's about the future!" That is the mantra in Christie Whitman's stump speech now. She says it wherever she goes. It doesn't mean much, but she delivers it well. Today she was in Trenton, campaigning along the Trenton Commons at lunch time, attracting much attention from the public, who recognize her now, and the media, who follow her like the proverbial 800-pound gorilla.

The best and worst of Whitman's campaign was on display today. At American Automobile Association headquarters in Robbinsville, outside Trenton, she gave her stump speech to no more than three dozen employees. The media had no idea why she visited this place; I thought it might be to talk about auto insurance, but she talked only about the economy and taxes, which is all she talks about now. A judge yesterday recommended fining the Florio campaign $10,500 for violating the campaign finance law, but Whitman never mentioned it, even though it was her campaign that filed the original charges. She stood under a Muzak speaker in the ceiling, which no one turned off, so the half-dozen radio and television crews covering her had Mantovani violins in their sound bites. The event was without rhyme, reason, or voters.

Then, she went to the Trenton Commons to shake hands and visit a food court, and somehow the urban setting, the many interested people, and the added media created energy. Whitman worked the crowd well. People peppered her with questions—about jobs for minorities, about her drunk-driving position, about cutting state government—and she answered each one patiently. Many of the people looked as if they hailed from the opposite end of the socio-economic spectrum from Whitman, but she tried to connect to each one. It was like a walking town meeting. Her aide, Jason Volk, kept trying to push her along, but more people had more questions, and the candidate wanted to answer them and explain herself. Retail politics, they call this. In 1981, Tom Kean drove his staff nuts by talking to people endlessly and getting way off schedule. Governor Florio comes into an event quickly and leaves quickly. Whitman today resembled Kean in '81.

The Whitman camp says its polls now show the race even, while the Florio camp says the gap is closing but still comfortable. "We have the momentum," Hazel Gluck told me today. "Everybody is very up." Brenda Bacon at Florio headquarters, on the other hand, talked about "getting nervous."

At NJN, we have been doing two packages a day since last week,

Sandra King and I now switching back and forth between the candi-dates. Yesterday I covered Florio, who went to Marcal Paper, a large mill in Bergen County which manufactures recycled paper goods, to get en-dorsed by the owners, the Marcalus family, and to talk about jobs and the environment. He was so happy and relaxed, I wondered what he knew that I didn't. Perhaps he was coming off the high of being endorsed by six newspapers on Sunday and the *New York Times* on Monday. Their words, in some cases, were glowing, while for Whitman there was mainly dis-dain. Today the New York *Daily News* became the ninth paper to go for Florio ("New Jerseyans are fortunate to have a genuine leader in their Statehouse."). Only the *Home News* of Central Jersey and the *Wall Street Journal* have gone for Whitman.

A Florio loyalist fears his candidate is overconfident and talks about "history repeating itself—not Byrne-Bateman ('77) but Florio-Kean ('81). The patrician (Whitman) is coming on!"

"Pride goeth before a fall," a Whitman supporter quoted from the Bible, saying Florio walks around all "puffed up" and warning it will backfire on him.

On the air, Whitman is finally responding to Florio's vilification of her. She has a TV spot on now in which she complains about a cheap shot. "I'm the mother of two teenagers. I know what it's like to worry on a Friday night about drunk drivers while my kids are out of the house. As governor, nobody will be tougher than me on drunk drivers. . . . And I'll continue to support the ban on assault weapons." She also has a radio ad in which sixteen-year-old Kate Whitman defends "my Mom" against all the "nasty things" Jim Florio has said about her.

Whatever question is asked of Florio these days, he tries to work into his answer guns, carjacking, drunk driving, welfare reform, and property taxes. Those are his mantras. Yesterday the NRA probably did him a favor by taking out full-page newspaper ads attacking him for using the NRA as a scapegoat for all the state's problems. Today Florio called a news conference to point out that recent NRA literature urged members to vote for Whitman, this despite Whitman's denials that she has anything to do with the NRA. Once again, he had a theme for the day; she just campaigned.

It's all guns.

Governor Florio today stood outside Caso's Gun-a-Rama, the Jersey City gun shop Christie Whitman wandered into in June, and mocked her for saying in Sunday's debate that Phillips-head screwdrivers kill people, too, so maybe the governor wants to outlaw them also. With the national president of the Fraternal Order of Police at his side, along with Officer Frank Sharkey of the Jersey City police, who survived an assault-weapon shot to his head eighteen months ago, Florio held up a picture of the Tech 9 that killed an East Orange girl in one hand and a screwdriver in the other. "This is the gun that killed Comisha Brown. This is a Phillips-head screwdriver. Anyone who doesn't know the difference doesn't deserve to be governor of New Jersey," he said.

"He has nothing else to run on," Carl Golden was quoted as saying in the *Record* this morning. "He's gonna ride this horse until it drops."

A lot of media are out with the candidates now in the final week. The protocol calls for the media to wait until the candidate finishes speaking, then to surround Florio or Whitman for a little press conference, a gang bang, as it's traditionally been called. The media jargon has overtones of sex and violence. "Where shall we get him?" the reporters or photographers might say. "Shall we do her over here?" "No, let's do her here."

In today's version of the gang bang, my body packed against other bodies, my arm outstretched along with other arms holding microphones and the little tape recorders that print reporters carry—a media octopus—I asked Florio why it's guns every day. Obviously polling or focus groups have told him that this is the issue. He answers by saying at his next stop he'll talk about guns but also about other things, like Mrs. Whitman's opposition to welfare reform and the inevitability of her raising property taxes. And to think, back in June I wondered if assault weapons would be a long-term issue in the race!

Several of us interviewed Frank Caso, the owner of the little shop that's become New Jersey's most famous gun emporium, who spoke disgustedly of Florio as a demagogue hell-bent on a wrongheaded crusade while all around him people are losing their jobs and hurting economically.

Whitman delivered her stump speech today at a few stops and fended off questions from Sandra King. Larry Stuelpnagel interviewed her for his weekend talk show, "On the Record."

"Want my take on Christie?" he asked me. "She's going through the motions."

Producer Retha Sherrod said she hadn't seen Whitman in person in a long while. "She looks thin."

Both candidates are going like whirling dervishes, especially Florio. He had six events today, beginning in Newark, then north to Bergen County, then Jersey City, then way down to Voorhees in Camden County, then back up to Trenton by dinnertime, then Newark again. He moves fast, with plainclothes State Police officers all around him. If out-thinking her isn't enough to insure victory, he'll outwork her.

While in Jersey City I talked to Bob Janiszewski, the Hudson County executive and a Florio ally, who predicted this election will become "a case study in American politics." As late as July, he said, Florio had an approval rating of 24 to 26 percent and a "hard disapproval" rating of 40 percent. Carville, Begala, and the others turned that around, he said. How? By reversing traditional logic: Instead of the incumbent defending his record and the challenger attacking it, they managed to "get Whitman almost into the role of the incumbent and turned the election into a referendum on her. She's been on the defense since Labor Day and before."

★ Thursday, October 28 ★

When Ed Rollins showed Christie Whitman a new TV commercial, she didn't like it. It was too harsh on Jim Florio, the music was too sinister, and the whole thing was typical fear-mongering and hype. "That's not me," she said to herself, and she told Rollins to rewrite it. She had him change the words, the music, and the announcer. Instead of a "talent voice," she wanted the voice of someone who sounded more like a real person. The footage of herself that comes on at the end had been used before; she told Rollins which new footage she preferred. "I made the ad harder in a way," she says. "They had it asking questions, like, 'can we afford four more years?' I said turn those into statements: 'we can't afford four more years.'" Rollins was supposed to be at a Trenton news conference with Ginny Littell and Republican national committeeman David Norcross to lay out the ethics case against Jim Florio, but Whitman told him to skip it and recut the ad.

I learned this while riding on the bus with Whitman today. I got on at the Statehouse, where she was endorsed by a handful of black ministers, and would ride with her to Merck headquarters in Hunterdon County, her next stop. She got on the bus and slapped a high-five with Johnny, the driver. It's become their thing.

For an hour, with just Kate Beach and Nancy Risque Rohrbach on board, plus the two aides, Keith and Jason, and an off-duty Jersey City police supervisor named Walter who provides security, I got a chance to learn some things. For example, Dan Todd never wanted the title of campaign manager, but Christie encouraged him to use it because, in his phrase as repeated to me by her, "somebody has to have the buffalo chip"—meaning somebody has to take the heat, be the point person. Replacing him with Rollins was not meant to be a big deal. Rollins was planning to come on full time anyway one week later, but then the *New York Times* poll came out showing a 21-point lead for Florio, and they all agreed something had to be done. "The point of it was to satisfy everybody," she said, meaning Republicans, who were unnerved by the poll.

When the press portrayed it as a firing, "it was very hurtful to him and to me—to him because you never want to be made to look like you couldn't do a job, to me because I wouldn't do that to my brother." He is still very much a part of the campaign, she said, and he and Rollins have had a good relationship all year. (Since the shakeup, Todd has been a little skittish, averting his gaze when you try to catch his eye, like a man nursing a wound.)

Of Jim Florio, she said, "As a governor he's been very bad. He's cost the people dearly." He's cost the children by not fixing education, she said. And he's done "long-term damage" by "pitching every issue so that somebody had to lose and somebody had to win." His style is divisive. And he has "denigrated the office of governor" in this campaign by implying things about her that aren't true. "You can rip into my economic plan all you want, but it's the whispering campaign that is really low." Such as? Implying there was something sinister in her 1990 tax return. Trying to get the press to write about her membership in a Florida club, the Key Largo Anglers Club, that the Democrats say excludes nonwhites. "They've tried floating that and floating that. A reporter eventually asked me, did you read the 1936 bylaws? I said, 'I joined the '90 club, not the '36.'"

She said Florio's use of "class warfare" had an "element of sexism" about it, as did the press coverage of the campaign. "It's okay for a man to be rich," she said. Linking her fitness for office to her wealth "wouldn't work if I were a man," so they wouldn't have tried it. She criticized the whole effort. "Start condemning people for their money, and it's not too far before you allow them to start condemning people for their color and their race." It was a "fear tactic" coming out of a "bunker mentality," and one that "lends itself to stereotyping."

As for the media, "I've detected a different level of questioning than he's received," she said. For example, on economic questions, "we've put out as comprehensive and thorough an economic plan as any challenger ever, and yet we're accused of not enough detail. Why don't reporters get affronted when he doesn't answer what he's going to do?" I tell her we've tried, many times, to get that answer but that he's very good at turning aside unwelcome questions. "After seventeen elections, he should be," she said.

"Maybe because I'm a woman, there have been subliminal questions about my not having enough toughness. The press wants to see me get up and attack him on something," she says, suggesting it's not really her style to attack. I asked her why she hadn't drawn more attention to the recent allegations about Randy Primas, Governor Florio's former cabinet officer, getting a big cut of recent state bond work, and she said it was because she didn't want to "turn the campaign into a witch hunt."

As the bus cruised through the beautiful west Jersey countryside on a bright, warm October day, Whitman confided there are two things she'd have done differently. One, she'd have put the bus in operation much sooner. "It would have been hard to ignore, and it would have addressed the notion that I took the summer off." Two, she would not have let Florio put TV ads on after Labor Day, ads that skewered her, and waited ten days to put on one of her own. "By letting him have that ten-day negative, he really burned that in."

I learned a few other things: that the idea of a tax cut didn't really start to occur to her until July, when the economic task force was formed; that "the economists" wanted a two-year 15-percent-a-year tax cut, the "political people" wanted something a lot less dramatic, and she chose 30 percent over three years because she firmly believes it's what the state needs, or so she says; that Carl Golden had indeed issued the welfare press release without her seeing it, and from then on she has insisted on seeing everything before it goes out. Above all, I learned there is not a lot of mystery about Christine Todd Whitman. What you see is what you get.

I sensed a candidate philosophical about either outcome: hoping for victory but prepared for defeat.

* Friday, October 29 *

"Are you doing another soft piece on Christie tonight?" asked Brenda Bacon, who's doing the scheduling for Florio's campaign now. That was on the phone yesterday afternoon. After finishing my piece around four o'clock, I dropped in at Florio headquarters, and Bacon was relentless. She accused me of giving Whitman a free ride night after night. I couldn't tell if she was serious or just needling me, but she never let up. We watched "NJN News" on a TV in the press office with Jo Glading and fund-raiser Karen Kessler. I had done a Whitman piece. When it came on, they seemed less interested in my fairness than in Whitman's demeanor. "She sounds down," Bacon said. "Was she down, Michael?" Glading wanted to know. Everyone is looking for signs in everyone else's face and voice.

From there I went to a women's rally for Whitman at the Brunswick Hilton. I chatted up John Whitman, who was very pleasant until we veered toward the subject of news coverage. "You guys never wanted her to win in the first place. And you've done everything you can to keep her from winning." He was speaking about the press in general but "particularly NJN." I told him Brenda Bacon had just said I'd been too kind to his wife. He guffawed. I felt vindicated. If both sides are unhappy, at least you're even.

About three hundred women attended the rally, perhaps half the number that attended the women's rally in July. Whitman has been criticized for not appealing more directly to women. Hazel Gluck has tried to encourage her in that direction, but Whitman says she is uncomfortable appealing on the basis of gender rather than on the issues. Polls show women going for Florio by as much as 50 percent to 30. Now, near the eleventh hour, Whitman has bowed to those who want to see her try to energize the women's vote, but the size of the crowd is not encouraging. The Florio camp countered by stationing women demonstrators outside the Brunswick Hilton, holding a Statehouse news conference featuring Florio's high-level women appointees, and issuing a fax attack on Whitman's record on women's issues. (The fax recounted her support of Clarence Thomas, accused her of helping to elect pro-life Republicans to the legislature, and included a copy of an Anna Quindlan *New York Times* column criticizing Whitman.)

Meanwhile, Florio on Thursday attended a ground-breaking for the New Jersey Performing Arts Center in Newark. The high-profile event could not have been timed better for Florio, and despite denials, the timing looks suspicious. Florio is using the government to help his re-election bid. He is hardly the first to do it.

He also unveiled a new "Most Wanted Deadbeat Dads" poster program. From now on, the ten noncustodial fathers most in arrears on their child support payments will have their pictures displayed in public like murderers on the FBI's most wanted list. A good move five days before the election.

Today Florio attended a rally at his alma mater, Trenton State College, where he started sounding visionary about the next four years. He also predicted the Democrats will take back the state senate on Tuesday, a sign of confidence. Whitman called a news conference in Newark, where a corruption-fighter from a bygone era, former U.S. attorney Herb Stern, came out and endorsed her because, he said, he was "appalled" by the Lyndhurst school controversy. Reporters in the room knew more about Lyndhurst than Stern, and the event was somewhat lame.

Then Whitman flew to Camden, where Jack Kemp was to join

her. First, though, she had to encounter Florio demonstrators. As her supporters shouted, "Christie! Christie!" the Florioites shouted "Go home! Go home!" It got a little rough. Whitman had to cancel a walking tour of a neighborhood. Then Kemp came and talked the Republican gospel of lower taxes.

Kemp raised $350,000 for the state Republicans at a luncheon yesterday. Lewis Katz, Steve Moses, and other Florio fund-raisers are still trying to raise last-minute dollars for the Democrats. Both Whitman and Florio "maxed out" weeks ago, meaning they raised the requisite amount to qualify for maximum public financing. They can't legally spend above that amount. The continued race for dollars is a sign that both parties will use loopholes in the spending caps to buy "generic" TV advertising, to pay for phone banking and literature drops, and to use as "street money" on election day.

Street money is a New Jersey tradition. The state parties give county and city political leaders thousands of dollars to get out the vote. The local people pay students and other workers $25 for a day of getting people to the polls. There is not a lot of accounting done on this money, but nobody complains about its being illegal or even unsavory because both parties do it and because, on its face, it is perfectly legal. The Democrats are reputed to be better at it and will spread around $600,000 or more among ten to twenty thousand people on Tuesday.

★ Saturday, October 30 ★

This morning Ed Rollins and other Whitman campaign people invited the press to see their new TV commercial featuring Tom Kean. Only three of us showed up. The rest of the press corps must have been out covering Whitman and Florio. Rollins and company seem genuinely to believe that they have a decent chance of winning. "This is a classic challenger race," media consultant Mike Murphy said. "You peak on election day."

For an hour, they and their pollster, Ed Goas of the Tarrance Group, gave us the lay of the land from their point of view, replete with lots of jargon about "driving up positives" and "negatives." Their nightly tracking polls had the gap going from 3 points a week ago to 5, to 3, and then 2 last night. They are spending a million dollars on TV advertising the final week, more, they say, than the Florio campaign's $600,000-plus and the Democratic State Committee's $200,000 combined (the Whitman camp's numbers). In Tom Kean, said Rollins, they have "the most popular figure in the state by far" pitching for Christie and for "change." "Change" is the buzzword in the three TV ads they are running now. They are spending $35,000 to buy one showing in the New York market of the Kean ad during "60 Minutes."

Rollins said the strategy had always been to peak late. He conceded that the campaign had had many imperfections, but the strategy was sound and had not changed. Make the election about Florio, aim for the undecideds, and save your money 'til the end, because undecideds make up their minds as late as election day. He praised "Florio and Carville" for doing what they set out to do, fog the issues, create confusion, cloud Christie Whitman, and put the onus on her. He called Florio's Washington helpers "the president's team," and said they were backed up "by as good a state team as you've ever seen." By comparison, he said, the Whitman camp is a "ragtag group" with very few experienced hands. (Rollins wants it known he's been outgunned, not necessarily outfoxed. He once said to me, "half the people in our campaign are debutantes and the children of fund-raisers.")

But the Whitman campaign had something else going for it, a candidate who "never freaked out," according to Mike Murphy. Most challengers lose because they get psychologically worn down, he said. In the kind of climate of criticism and bad poll numbers that hit Whitman this past month, weaker candidates panic. They waste resources. "She never lost her cool," Murphy said, with genuine admiration.

"No candidate I've ever been around has risen to the occasion the way she has," said Rollins, who has been around quite a few, among them Ronald Reagan. He said he pulled Whitman aside two weeks ago, told her to "look into the abyss" and see that she could very well lose this race unless she gave it everything she had. "She was quiet for awhile. Ten minutes later she said, 'let's do it.'"

As Hazel Gluck, Carl Golden, and other Whitman operatives listened in the conference room of Gluck's son's law firm in Lawrenceville,

Rollins said with a straight face, "We are in a dead even race with the final weekend going on, and I'm very confident."

Meanwhile, the candidates pushed their tired bodies through the state one more time. Whitman's bus barnstormed Central Jersey on a raw, wet day. Hillary Clinton flew into a small airport in North Jersey for Florio, stood in a hangar with the governor and twenty-five Democratic women, and said, "Anybody can get on a bus. The trick is to figure out which direction you're going in."

★ Sunday, October 31 ★

This morning's final *Star-Ledger*/Eagleton poll has Florio up by 9 points. The *Record* has him up by 10. But the *Asbury Park Press* has the race dead even at 38 to 38 with 22 percent undecided. The *Press*'s poll is the least respected of the three, but if somehow it's true, Whitman is surging. That possibility is making the Florio people nervous. "I'm a nervous wreck," said Rich Gannon, the deputy campaign manager. "When you've been in the gutter for three years, of course you're nervous," said Carl Van Horn, Rutgers professor and Florio advisor.

They were at a rally for Florio on the Rutgers campus this afternoon. About five hundred students and Democratic politicos turned out for a good, old-fashioned, noisy rally. Jon Shure said the nervousness felt by those inside the campaign is natural, and he dismissed the *Asbury Park Press* poll. "When you've got a poll that shows 22 percent undecided two days before an election, you throw it in the garbage," he said.

On hand to boost Florio and build up spirits were Bill Bradley, Frank Lautenberg, and Congressman Bob Torricelli, along with the woman he has been seen with a lot lately, Bianca Jagger. Bradley asked the crowd to think of Florio as a boxer who may have been down for a nine-count but never stopped fighting. Florio echoed the line. "If there's something worth doing, it's worth fighting for," he said, offering a maxim for himself. He said this morning's papers contained good news: not the polls, although they were good, but the fact that 10,000 jobs were created in September and that crime stats were down again in the seven top categories (Whitman has said the state lost 10,000 jobs in September). Florio's speech was all issues. Here is what I've done. Here is how I differ from what "some people" would do (he no longer speaks of Whitman by name). "It is always easier to tear things down than to build things up," he tells the crowd. He makes a strong case for electing him on the issues—guns, crime, jobs, the Shore, welfare, property taxes, tuition assistance, education, job training, mortgage assistance—and he tells them the election is important.

Afterwards, surrounded by media asking about the polls and how he feels, Florio repeats standard phrases about being "comfortable" and working as hard as he can. This is his seventh stop of the day; he is literally charging up and down the state. "I'm satisfied we've done everything we can do," he says, and there is the slightest hint in that answer of its perhaps being not quite enough. Standing a foot away from him and off to one side, I see a softness in his face, in his cheek. Normally the Florio visage appears hard as granite. Today I see a glint of vulnerability.

The *Star-Ledger* became the sixteenth newspaper to endorse him today, to five for Whitman. The case for Florio as rendered in the newspaper editorials is a powerful one, and in fact those editorials form the basis of the two TV commercials he has put on this week, one full of laudatory comment, the other pitting what they said about him against what they said about her. The *Star-Ledger* dismissed her in two paragraphs as inexperienced and offering a tax cut promise that's not credible.

But Senator Bob Dole finds it credible. The U.S. Senate minority leader stumped with Whitman today in Essex and Bergen counties, another cold, rainy day. Dole said a Whitman victory would send a signal that will be heard in the White House. "It'll be heard by Bill and it'll be heard by Hillary, and they'll understand the people of New Jersey are saying we don't want more taxes, let's not Florioize America."

All week I've been asking Jo Glading for a chance to ride with Florio, as I rode with Whitman, and interview him for this journal. She has put me off. It dawned on me that perhaps, like Brenda Bacon, others in the Florio camp think I've been too soft on Whitman. At the rally I pulled Jon Shure aside and asked him if that's why I wasn't getting my ride with the governor. He said he doubted it, but acknowledged that some in the Florio campaign think I've been soft on Whitman. "Do you?" I asked. He flinched for an instant, then said, "No." People in the final stages of a campaign can get a little overly partisan, he said by way of explanation. But he did not think Jim Florio would want company in the car tomorrow. "He'll want to think about what he has to do at the next stop."

★ **Monday, November 1** ★

The strategizing is over. The talk about issues is over. Everyone close to both campaigns understands that the election is out of their hands now, except for tomorrow's execution of get-out-the-vote plans.

Still, the candidates barnstorm. Governor Florio was in Blackwood, Camden County, his old home town, at eight this morning, meaning he left the governor's mansion by seven. He spent the morning in South Jersey, the noon hour in Central Jersey, the afternoon and early evening in North Jersey, then did a quick hit in Central Jersey before heading back down south for a big rally at Garden State Park hosted by the Camden County Democrats. You can do all that by car in this small state, but it's grueling.

Christie Whitman took her bus into Ocean County for the afternoon—an important Republican and senior citizen area—before ending with a nighttime firehouse rally in Hamilton Township, Mercer County.

I covered Florio today. He was buoyant, foucsed, a little giddy. His wife has been at his side holding his hand the past four days. "Are the eyes of the nation on this race?" I asked him at one of several gang bangs I participated in, borrowing the headline on page one of today's Trenton *Times.* "Are the eyes of the nation on this race?" he repeated back to me. "How about the world? How about the universe? Let's see, 'Florio proclaims eyes of the universe are on this election!' Does anyone have a serious question?" he asked as he broke ranks and started walking away. I guess he is too intent upon winning to bother with the implications for anyone other than himself and this state.

His aides don't have a lot to say. Reporters have run out of intelligent questions to ask them. There is only one question left—who's going to win? or, "how's it look?" as I put it to Harold Hodes, who's been travelling with Florio, Lucinda, and Jon Shure the past few days. "What d'ya mean?" he said, as if he didn't know what I could possibly be inquiring about.

At another stop I mentioned to Doug Berman that the Whitman camp is claiming it outspent the Florio campaign on television in this final week. "That's a bunch of bullshit," he said, arguing the Florio camp bought 1,200 "points" for the final week compared to the Whitman camp's likely 800, and explaining how you buy TV time. A gross rating point means 1 percent of all the homes in a market. You need to buy about 700 points to make sure an ad sinks in. A point costs about $600 in New York and in Philadelphia. So to make sure an ad is seen in one market costs about $420,000. It was a safe topic of conversation.

Meanwhile, the Whitman camp tonight still thinks it can win. Hazel Gluck says that in last night's tracking polls Whitman passed Florio for the first time—by 2 points. Carl Golden calls that "the inevitable consequence of the trend line we've been seeing. People have been peeling away from the governor." What's the attitude among Whitman people about the likelihood of victory? "It's pretty high," he says.

James Carville is on New York news tonight saying that when one side tells you about their tracking polls, they're usually trying to sell you a line.

★ Four p.m., Election Day ★

In six or seven hours it will be over. This is nervous time for everyone. Turnout around the state is said to be heavy. The weather is good.

This is the moment of truth for Jim Florio. In recent days he has been citing Harry Truman's dictum that if you do what is right, things will turn out alright in the end. Florio says he believes in that. It is a 1960s, karmic approach to politics: zen and the art of getting re-elected. Florio has never publicly doubted that he did the right thing when he raised taxes three and a half years ago. He gets the public's verdict tonight.

For Christie Whitman, the stakes are different. She is not expected to win now. If she does, it will mean the Whitman mystique is real and powerful. She will have come back from the dead (something they also say about Florio, except he was "dead" much longer ago). If she doesn't win, she will be blamed for mistakes but also credited with having righted herself in the final weeks of the campaign.

Prior to the 1947 constitution, New Jersey governors were not allowed to succeed themselves. Since then, all five governors who have stood for re-election against a nominee of the opposite party have won: Driscoll, Meyner, Hughes, Byrne, and Kean. (William Cahill lost in a GOP primary in 1973.) Florio would be the first incumbent to lose in a general election. Complicating the picture tonight is the presence on the ballot of seventeen independent, fringe, and kook candidates, a record number. If they pull 3 or 4 percent, those are votes that could have gone for Whitman, according to the conventional wisdom. But Whitman's pollster argues that most of the people leaning toward independent candidates are registered Democrats.

The politics of ridicule coming out of the Florio camp has continued up to the last minute. Whitman was on "The Howard Stern Show" yesterday morning, engaging in light banter. The Florio camp took what she said about having once tried marijuana and about the right to bear arms, and put them into a blistering fax attack. I don't know how many of the Florio people have ever owned guns, but the other sin they shouldn't be criticizing.

For weeks, politicians and pundits have been saying the New Jersey electorate is unenthusiastic about the choice being offered them this year. They will choose the lesser of evils, people like Rutgers professor Cliff Zukin keep saying. I like both candidates. I am on my way to vote for one of them, and then to Florio election night headquarters to begin a night's work. I give Florio a three-in-four chance of winning tonight, Whitman a one-in-four chance of an upset. That's not exactly going out on a limb, but it's as close as I feel comfortable to making a prediction right now.

You, dear reader, have known since you picked up this book what I learned just nine hours ago. Christie Whitman is the first woman in a line of New Jersey governors that dates back to 1624. I confess, I am surprised: not shocked, but surprised. As you know from having read this far, I and most everyone else thought the Florio campaign out-performed, out-thought, and out-worked the Whitman campaign. Polls kept reaffirming that judgment. But one of the marvels of American democracy is how unpredictable a mass of people can be. We were wrong about Florio and Whitman, at least in the final days when the race tightened. We may have been wrong for months.

Florio election night headquarters was not a happy place last night. Early exit poll returns had shown the governor with a small lead, but by eight o'clock that evaporated. The network affiliates, who pooled the cost of the one exit poll undertaken, said the race was too close to call at 50.3 percent for Florio to 49.7 for Whitman.

When actual returns started coming in, Whitman was on top. She stayed there most of the evening. With 43 percent of the vote in, she led by 52 percent to 48. On the air, I reminded viewers that this was the point at which her lead over Bill Bradley on election night 1990 put us in a state of near-apoplexy and then disappeared. But when she still held the lead over Florio with 56 percent of the vote in, the grim reality started to set in on a subdued ballroom full of Florio supporters. At 65 percent, the gap narrowed to 50 to 50, Whitman ahead still by ten thousand votes, and the crowd perked up a bit. But the sense of loss still hung in the air like a thick vapor.

Upstairs, on the eleventh floor of the Brunswick Hilton, the same hotel in which he'd declared victory four years ago, Florio watched television with his wife and his three children and two grandchildren. His inner circle of advisors was in another suite, watching the returns on TV and working the phones in a frantic effort to learn which areas had not yet been heard from. In 1989, then-campaign manager Doug Berman had the pleasure of walking in to Florio's suite and telling him he'd won. Last night, with 97 percent of the vote counted and Whitman clinging to a 30,000 vote lead, it fell to Berman to enter Florio's suite and tell him he lost. After nearly thirty years in politics, the governor didn't need to hear it from a confidante. He knew.

Over at Whitman headquarters, at the Princeton Marriott in Plainsboro, I could see jubilation on the TV monitor I was using. Around twelve-thirty, by a bad stroke of timing, or perhaps deliberately, Florio entered the room to give his concession speech at the moment Whitman was about to declare victory. NJN had to split-screen the two events and play audio from both, until someone decided the victor should be heard and the network cut away from Florio. "We did it!" a triumphant Christie Whitman yelled to a roomful of whooping, hollering Republicans.

Surrounded by family and staff, Florio couldn't have been much classier in defeat. Jon Shure and Doug Berman had written some remarks for him that afternoon, just in case. In them, Florio promised Whitman a smooth transition, reaffirmed the principles he said he had fought for, said he was proud of what they had all done together, and stuck with the Harry Truman line that in the long run, if you do right it will turn out alright. The smile that kept breaking into his face looked as real and as genuine as any I'd ever seen. In defeat, he looked more relaxed and un-guarded than usual.

I had many questions prepared for the two interviews I'd ex-pected to get with him, but he left the ballroom without running the gauntlet of fifteen TV camera positions set up in the middle of the room. Reporters were probably just as relieved not to have to interview him at this moment of crushing disappointment. Carville, Begala, Berman, Shure, and others gave interviews around the room. Carville took the blame for the loss and declined to be drawn into instant analysis. A number of women staffers were crying.

Two images stay with me this morning, in addition to Florio's strength and graciousness at the podium. One is the image I saw on our six o'clock news of Whitman, accompanied by John and Danny, as she calls her brother, riding to their Tewksbury Township polling place yesterday morning on bicycles. It was a powerful image of healthy, wealthy, unpretentious landed gentry riding to do their civic duty. The son of the shipyard worker rode to his polling place in his big blue state-issue Cadillac limousine; the millionaires pedaled down a country lane.

The other image is of a woman in her late fifties or sixties who came up to me at the end of our broadcast last night with a Florio sticker on her dress and tears in her eyes. She clutched my arm and begged me to tell her why it happened. "He was the greatest governor we ever *had*," she said, incredulous, stricken, the tears welling up in her eyes.

★ Thursday, November 4 ★

Why it happened. There are dozens of reasons. Before I get into them, I should say that the New Jersey electorate basically split. Unofficially, Whitman got 1,236,000 votes or 49 percent of the total; Florio got 1,209,000 or 48 percent; the independents got the rest. This was not a mandate for Whitman or an outright rejection of Florio. As Jim McQueeny pointed out on NJN last night, it averages out to a difference of six votes at each polling place.

It happened because the people don't know about all the good *little* things Jim Florio did as governor, and the Florio campaign was so busy attacking Whitman that it failed to tell them. The decision appears to have been made early on that you cannot lift Florio's "positives" so you must build up Whitman's "negatives." You will never make Jim Florio warm and fuzzy, one kept hearing from Democrats. Maybe the public expects a long list of accomplishments from any governor, but the Florio campaign never offered such a list, except in some of the governor's stump speeches, where, coming out of his own mouth, it fell flat.

It happened also because Christie Whitman promised to cut taxes by 30 percent, and even if the public choked on that at first, eventually the idea sunk in that if she could not deliver the entire package, a part of it would still be welcome. New Jersey became tax-phobic after June 1990. The Republicans have been wringing that cloth in every election since, and we thought there was not much water left in it. But there is. The tax cut became Whitman's message. Prior to her unveiling it, pundits were writing she had offered no reason for her candidacy. Suddenly, there was a "there" there. Not only that, but it was a sharper and more foucsed message than Florio's. Hear the name Whitman and you thought "tax cuts." Hear the name Florio and you thought "tough decisions," "leader-ship," "competence," "continuity," all broader and more diffuse notions.

It happened because when people got into the privacy of the voting booth, personality came into play. I remember a few months ago hearing someone say, whatever Florio's numbers are in the final Sunday polls, subtract three for those who go into the voting booth and just can't bring themselves to vote for him. It became accepted wisdom that people "hated" Florio after the 1990 tax hikes. The anger has "dissipated," we kept hearing this year. But, as Neil Upmeyer, editor of *New Jersey Reporter* magazine, put it on NJN's election night broadcast, there are still "reservoirs of antagonism" toward the governor. A veteran lobbyist attending Whitman's victory press conference at the Statehouse yesterday put it more bluntly: "People got into the voting booth and said, 'I hate this guy.'" A politician who had generated enormous personal good will might have been able to survive the tax anger and the bad economy, but Florio generated respect in some quarters, admiration at best, and never love. Contrast that with Whitman, who, if not yet loved, nonetheless comes across as down-to-earth, sincere, pleasant, and more expansive than Jim Florio. A male TV reporter, remarking upon the difference between the two, said to me on election night, "I'd rather have a beer with her than with him." It was a comment that touched ironic echoes, because in 1981 Tom Kean started closing in the polls against Florio after he staged an event in a bar to prove he could "have a beer with the boys in Bayonne," as the knock against him had been phrased.

It happened because the corruption card helped delineate Florio's darkness from Whitman's lightness, although Whitman did not play the card as heavily as she might. If people like Joe Salema were getting rich off of their associations with Florio, it meant that Florio's cronies were in the back room, wheeling and dealing, while their boss was out front being political. With his security detail whisking him in and out of campaign events, and all government decision making seeming to emanate from his office, Florio sometimes gave off an imperial air. The aura was one of guardedness, secrecy, and deal making. Contrast that with what appeared to be Whitman's openness and freshness—even naïveté—and you get another part of the appeal.

It happened because Florio's embrace of the gun issue may also have put some people off. Although it became a potent political weapon— underscored by the president's and the First Lady's homages to its effect on their thinking—Florio was so quick to use it and so often raised it that even the average voter began to notice and wonder, is this all the guy has to talk about? Like Bill Bradley's refusal to talk about state taxes in 1990, Florio's insistence on trotting out his Uzi's and Tech 9s at every stop could be taken as a sign of arrogance: an unwillingness to address what's on the public's mind, a stubbornness about sticking to one's political script.

And it happened because of the desire for change. I scoffed at Cary Edwards a year ago on election night when he called Clinton's victory over Bush a harbinger of the challenger's dumping the incumbent in the '93 New Jersey race, but he turned out to be right. The economy is what people are worried about first. It's been poor through most of Jim Florio's term. It shows signs of getting better, but not much. In that context many people say let's try something new. I was wrong to think that Whitman's glass-half-empty description of the state contradicted people's realities. In many cases, it must have spoken to them.

The turning points for Whitman were the arrival of Ed Rollins as day-to-day campaign manager, and then the bus. Rollins is a cool professional who inspires trust. The decision to put him in charge, I've learned, was made not at Kate Beach's house in Washington, as I have written, but right afterwards, in Rollins's car, on a twenty-minute ride to the Holocaust Memorial. Christie and John Whitman were in the back seat. Rollins told them what had to be done: Dan Todd needed to be replaced by Rollins. The Whitmans saw the light, and the question became, who would tell Danny? Who would "pull the trigger"? as the person telling me the story put it. Christie decided she would have to do it, and the next morning, back in New Jersey, she did.

From then on, things seemed to right themselves. The candidate stopped trying to manage her own campaign and got out more and *campaigned*, which is what a candidate is supposed to do. Then came the bus, the idea of all-purpose aide Keith Nahigian. It worked so well that two days after the election Governor-elect Whitman is still riding it—*today*, all over the state, on a victory tour. It's almost embarrassing that an irrelevancy as mundane as a bus can so captivate the media and tickle the public. But politics is part marketing, and the power of symbols in marketing is well known.

In the final week of the campaign, Rollins and Mike Murphy ran four different TV commercials. One of them reminded voters of how much they disliked the Florio tax hikes. Some in the Florio camp think that powerful negative helped close the gap at the end. More powerful, I think, was the way the commercials ended: with the same slow-motion shot of Christie on a Shore boardwalk, wearing a blue t-shirt, leaning over to a young girl and giving her a hug. Soft and warm, it was the best shot Mike Murphy put on the air, and he was smart enough to know how good it was. New Jersey, vote for Christie and you get a mother. Reject her, and you keep that hard-edged fighter.

Florio wanted to be the underdog. All year he kept saying he was. But Whitman became the underdog when the polls, the pundits, and the media started writing her off. People are naturally sympathetic to underdogs. And when the underdog does not give up, does not crack, does not even show signs of panic, some people take notice. Whitman's composure in the face of near-collapse impressed insiders and Republicans and was probably another factor in convincing people to "take a second look," as Ed Rollins liked to say. Her brother says she won "because everybody said she's *not* gonna win, and she's a spoiler, she's a fighter."

You have to wonder whether the constant drumbeat of negativity by the Florio campaign also created a sympathy vote for Whitman. Once people saw she was not as out to lunch as the Florio campaign asserted—and once she started defending herself in TV commercials— the attack itself may have come to seem unfair. The politics of ridicule was something new in New Jersey this year. We've had negative politics for years, but the note struck this year came out of a different place, out of "Saturday Night Live" and "Late Night with David Letterman." It wasn't dirty or below-the-belt; it was just so incessantly mocking. One assumes James Carville had a lot to do with setting that tone. It probably worked against George Bush, who had been the subject of professional lampooning for a decade. It didn't work as well against the newcomer woman who promised to bring, as she called it yesterday at her victory news conference, an "honest, direct, and up front" approach to government.

Maybe you had to tear down Whitman's credibility in order to win with a candidate despised by 40 percent of the public. Maybe it was the best strategy. But it didn't work. Commenting last night on why

Whitman won, Roger Bodman, NJN's Republican analyst, reduced it to two words. "Credibility and likeability," he said.

Later, off camera, his Democratic sidekick, Jim McQueeny, conceded of Florio, "He had the best team in the country trying to convince people that black is white." They almost did.

The polls certainly threw us off. The *Star-Ledger*/Eagleton poll had Florio ahead 48 to 43 in June, 47 to 38 in September, 52 to 40 in early October, and 48 to 39 this past Sunday. Either the polls failed, or the Whitman surge really didn't happen until the very end. Carville once quoted British prime minister Harold Macmillan to the effect that in a political campaign a week is like a year. That truism was certainly borne out in this election.

Another truism that survived was the line heard all year that, with Florio so unpopular, Whitman need only present herself as a "viable alternative" to win. We in the media thought her missteps and Florio's attack had destroyed her viability. We were wrong by a percentage point.

Hindsight is easy. Let me jump forward and engage in a little fantasy. I had planned to end this journal with a playful thought about Jim Florio's possible political future as envisioned by his closest associates, the people who *do* love him. After presiding successfully over New Jersey for another four years and perhaps becoming the national leader in a crusade to cut down on handguns, he plots a course toward the White House in the year 2000. If today's scuttlebutt becomes reality, maybe he even runs up against Hillary Clinton in the Democratic presidential primary. We must scratch that fantasy now, but we can replace it with another. Say Christie Whitman presides successfully over New Jersey for a term and a half, becoming nationally recognized for streamlining government humanely and without hurting education. In 1999 she gets recruited to run for president by moderates in the national Republican party. It's not that far-fetched; this morning's *New York Times* ends its front-page Whitman piece on the same whimsical note, a voter musing, "if she governs the state well, she's presidential material." Who knows? It could even be Christie Whitman against Hillary Clinton in 2000. A rematch between Rollins and Carville! A race I'd like to cover.

As my publisher was preparing this manuscript for the printer, Ed Rollins, in an act of colossal self-destruction, set off a firestorm of controversy that rages as I write.

At a breakfast meeting with reporters in Washington last Tuesday, Rollins boasted that the Whitman camp had beaten the Democrats at their own game, using $500,000 in street money to suppress the black vote. The money, he said, had been funneled to the "favorite charities" of black ministers, to keep them from energizing the electorate in their sermons the Sunday before Election Day, and to Democratic street workers, who were asked what amount the Democrats were paying them to get out the vote and were given a matching amount to "go home, sit, and watch television."

Rollins must have a blind spot when it comes to race. He was the one who thought that hiring Larry McCarthy, of Willie Horton–ad fame, would be a "one-day story." Now he has set off a most extraordinary chain of events. He apparently didn't realize that the idea of using street money to keep a minority group from going to the polls would strike many people as the antithesis of how democracy should work.

Christie Whitman now has a controversy on her hands that makes illegal aliens and missed school board votes look trivial. She denied Rollins's story and got him to recant it. But the damage has been done. Even though Rollins faxed Whitman an apology, for her to make public, saying he had grossly exaggerated ("my desire to put a spin on events . . . left the impression of something that was not true and did not occur"), people find it hard to believe that he made the entire thing up. Most people I've spoken to assume that what he talked about did happen on some small scale, but nowhere near $500,000 worth. The fact that both

Dan Todd and Carl Golden were discovered to have made comments about "voter suppression" in the days following the election adds credence to this view.

The story is getting enormous state and national media attention, including page one of the *New York Times* for three of the last four days, a segment on "The MacNeil-Lehrer Newshour," plus steady coverage in the *Washington Post* and *Wall Street Journal*, not to mention multiple page-one stories every day in the Jersey papers. President Clinton jumped right into the fray, saying on Wednesday that if the allegations are true, what the Republicans in New Jersey did is "terribly wrong." The black clergy in New Jersey is outraged; Rollins's story implies that black ministers will sell out their parishioners for a large donation to their pet projects. When Jesse Jackson and Al Sharpton announced they were coming to New Jersey to protest, the furor took on a *Bonfire of the Vanities* cast—a conflagration made of four elements: media, money, politics, and race.

"The attack by Mr. Rollins was an arrow aimed at the heart of our church, our moral oasis," Jackson proclaimed yesterday, standing with Whitman, Sharpton, and a dozen black churchmen inside her transition headquarters in Trenton. The very *idea* that Jesse Jackson would be in New Jersey, involved in the gubernatorial election, at the side of Christie Whitman would have been utterly unthinkable six days ago.

Suddenly, five legal actions are going on simultaneously. The U.S. attorney is conducting a federal criminal investigation, the state attorney general has launched a state criminal probe, the Election Law Enforcement Commission is investigating how public matching funds were used, the Democratic National Committee and Democratic State Committee have filed a federal lawsuit seeking to overturn the election, and Jackson and Sharpton are filing a class-action defamation suit against Rollins and the Republican State Committee for besmirching the state's black clergy. They dropped Whitman from the suit after meeting with her yesterday and seeing that she appears to be as genuinely outraged as they are.

"It did not happen," Whitman keeps saying. "It's a flat-out lie." The day the story broke, she called it "inconceivable" that such a thing could have occurred and said, "I find this whole thing, everything that was alleged, degrading—degrading to the voters of New Jersey, to the African-American community, and, frankly, to me."

Jim Florio called Rollins's story "very troubling" and said it was "obscene" for Rollins to have said that paying people to suppress voter turnout "is the way the game is played in New Jersey." But beyond reading that one statement, the governor has been silent. James Carville, however, is saying the election is now "tainted" and he would be "appalled if Mrs. Whitman would now take office with this cloud hanging over her head." The state NAACP yesterday added its voice to those urging Whitman not to accept official certification of her victory until the controversy is resolved.

Governor Florio lost by 25,628 votes out of about 2.5 million cast. Low turnout in the cities was cited as a factor in his defeat even before this week's revelation. Whitman said yesterday that if it turned out that secret payments to suppress the black vote could be shown somehow to account for the outcome, she would consider resigning and holding a new election.

But there are other factors that explain why Jim Florio didn't do as well in the cities this year as he did in 1989, among them his de-emphasis of urban issues as he appealed for middle-class suburban votes. Furthermore, no black minister or urban Democrat has come forward yet to say he or she was offered money by Republicans to keep quiet or to stay home on Election Day. The FBI has set up a 24-hour telephone hotline in hopes of gaining pertinent information.

All over the state people are asking why Rollins opened his mouth, which of his versions to believe, and how wrong is what he confessed to and then retracted. If it is okay to pay people to get out the vote, is it okay to pay people *not* to get out the vote? This is the nub of the issue, as some frame it. A poll out today suggests two-thirds of the public think it's terribly wrong. Others see it more in racial terms, as an affront to African-Americans. President Clinton said, "People have died in this country to give other people—especially African-Americans—the right to vote." By his logic, to discourage them from voting is immoral. But is it a crime to pay someone to refrain from saying something he may or may not have planned to say in a church sermon? The Justice Department has already announced it will concentrate its investigation more on alleged

payments to Democratic street workers than to black ministers. Government lawyers at the federal and state levels are looking at the statutes that
pertain to bribery, uses of public money, and improper inducements to
voters.

For Christie Whitman, who began her campaign amidst a barrage of tough questions about illegal aliens and then faced scornful
questions all year about campaign disarray and missteps, this twist of fate
is cruel and maddening. It puts a cloud over her governorship. It para-
lyzes her transition effort. It strains her relationship with the African-
American population. At this writing, it's possible to imagine its even
costing her the election, though I consider that prospect highly unlikely.
Whitman came through a year of gaffes and crises upright and triumphant. She is weathering this mega-crisis with the same pluck she has
shown all year. (This morning she attended services at two black churches.)
But the mere fact that she is embroiled in yet another crisis makes you
wonder if her governorship will be a continuation of the pattern. "The
Misadventures of Governor Whitman"—is that the theme for the next
four years?

Ed Rollins has not been heard from since Whitman read his
retraction to a crowd of newspeople last Wednesday. If you got to know
him professionally, as I did this year, you have to feel sorry for him. He
was on top of the world last week. This week he is a pariah. His three
careers—political consultant, corporate public-relations strategist, and
television commentator for NBC—are all in jeopardy. Last Sunday
assembly speaker Chuck Haytaian proudly announced Rollins would help
his 1994 U.S. Senate campaign. By Wednesday Haytaian wanted nothing to do with Rollins. Psychologists would say Rollins has a self-destruc-
tive streak, and dramatists would say he committed the sin of hubris.
Apparently, he was so eager to show off how cleverly he and the Whitman
campaign had outfoxed Carville and the Democrats that he confessed to
his own dirty tricks! Not only that, but he probably exaggerated them by
a factor of five, ten, twenty, or even fifty, enlarging by an equal amount
the size of the bullet wound in his foot.

The way the media are swarming over it, the story is almost as
big right now as the story of the election itself. Unfortunately, I have to
leave off here so that my publisher can get this book out by Inauguration

Day, as planned. My imagination is leaping from one possible ending to another—one that you already know, but I don't. Or, maybe the bonfire will just simmer down and burn out.

The Democratic party is eager to get Ed Rollins and Dan Todd into court and under oath. Their federal lawsuit is being heard tomorrow morning at 8:15 in the Newark courtroom of U.S. district judge Dickinson Debevoise. I'll be there.

THE EDWARDS CAMP

Pete McDonough, campaign director
Jeff Michaels, campaign manager
Greg Stevens, consultant

THE WHITMAN CAMP

Hazel Gluck, senior advisor
Carl Golden, press secretary
Joe Justin, press secretary for the primary
Ginny Littell, New Jersey Republican state chair
Dave Marziale, press secretary for the primary
Mike Murphy, media consultant
Dave Murray, campaign manager for the primary
Ed Rollins, consultant and second campaign manager
Webster B. (Dan) Todd, Jr., brother and first campaign manager
John Whitman, spouse and advisor

THE FLORIO CAMP

Jim Andrews, campaign manager
Brenda Bacon, senior advisor
Paul Begala, consultant
Doug Berman, strategist
James Carville, consultant
Jo Astrid Glading, campaign press secretary
Harold Hodes, lobbyist and advisor
Ray Lesniak, New Jersey Democratic state chair
Joe Salema, governor's former chief of staff
Jon Shure, governor's communications director
Rick Wright, governor's chief of staff